W9-CLK-301

THE UNDISPUTED GUIDE TO PRO BASKETBALL HISTORY

BY THE SAME AUTHORS

The Macrophenomenal Pro Basketball Almanac

FREEDARKO PRESENTS

THE UNDISPUTED GUIDE TO PRO BASKETBALL HISTORY

BLOOMSBURY

NEW YORK BERLIN LONDON

Published by Bloomsbury USA, New York

All papers used by Bloomsbury USA are natural, recyclable products made from wood grown in well-managed forests. The manufacturing processes conform to the environmental regulations of the country of origin.

LIBRARY OF CONGRESS CONTROL NUMBER: 2010906591

ISBN: 978-1-60819-083-6

First U.S. Edition 2010

10 9 8 7 6 5 4 3 2 1

Typeset by Jacob Weinstein
Printed in China by C&C Offset Printing Co., Ltd.

CONTENTS

INTRODUCTION

Following a sport from season to season is full immersion. That's why our first book, *FreeDarko Presents: The Macrophenomenal Pro Basketball Almanac,* in many ways wrote itself. That's not to suggest that putting it together was quick or easy. But those words, ideas, and images came right out of our relationship with the present-day NBA. The material may have been abstruse or silly at times, but it was ours.

Fans, even those as abstracted as us, live this shit in a way that's distinct from reporting or research alone. Whether the *Almanac* registered as sportswriting, cultural journalism, blogging, or pop art is beside the point. It was what happens when years' worth of closely held ideas and intuitions run like hell for the outside world. It may not have been a complete view of the NBA, but it was a way of looking at it. There is no monolith.

The Undisputed Guide to Pro Basketball History is our attempt to tackle the past. On the face of it, this is a simple task. The preferred method? Good, clean history, the kind the Germans once dared consider a science. You exhume all sources, track down the survivors, review evidence, consult the experts, and craft a footnote-riddled tale of what was.

But we didn't come up with the *Almanac* by staying calm and checking names off lists; nor is it how we were consuming the NBA when FreeDarko first crawled out of the muck of a fantasy-league message board. So why should we consider the game's past that way? This book is our attempt to go back in time, to make the game feel as alive, and as overwhelming, as it does when we watch it today. We didn't try to reconstruct everything that happened; that's been done several times over. Instead, we were interested in ourselves. Given our focus on personality, style, aesthetics, race, and politics, why should basketball history matter to us? What would FreeDarko have cared about back then?

This might be unrealistic or come off as a cop-out. Typically, the goal for historians is to prove they know it all. However, we have never really gone for this kind of credibility in the present. It may be a gamble, but we believe there's no reason we need to change our tune just because we found a time machine by the side of the road and tried to crawl inside of it.

All of which lands us right back at method, if you can even call it that. How did we go about this lopsided task? Mostly, we did it by wandering through books, video, and other material culture with no clear goals in mind. We emptied our minds and let it all wash over us. At least initially, player bios or memoirs from the wild-and-woolly seventies or magazine articles from that era (*Sports Illustrated*'s online Vault is absolutely indispensable) were key in helping us get a feel for how the sport was talked about at the time. They also helped us recover ideas and impressions that have been buried over the years. While ESPN and NBA TV have been solid sources of old game footage for some time, YouTube blew the business of pro-ball archiving wide open. All of a sudden, you could watch a 1970 Hawks-Suns game—Pistol Pete Maravich versus Connie Hawkins—in full. Grainy footage of the ABA mysteriously appeared, like basketball's answer to the Dead Sea Scrolls.

Yet that's not to say that this project was a delirious, decentralized mess. There were some stone classics that we returned to again and again. Many are now as much artifacts from the past as documents of it. David Halberstam's *The Breaks of the Game* is the gold standard when it comes to conveying the nuance of basketball-as-it-happens and then extrapolating broader themes; his later *Playing for Keeps: Michael Jordan and the World He Made*, while more conventional, is a treasure trove of information on His Airness. Bill Russell's *Second Wind: The Memoirs of an Opinionated Man*, from 1979, is easily among the most thoughtful books about sports, race, culture, and life ever written. That it was penned by one of the NBA's greatest players makes it all the more profound a statement. Fittingly, Wilt Chamberlain's *Wilt: Just Like Any Other Black Millionaire Who Lives Next Door* is more outlandish, and certainly more entertaining, but—while deeper than you'd expect—ultimately less substantive.

David Wolf's *Foul!: The Connie Hawkins Story* chronicles one of the game's great tragic figures, but it offers a far richer, and more expansive, look at the times than its title would suggest. Bill Bradley's spare, literate *Life on the Run* and Walt Frazier's convivial *Rockin' Steady: A Guide to Basketball & Cool* are as different as their authors, and yet both get to the heart of those beloved championship Knicks.

There's also *Tall Tales* and *Loose Balls*, Terry Pluto's invaluable oral histories of the sixties NBA and the ABA, respectively; hearing the players' voices, however mediated, always allowed for that contact point we sought. More roll call: Vincent Thomas's *They Cleared the Lane*, an account of the early black players in the league; Robert W. Peterson's *From Cages to Jumpshots*, the definitive book on pre-NBA pro ball; Charlie Rosen's quirky meditation on seventies ball, *God, Man and Basketball Jones*; and Nelson George's *Elevating the Game*, the rare polemic that never has to force its issue. And while Bill Simmons's *The Book of Basketball* sent us scrambling, it did a lot to help us firm up exactly what we were trying to accomplish ourselves.

The above isn't intended as a lit review. We just wanted to give credit where credit was due, as well as point to writing that helped us figure out what the hell we were doing. It isn't a justification, either: Soon after beginning work on this *Guide*, we realized we really didn't have any other choice. Staying true to what we love about this game required believing it possible to stumble through the past as if we'd known it all along. While we haven't come through with any easy answers, we at least like to think we've gotten a few new scabs along the way. —*B.S.*

NOTE ON AUTHOR CREDITS: All essay authors are indicated by two-letter bylines, e.g., "B.S." for Bethlehem Shoals. All sidebar text was written and researched by Brown Recluse, Esq., and Eric Freeman. All illustration and design by Jacob Weinstein.

DATES AND DATA: Unless otherwise noted, all statistics have been taken from www.basketball-reference.com. When a season is referred to as a single year in a graph or chart, it refers to the ending date of that season. (For example, '90 refers to the 1989–1990 season.)

CHAPTER
0

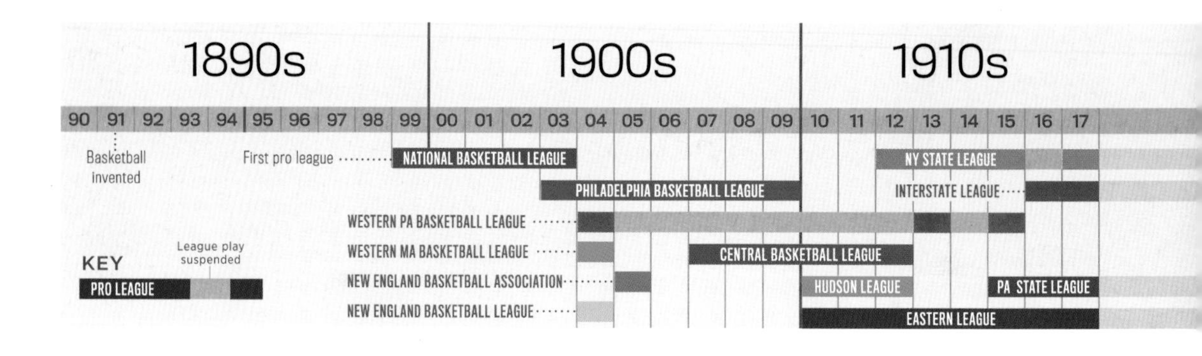
1890s
1900s
1910s
90 91 92 93 94 95 96 97 98 99 00 01 02 03 04 05 06 07 08 09 10 11 12 13 14 15 16 17
Basketball invented
First pro league
NATIONAL BASKETBALL LEAGUE
PHILADELPHIA BASKETBALL LEAGUE
WESTERN PA BASKETBALL LEAGUE
WESTERN MA BASKETBALL LEAGUE
NEW ENGLAND BASKETBALL ASSOCIATION
NEW ENGLAND BASKETBALL LEAGUE
CENTRAL BASKETBALL LEAGUE
HUDSON LEAGUE
EASTERN LEAGUE
NY STATE LEAGUE
INTERSTATE LEAGUE
PA STATE LEAGUE
KEY
League play suspended
PRO LEAGUE

UP FROM THE WATERS

1891–1946

In 1891, basketball was born; it then took more than fifty years to mature. The sport began humbly, as a solution to a crisis in one school's phys-ed curriculum. Then, as it spread from its Springfield, Massachusetts, epicenter, the first leagues began to form. However, "league" was a relative term for much of this early, rough-and-tumble period. First there were networks of local clubs; then, regional operations where teams didn't always agree on the rules; barnstorming squads who roamed the country playing whatever competition presented itself; and, periodically, attempts to bring order to the chaos—all against the backdrop of low, low pay, seismic shifts in the style of play, and the quest for recognition as a legitimate professional sport. But while it's easy to dismiss the decades between James Naismith's eureka moment and the NBA's formation, they were also a heady, colorful time. Those playing were competitive as hell, daring to love the sport when nobody else could be bothered, and, however slowly, marshaling the development of the game.

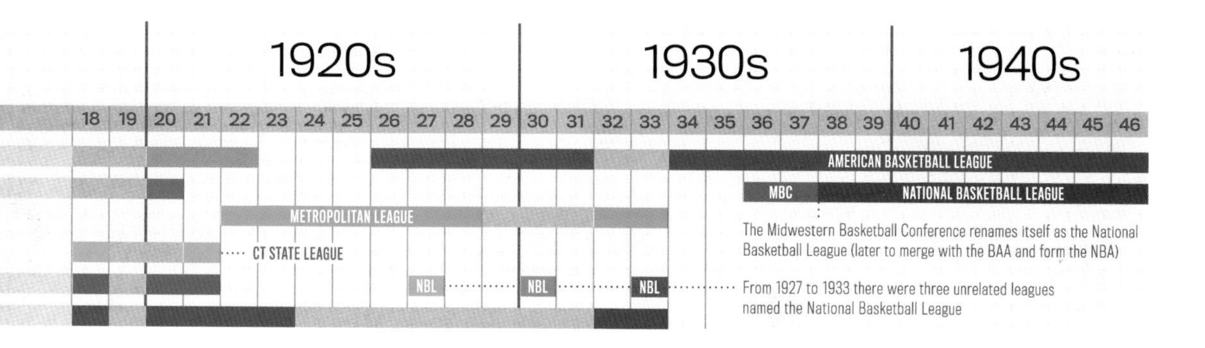

BASKETBALL
I
II
III
IV
V
VI
VII
VIII
IX
X
XI
XII
XIII

DOWN BY LAW

James Naismith, the Peach-Basket Patriarch

Basketball, unlike the other major sports, was invented. It didn't evolve out of other pastimes; it was handed down to the people in Springfield, Massachusetts. And its Moses, its law-giving father, was James Naismith, a Canadian physical education teacher just trying to keep his students engaged.

In the fall of 1891, Naismith was an instructor at the YMCA International Training School in Springfield. Naismith was a devotee of muscular Christianity, a doctrine holding that physical fitness and the purity of the body were as key to salvation as the state of the soul. During the harsh New England winter, Naismith's classes were confined to the indoor gym. The only approved indoor activities were calisthenics and gymnastics—no one's idea of fun, but an especially bad match for an older, fractious bunch known as the Incorrigibles, who had little patience for marathon stretching routines. Things were getting tense, and the class increasingly restive. There was no choice but to act.

Dr. Luther Glick, Naismith's boss, tasked the mild-mannered Canadian with developing an indoor game to get his students, and him, through the next few months. In December 1891, Naismith came to class armed with thirteen rules for a new sport in which players passed the ball around while attempting to get a clear shot at a raised goal. He tacked them up on the bulletin board, let everyone have a look, and motioned toward the peach baskets mounted at either end of the gym. Admittedly, this sport had no name, and its architect had to step in and guide play at first. But Naismith had given them an indoor sport where before there had been none. The law had been received.

As the game caught on locally and spread to other YMCAs, Naismith decided to introduce it to the public. That January, its rules were published in the *Triangle*, the Springfield student newspaper. While his pupils encouraged Naismith to name the sport after himself ("Naismith ball"), he opted for "basket ball."

NO PATENT NECESSARY: Of all the major sports, basketball alone can claim its very own Big Bang. Football developed out of rugby, soccer was played in various forms throughout England for decades before the Football Association's 1863 "Laws of the Game," and hockey came from a combination of Native Canadian games and European innovations. And while baseball has its own creation myth of Abner Doubleday, the game is actually a descendant of various bat-and-ball games such as rounders and cricket.

BABY STRETCHER: Naismith theorized that since "the body is more or less elastic," it could be lengthened by 2 inches by "stretching the body 30 minutes a day for six months." He thought the best time to stretch people was when they were infants from five months to a year old. He was worried that if done at a later age, an individual might keep growing and there would be no way to stop it.

LAND OF THE RISING ROUND-BALL: One of the first people to play a game of basketball was a Japanese exchange student named Genzaburo Ishikawa. He was enrolled in Naismith's gym class when the game of basketball was first introduced. Basketball has stayed in the family, as his descendant Takeshi Ishikawa is the current executive director of the Japan Basketball Association.

CHUG! CHUG! CHUG! Even James Naismith was not immune to the power of peer pressure. While a student at McGill University, Naismith played on the rugby team, and at the team banquet, at each place around the table sat a glass of white wine, a glass of red, one of whiskey, and one of brandy. Naismith held true to his moral beliefs against drinking alcohol, but later wrote of that night, "I spent two hours in hell, thinking that everyone at the table was thinking I was a sissy. But the banquet ended and the glasses were untouched."

He had devised a form of recreation based on throwing a ball into a basket—the point had never been to make a name for himself. Moses, too, would likely be shocked to hear the Commandments referred to as "Mosaic Law." It was the tablets that did all the work.

But Naismith and his thirteen rules are also analogous to another seminal moment in religious history (a moment that actually happened outside the realm of myth, at that). The rules of "basket ball" weren't a divine blueprint handed down in a cloud of smoke, after all; they represented reform, a solution to a seemingly insoluble problem: What the fuck to do when it's ten below outside? Basketball began with handwritten theses nailed (tacked, rather) to a door (er, bulletin board). Naismith didn't intend to alter the course of athletic history any more than Martin Luther wanted to bring down the church. Basketball was a corrective measure, just as the Ninety-five Theses were intended to be. The latter was a reaction against ecclesiastical simony, a debauched papacy, and the sale of indulgences; the former was the curriculum's response to, well, winter. Both Protestantism and the NBA came much later. Naismith in 1891 could no more have imagined the sport as a multibillion-dollar business than Luther could have foreseen Sarah Palin and snake handling.

Luther's ideas, at least in the Ninety-five Theses, did not for the most part extend beyond a reaction to church shortcomings; he wasn't proposing solutions so much as pointing out the problems. Naismith, however, took the next step, from critical reaction to reasonable prescription. He went one step past Luther, two past ol' cranky pants Moses and his raging edict. The way in which Naismith did so not only rescues him from myth, it also marks Naismith—and basketball—as very much of their time. He cooked up basketball efficiently, even scientifically, by taking a survey of other sports, determining what made them viable and enjoyable, and then synthesizing their best qualities.

As Robert W. Peterson explains in *From Cages to Jumpshots*: "He first decided that the new game must use a ball, since all popular team sports had one. A large ball or small? Sports that used a small ball required intermediate equipment—bat, stick, or racket—and Naismith was striving for simplicity. The choice was easy: It would be a large ball." The indoor setting brought about another crucial determination. Naismith was first and foremost a rugby man. But the hard floors of a gym made tackling out of the question, especially for those zany Incorrigibles. The ball would be moved, then, only by passing, a rule that has obviously changed with time. That still left the matter of scoring. Since Naismith was trying to discourage rowdiness, placing the goal on the ground was out of the question; using hockey or soccer as a model would insert force into the equation. Searching for other options, he recalled a Canadian schoolyard game called Duck on the Rock, in which participants used a ball to try to knock a "duck" (a smaller rock) off of a larger rock. A "guard" tried to keep the duck safe; the best way to get past the guard was to arc it. Touch and finesse would be at a premium if the goal made an upward, arcing shot necessary. That's how the basket ended up in the air.

It was, as solutions go, an extremely elegant approach. By engineering a sport, Naismith may not have set out to create the perfect indoor pastime, but he certainly hoped to come up with something that his students would stick with. It was a matter of results, and to this end, he had to work backward from empirical fact. There was nothing mystical or dogmatic to it. Naismith's faith lay not in his rules but in the process by which he had arrived at them. Even though James Naismith's invention of basketball readily lends itself to mythic or religious analogies, the man's methods were unmistakably rational.

Or were they? Naismith worked his way through this chain of reasoning in a single night, under a strict deadline. His process may have been rational, but nevertheless there was a tinge of inspiration—if only of the Romantic variety—in this unassuming man scribbling down basketball's rules by candlelight. His ingenuity was responsible for a game that would become wildly popular in Springfield within weeks and, before long, that would spread across the entire nation, all because of a few surly students and an unforgiving chill.

Naismith defies our need to assign grandeur to the creators of things that matter. In biography, he is equal parts glorious and mundane, generative and curiously finite. To some extent, this captures the spirit of his own act of creation. In that fevered attempt to fuse rationality and inspiration, and looking now at what the sport he created has become—a game that embodies this country's best and worst qualities—it's hard not to see Naismith as another sort of historical figure, a secular one: the Founding Father of the only American sport with a Constitution. Not bad for a Canadian. —*B.S.*

EACH ONE TEACH ONE:
Naismith's coaching lineage is usually thought of as a college thing, but it also has its professional progeny. Naismith would eventually head to Kansas, where he coached Forrest "Phog" Allen, and although Naismith discouraged him from pursuing a career in coaching ("You can't coach basketball; you just play it"), Allen went on to a long and successful career. Dean Smith and Adolph Rupp were both assistants under Allen; in turn they begat their fair share of NBA notables. Smith coached Larry Brown, Doug Moe, and George Karl, while Rupp sired Pat Riley.

Go Forth and Dribble

Basketball's First Great Age of Expansion

Early pro leagues sprouted up across the Northeast within years of Naismith's inventing the sport in 1891. These leagues were anything but organized, with wildly differing rules and styles of play, and it would be a long, hard road from Springfield to the first NBA game in 1949.

MICRO LEAGUES

1898–1909

STRUCTURE: More like DIY community groups than anything we would recognize as a professional sports league today, the first pro teams were totally informal, growing out of YMCAs, high schools, settlement houses, and often consisting of several teams from the same city.

VENUES: Games were played anywhere and everywhere; the earliest pro team, from Trenton, New Jersey, played its home games at the local Masonic Temple. In one of the first of many schisms between the pro and amateur game, the professionals decided to enclose their courts with wire-mesh cages in order to keep the ball in play and speed up the game, and for years professional basketball players were dismissively referred to as "cagers" by the press.

STYLE OF PLAY: Violent and, by today's standards, totally unrecognizable. Teams fielded seven players, shooting was limited to the layup and the two-handed set shot, and, as tall dudes were used only for the center jump after every basket, few players stood over 5′10″. The whole affair more resembled a mixed martial arts contest performed by a troupe of midgets than a modern basketball game.

INNOVATIONS: Developments at this stage were so primitive they can hardly be called innovations, but perhaps the first great breakthrough by the pros was the invention of the dribble. Nowhere in Naismith's original rules does the word "dribbling" even appear. But pro players who were trapped by their defenders soon realized that by intentionally fumbling or dropping the ball away from themselves, they could escape the trap. Each dribble was thus originally a sort of controlled loss of possession. The YMCA quickly moved to outlaw dribbling in 1898, but the pros continued to refine the mysterious art.

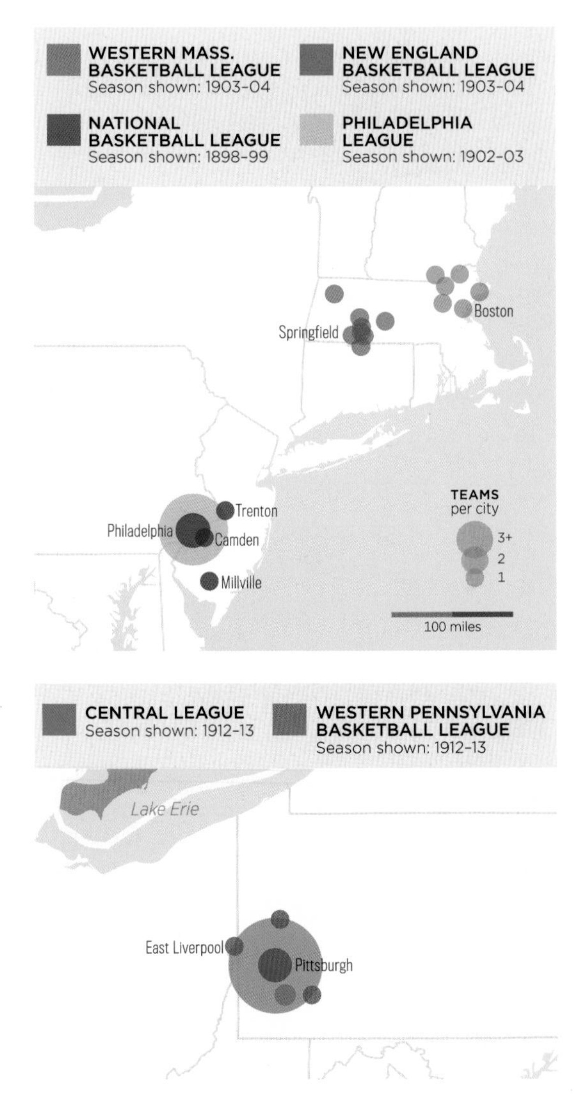

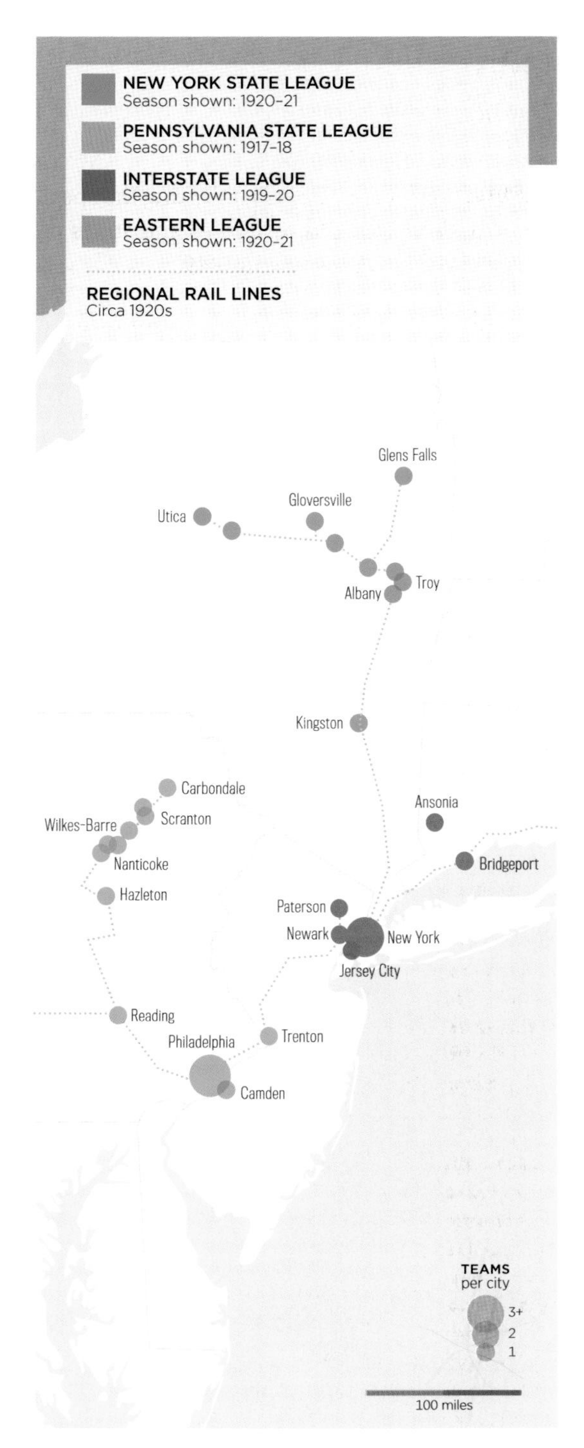

REGIONAL LEAGUES

1910–24

STRUCTURE: By 1910 there were several pro leagues built around regional railroad lines. Since there were no formal contracts, these leagues were wildly unstable, with players constantly jumping from one team to another. Some players were on as many as five different rosters at a time, selling their services to the highest-bidding team on a daily basis.

VENUES: In the New York State League, nearly all games were played in local armories. This meant players had to join the National Guard just to get on the court—only to be discharged at the end of the season. In Nanticoke, Pennsylvania, the court was lined with burning-hot steam pipes that players gleefully threw their opponents against. The dimensions of the courts still varied, with most being only two thirds the size of the modern NBA court.

STYLE OF PLAY: Very violent. Head-butting, pushing, and slamming opponents into the wire cages surrounding the court was all considered fair play. Joel Gotthoffer, who moonlighted in the Penn State League, said, "You could play tick-tack-toe on everybody after a game because the cage marked you up . . . if you didn't get rid of the ball you could get killed." As players could double dribble, games were dominated by one-on-one play, with the dribbler acting like a football running back and bowling over defenders by head-butting them. As each league used different rules, there was also a great flowering of regional styles. For example, while Western players commonly took bank shots, most East Coast players practiced a "clean" set shot since most New York leagues did not use a backboard.

INNOVATIONS: Since team rosters were so volatile and players were so often traveling, there was seldom time or reason to practice set plays. But while teams might barely last a season intact, pairs and groups of players often stuck together for years, and their familiarity with each other led to the development of the pick and roll, or, as it was known at the time, the buddy system. The most accomplished practitioners of the early two-man game were Barney Sedran and Max Friedman, who were known as the Heavenly Twins. Other innovations of the era were the fast break and the bounce pass. Interestingly, the dunk appears to have been invented as soon as there was a man who could jump high enough to perform the feat, but since dunking was considered hot-dogging and unsportsmanlike during the early years, its development was stymied until the 1960s.

BIG LEAGUES 1925-37

STRUCTURE: In an ambitious attempt to form the first "national" league, the American Basketball League was founded in 1925. The ABL introduced exclusive written contracts for the first time and was thus remarkably stable and successful, until it crashed and burned along with the stock market in the early 1930s. The Great Depression decimated the pro leagues, forcing most of the remaining teams onto the barnstorming circuit. The ABL attempted a modest comeback as an Eastern regional league in the late 1930s, but it would be fifteen years before another national league was attempted. The other important league of the era was the Midwestern Basketball Conference, the grandfather of the modern NBA, which was founded in 1935. MBC teams were backed by local factories that provided financial stability and fanciful team names such as the Akron Firestone Non-Skids, the Chicago Duffy Florals, and the Fort Wayne Zollner Pistons (much later to become the NBA's Detroit Pistons).

VENUES: While the Indianapolis Kautskys (MBC) often rented the 15,000-seat Butler Fieldhouse, most other teams were still toiling away in armories, high school gyms, and random venues such as fire stations. During the 1930s there was also a brief fad for playing games on theater stages, with teams like the Brooklyn Jewels playing in the Brooklyn Paramount Theater, and the Kate Smith Celtics playing in Manhattan's Hippodrome.

STYLE OF PLAY: The ABL made significant attempts to clean up and speed up the game by outlawing the double dribble, cages, and gambling, and also instituting harsh fines for misconduct. Later, the ABL also adopted disqualifications after five fouls and invented the three-second rule in an attempt to open up passing lanes. But by modern standards, the game remained wacky and untamed. New York's Metropolitan League was still playing gladiatorial cage matches based on bulk and strength, and even in the ABL and MBC there was still a center jump after every basket and teams played a possession-based game, with scores hovering between the 30s and 40s.

INNOVATIONS: Due to the outlawing of the double dribble and an influx of college players to the pro ranks (bringing with them the college game's emphasis on passing), there was a shift from the one-on-one style of the early 1920s to a more team-oriented style, best exemplified by the New York Renaissance and Original Celtics barnstorming teams. These teams played a controlled game—later proselytized by former Celtics-turned-coaches Nat Holman and Joe Lapchick as "scientific basketball"—which was characterized by hard-nosed man-to-man defense and short, crisp passing for high-percentage shots. This new emphasis on teamwork helped lead to the development of the pivot play, set plays for out-of-bounds balls, and switching on defense.

MAJOR LEAGUES 1938–50

STRUCTURE: In 1938 the MBC unimaginatively rechristened itself the National Basketball League (it would be the fifth professional league to use that name), and for the next decade the NBL ruled the sport, despite its franchises being located almost exclusively in small and medium-sized Midwestern cities. Sensing an opportunity, a group of fat-cat hockey team owners formed the Basketball Association of America in 1946, hoping to fill their empty arenas with basketball games while their hockey teams were out of town, and, by taking control of the major-market cities, force an eventual merger with the NBL.

VENUES: These hockey arenas were the BAA's great strength and the bargaining chip that led to the formation of the NBA. Professional basketball still suffered an image problem in the 1940s, and NBL teams were not welcome in the nation's major arenas even though college basketball teams as a rule were. The BAA changed all of that by opening up marquee arenas such as Madison Square Garden and Chicago Stadium to the pro game. In 1948 four NBL teams jumped ship to the BAA, and the following year the BAA and the now weakened NBL formally merged to create the NBA. Since the NBA traces its official history through its BAA parentage, the contributions of the NBL are often overlooked, but the best teams and players in the early NBA can all be traced back to the NBL side of the family tree.

STYLE OF PLAY: In 1937 the center jump after each basket was eliminated. This both sped up the game and forced big men to learn real basketball skills if they wanted to keep their jobs. With big men now becoming more involved in the offense, and the average height of players increasing in general, offensive rebounding and put-backs became integral to the game for the first time. As usual, old-timers didn't like the new developments, and demands were made to raise the hoop or remove the backboard entirely to eliminate rebounds.

INNOVATIONS: Much as the movie camera was preceded by an endless stream of zoetropes, stroboscobes, and praxinoscopes, the jump shot is one of those inventions that came into the world all at once, but with its instructions scattered across the globe. The first ingredient was the running one-hander, used to great effect by Stanford star Hank Luisetti in the mid-thirties. But Luisetti's feet barely left the floor when he shot, and it seems the true jump shot was developed independently and almost simultaneously by multiple players across the country, including Myer "Whitey" Skoog in Duluth, Minnesota, and Kenny Sailors in rural Wyoming. But it wasn't until "Jumpin' Joe" Fulks led the BAA in scoring during its first season that the shot with his name finally gained national acceptance. Within a decade the jumper would become the weapon of choice for the modern player.

Only the Ball Was Orange

Early Barnstorming Teams, Ethnic and Otherwise

The early pro leagues were such a mess that the best teams in the country often bypassed them altogether, instead choosing to organize individual games themselves while traveling the nation's barnstorming circuit. Frequently playing more than a hundred games a year, the barnstormers were some of the era's best teams while at the same time blurring the boundaries between entertainment and sport. For some, barnstorming was a financial consideration, as teams like the Original Celtics could earn more money promoting their own matches than they could in regional leagues. But for other teams, generally those made up of minorities, nomadism was the only option available. Like much of America's society in the early twentieth century, these teams fell along ethnic and religious fault lines. But they simultaneously fell into and subverted stereotypes, working as marketing ploys and as means of asserting ethnic pride.

BUFFALO GERMANS

Shrouded in mystery, this team of creepy teenagers from Upstate New York was forced into barnstorming by geographic isolation. Founded in 1895 at the German YMCA in Buffalo, the team is legendary for having once won 111 consecutive games, though this accomplishment is somewhat diminished by the quality of its opponents: YMCA teams, college teams, and local yokels. (Their epic win streak was finally snapped when they ran up against another pro team, in 1911.) As a team, the Germans' defining trait was their sadism. In an era when teams commonly averaged 20 points a game, the Germans mercilessly crushed their overmatched competition, running up scores like 111–17, 104–8, and 104–13, and once eviscerated Hobart College 134–0.

ORIGINAL CELTICS

Founded in 1914 as the New York Celtics, the team first consisted of Irish teenagers from a Hell's Kitchen settlement house, but would soon drop both the New York from their name and their Irish bias, picking up local stars such as Joe Lapchick (Czech), Nat Holman (Jewish), and Henry "Dutch" Dehnert (Dutch, duh). The Celtics would go on to become the most famous pro team of the 1920s, playing in several leagues as well as barnstorming. In their prime, they are estimated to have won 90 percent of their games, one season finishing with the confounding record of 193–11–1. Known for their ball movement and tenacious defense, the team is often credited with developing the give-and-go, switching on defense, and formalizing the pivot play.

THE RENS

There were many all-black pro teams during the early twentieth century, but the first and greatest was the New York Renaissance. They were also better than all the white teams. Founded in 1923, the Rens took their name from the Renaissance Ballroom in Harlem, where the team played on the dance floor between sets by the house orchestra. After the Depression shut down the ballrooms in the 1930s, the Rens—who were forbidden from joining the all-white pro leagues—were forced onto the barnstorming circuit. In 1933 they posted an 88-game win streak and from 1932 to 1936 had a 497–58 record. The Rens became the first all-black pro team to win a world title in any sport when they prevailed at the World Pro Tournament in 1939. They also won in 1943 as the Chicago Bears.

THE HARLEM GLOBETROTTERS

On one hand, the Globetrotters are a classic American success story. The operation started in the late 1920s as six men touring the Midwestern hinterlands in the dead of winter in a cramped, unheated Model-T Ford, often making just enough money to get to the next town. By the 1950s the team was a national institution, playing before record-setting crowds on multiple continents and starring in Hollywood movies. On the other hand, the relationship between black players, their white audience, and the Jewish owner-promoter Abe Saperstein is another sort of American story, a typically twisted tale of friendship, betrayal, and outright exploitation. But what's often buried beneath the rags-to-riches narrative, the racial politics, and the banana cream pies is that for over two decades the Globetrotters were a legitimately awesome basketball team. After years of playing second fiddle to the New York Renaissance, the Globetrotters would defeat the defending-champion Rens in the 1940 World Pro Tournament and, later, to much fanfare, would defeat George Mikan's reigning-champion Minneapolis Lakers in both 1948 and 1949. Stars like Runt Pullins and Marques Haynes were the best ball handlers of the era, and goofy big men Goose Tatum and Nat "Sweetwater" Clifton could pass and dribble like players half their size. After overtaking the Rens, Saperstein enjoyed a virtual monopoly on black talent until 1950, when the NBA finally broke his stranglehold by selecting Chuck Cooper and Earl Lloyd (both signed to the Trotters) in the NBA draft.

THE SPHAS

The Sphas—an acronym for South Philadelphia Hebrew Association—were organized in 1917 by a teenage Eddie "the Mogul" Gottlieb, the legendary promoter who would later own the Philadelphia Warriors. Gottlieb promised "a fight in every game, guaranteed," and the rough-and-tumble Sphas defeated both the Celtics and the Rens in best-of-three exhibition series in 1926. Paul Gallico, sports editor of the *New York Daily News*, mused, "The reason . . . that basketball appeals to the Hebrew . . . is that the game places a premium on an alert, scheming mind, flashy trickiness, artful dodging and general smart aleckness." Though Jews soon faded from the courts as players, these traits continued to serve them well as they moved into coaching and managerial positions in later years.

HONG WAH KUES

A Chinese American team from San Francisco, the Hong Wah Kues burst onto the barnstorming circuit in 1939, only to disband two years later due to the start of World War II. Managed for a time by Abe Saperstein, the team was required to speak Cantonese on the court (although they could speak fluent English) and played at least one game a night and two on Sundays, often in Podunk towns such as Grangeville, Idaho, where the match was promoted with flyers announcing, "WAR! Grangeville to be attacked! These are the Chinese invaders!" With no player standing over six feet, the Kues played an up-tempo game marked by crisp passing.

CARLISLE INDIAN INDUSTRIAL SCHOOL

Founded in 1879, the brutally oppressive Carlisle School's official mission was to "civilize" Native American children, but its unofficial motto was "Kill the Indian, Save the Man." The school emphasized athletics and fielded the most heralded Native American basketball team of the era. In his book *Basketball: Its Origins and Development*, the ever-observant Dr. Naismith noted that the team's "ability to move quickly and their art of deception overcome the disadvantage of their height." There were also several Native American barnstorming teams, such as the Sioux Travelers-Warriors, which featured South Dakota all-state players Chub Bear and Suitcase Little, who were tastefully promoted with posters declaring, "Indians on the war path . . . after every club's scalp."

OLSON'S TERRIBLE SWEDES

The Terrible Swedes were founded in 1920 by the titular C. M. "Ole" Olson, who played on Nordic stereotypes by fielding what was for the time a team of "giants," with the average player standing more than 6′5″ tall. Based in Cassville, Missouri, with players pilfered from the Midwestern AAU ranks, the Swedes were one of the hardest-working teams on the barnstorming circuit, playing nearly as many games as the Celtics and Rens. The Swedes mostly played straight basketball, but Ole Olson, who was a player as well as manager, was known to break out behind-the-back passes and one-handed trick shots to add a little razzle-dazzle to the show. In 1935 Olson founded his second barnstorming team, the All American Red Heads.

THE ALL AMERICAN RED HEADS

At a time when most women's teams still played six-on-six, half-court basketball, the Red Heads played by men's rules against men's teams. Touring the country in a station wagon, and later a limousine, the Red Heads played 200 games during a seven-month season, exhibiting special ball-handling routines and trick shots. At the height of their popularity, they were featured in *Life* and *Colliers* and had a spin-off team called the Ozark Hillbillies. Unless a player was naturally redheaded, she was obligated to dye her hair upon joining the squad. The team continued to tour until 1986, though its popularity steadily diminished after 1973, when Title IX finally forced colleges to field women's sports teams.

HOUSE OF DAVID

By far the weirdest weirdos on the already very weird barnstorming circuit, the Israelite House of David (not Jewish) was a religious commune in Michigan that fielded a semipro basketball team in addition to its more famous semipro baseball team. Required to refrain from sex, haircuts, shaving, and eating meat, the House of David players all sported full beards and flowing locks and were often billed as the Bearded Aces. The team was a big draw on the road and inspired several imitation teams such as the Colored House of David, featuring black players with fake beards. Despite their novelty, the team was taken seriously enough to be invited to the World Pro Tournament in 1939 and 1940 and continued to play well into the 1950s, even touring Europe with the Globetrotters in 1954.

	1947	1948	1949	1950
BAA/NBA FINALS CHAMPION	PHILADELPHIA WARRIORS	BALTIMORE BULLETS	MINNEAPOLIS LAKERS	
FINALS LOSER	STAGS	WARRIORS	CAPITOLS	NATIONALS
NBL FINALS CHAMPION	CHICAGO AMERICAN GEARS	MINNEAPOLIS LAKERS	ANDERSON DUFFY PACKERS	
FINALS LOSER	ROYALS		ALL-STARS	

Minneapolis and three other NBL teams join BAA

BAA and NBL merge to form NBA

A MORE PERFECT UNION

1947-1956

The National Basketball Association was formed in 1949, when the country's two major pro leagues, the Basketball Association of America and the National Basketball League, formally merged, bringing together the East Coast BAA's big-city arenas and the Midwestern NBL's corn-fed talent. The formation of the NBA meant that at long last all of the nation's major pro clubs were competing under a single umbrella. Center George Mikan really made big beautiful, and the introduction of the shot clock in 1954 placed a premium on a player's ability to quickly get up and down the court. In 1950, integration opened the doors for African Americans, even if opportunities for them would remain limited until the mid-fifties. Mikan's Minneapolis Lakers were the first dynasty, winning five titles in the NBA's first six seasons. And as the game changed, stars Bob Pettit, Neil Johnston, and Paul Arizin began putting up big numbers, making the days of YMCAs and cage matches seem primitive by comparison.

	1951	1952	1953	1954	1955	1956
Champion	ROCHESTER ROYALS	MINNEAPOLIS LAKERS	MINNEAPOLIS LAKERS	MINNEAPOLIS LAKERS	SYRACUSE NATIONALS	PHILADELPHIA WARRIORS
Runner-up	KNICKS	KNICKS	KNICKS	NATIONALS	PISTONS	PISTONS

	1952		1953		1954		1955		1956	
POINTS per game leader	Paul Arizin	25.4	Neil Johnston	22.3	Neil Johnston	24.4	Neil Johnston	22.7	Bob Pettit	25.7
REBOUNDS per game leader	George Mikan	13.5	George Mikan	14.4	Harry Gallatin	15.2	Neil Johnston	15.1	Maurice Stokes	16.3
ASSISTS per game leader	Andy Phillip	8.2	Bob Cousy	7.7	Bob Cousy	7.2	Bob Cousy	7.8	Bob Cousy	8.9

MIKAN AND MODERNITY

Time, Space, and the Basketball Subject

HOME COURT ADVANTAGE: Even after the NBA standardized the length of the game and the size of the court, many early arenas still offered their own version of time and space. The Boston Garden in particular was a fun house of temporal dislocation. Built directly over Boston's North Station, years of rumbling trains caused numerous cracks and dead spots in the trademark parquet floor. K. C. Jones claims the Celtics would intentionally force opponents toward these dead spots to create turnovers. Even more confounding was the Garden's complicated hockey clock, which was marked at 15-, 30-, and 45-minute intervals, even though basketball is played with 12-minute quarters. Visiting players constantly misread the clock and were then baffled when the buzzer sounded earlier than expected.

Without a fixed sense of time and space, it's hard to sustain a sport. In his original rules, Dr. James Naismith stipulated the length of periods; the height of the goal and size of the court were, well, a function of his gym in Springfield. Before long, though, enthusiasts saw fit to try out different durations for games and periods. And the more popular the game became, the more places it was played. Time and space fell into flux, and the game entered its long period of chaos.

The variations in time suggested that, as the game changed, Naismith's calculations just didn't make sense anymore. The issue of space was, from the beginning, almost inherently problematic. Naismith had mounted the baskets on the gym's overhead track—a purely heuristic decision. That put them at ten feet, which remained more or less the height of choice. Yet by not codifying this measurement, Naismith set the sport up for spatial uncertainty. The same went for his failure to specify the dimensions of the court. For the next five decades, then, the placement of the hoop, the court's size, and even the division between audience and participants would vary depending on circumstances. A game played in a gaslit basement would be cramped; a cavernous armory, the opposite. The goal was mounted wherever it made sense to put it. Fans seated directly above the hoop sometimes knocked away shots. The backboard solved this problem, but itself further altered the geometry of the goal. Time and space wobbled because the sport lacked a strong institutional culture, and pro basketball remained primordial for decades.

The ABL recognized the importance of uniformity in 1925, when it insisted that all its teams honor the same set of rules. The league saw such regulation as the key to making the sport legitimate; it also made players sign exclusive contracts, which, implausible as it may sound, was a radical shift away from the way pro basketball had worked before. But the ABL didn't last, and this uniformity would not be realized for another twenty-five years. The very idea of the NBL-BAA merger that formed the NBA in 1949 was to create a single league that would provide the definitive version of the pro game. Problem solved, sport official, let history begin in earnest.

But just as the NBA allowed for an assertion of absolute time and space, it found itself dealing with two factors that posed serious challenges to this fixity. The first one came in the form of a single player, George Mikan. Mikan wasn't the first really tall person to play basketball. They had been around for some time, but teams carried them for jump balls and little else. Moves like the set shot assumed that size, and to some degree speed, would not figure into a player's effectiveness; the pivot was more about shiftiness than size. Furthermore, tall, uncoordinated bumblers were liabilities in this hunched and violent era.

Mikan broke the mold. He was a legitimate basketball player who happened to be stretched to comic proportions. Light on his feet and coordinated, he showed that a big man could capably handle the flow of the game. When he began at DePaul University in 1942, his height marginalized him. However, coach Ray Meyer took it upon himself to develop Mikan's overall athleticism (in the most basic sense) through activities like rope jumping and dancing lessons. Meyer also helped Mikan to think of his height as an asset and himself as a noble giant—not as an inferior non-factor whom no team would ever love. His hook shots under the basket were next to unguardable, and on defense, Mikan could displace a field goal attempt just above the hoop.

When Mikan joined the pros as a member of the NBL's Chicago American Gears, the challenges posed by the 6′10″ star were undeniable. No longer was an irregularity of space something that could be corrected through a strong governing body. It now arose not from the field of play, but from the differences between the players on it. Mikan led the NBL in scoring for six straight seasons; basketball's best player was also its most unique.

Goaltending was soon prohibited at the college and pro levels because of Mikan, and the lane was widened from six to twelve feet so he and future big men couldn't camp out directly under the basket without drawing a three-second violation. Yet there was simply no way to legislate Mikan out of existence. He forced the issue of individuality, opening up a breach in the newfound uniformity of competition. From this point on, players and teams

GET THAT OUTTA HERE: Although George Mikan is often portrayed as a four-eyed geek and a gentle giant, he was actually one of the game's first intimidators. In addition to his imposing size, he was certainly not above a well-timed elbow or engaging in trash talk. Opponents recall him often saying things like "Hey, man, this is my territory. Don't come around the basket." Once, after delivering a hard foul to opposing guard George King, he said, "I'll teach that son of a gun."

OTHER EARLY NBA NOTABLES:

JOE FULKS: The NBA's first great scorer and the first pro to perfect the one-handed jump shot, "Jumpin' Joe" held the record for most points in a game (63) until Elgin Baylor's 64 in 1959. Fulks averaged 23.9 points over his first three seasons at a time when teams rarely topped 70 points.

BOB DAVIES: Davies was the league's first great point guard and popularized the behind-the-back dribble, although Bob Cousy usually receives the credit. His best years were played in the NBL, where he led the Royals to a title in 1946 and was named league MVP the following year. Davies went on to lead the NBA in assists during the 1949 season.

PAUL ARIZIN: An early innovator as a scorer, Arizin refined and expanded on his teammate Joe Fulks's line-drive jump shots. Over ten seasons with the Philadelphia Warriors, Arizin averaged more than 20 points per game nine times, led the league in scoring twice, and made the All-Star team every season. Cursed with both asthma and a sinus condition, he panted audibly as he came down the floor.

had to be considered on a case-by-case basis; Mikan represented nothing less than a Copernican shift, opening the door for player individuality as we know it.

In the short term, teams responded to Mikan by tinkering with the passage of time. As the NBA dawned in 1950, stalling was accepted as the best way to win basketball games. It was in the interest of the defense to keep the ball away from the other team and protect the lead if they managed to get it, especially if Mikan was wearing the other jersey. This made for conservative, offense-as-defense basketball that was unbearable to watch, resulting in too few baskets to keep the audience engaged and too little action to build meaningful suspense around the rare points that did go up on the board. It also could not have come at a worse time.

With the formation of the NBA, pro basketball finally seemed ready to be taken seriously. Certainly, it didn't hurt that college basketball was rocked by a major point-shaving scandal in 1951. But the professional product was still inferior to the college game, preoccupied with toughness and not nearly as studied in ball movement and overall fluidity. That's when Syracuse Nationals owner Danny Biasone devised the shot clock. Limiting the amount of time a team could hold the ball forced them to shoot, making for more possessions, a faster pace, and a more exciting game. It also meant that a team couldn't wait until, say, George Mikan was in position to score.

As with Mikan's play, the implications shook the game to its very foundation. The pace of action and length of possessions were freed up to vary over the course of a game. Teams had choices to make; those that didn't were at a disadvantage.

The combined impact of Mikan and the shot clock (a response to both the big man and the strategy employed to stop him) worked to put time and space at the mercy of players and coaches. What made basketball modern was the notion that players and play itself were anything but uniform. This assertion of subjectivity opened up a host of possibilities; the parameters of action could now be manipulated and not merely accepted.

If you want a snapshot of the immediate post-Mikan, post-shot-clock era, look no further than the career of Bob Pettit. Pettit had the size of Mikan but with a diversified skill set that matched the changes afoot. Pettit wasn't simply an assertion of the value of difference—he cultivated it in his game. A tireless worker, he had starred at LSU but was considered too scrawny to amount to much as a pro center. Pettit landed with the Milwaukee Hawks, who already had 6′11″ Charlie Share in the starting lineup.

If Pettit was to have a chance at starting as a rookie in 1954, he would have to convert from center to forward. Surveying this brave new league, Pettit saw the upside of switching positions. He could alter his game, introducing an element of unpredictability that posed a new kind of challenge for defenders. As a center, he had played a back-to-the-basket game, but now he added a jump shot with range to spare. Pettit also turned himself into an impressive ball handler, whether going to the basket or on the break. He was a self-made superstar, one who worked to perfect a style suited to a league that was both bigger and faster than before. This understanding of how to exploit the new shifts in time and space also made Pettit a rebounding machine, pulling in 20.3 per game in 1960–61.

Pettit played eleven seasons, all for the Hawks, and made the All-Star team in each. His Hawks won the title in 1958, and Pettit himself was voted MVP twice. He retired in 1965, only thirty-two years old and still at the height of his powers—in his final season, he averaged 22.5 points and 12.4 rebounds. But Pettit claims that his career wasn't unusually short for his day; he has mused that "it was just time for me to move on, so that's what I did."

And in a sense, he was right. Pettit was the ideal weapon. But the game would soon change again. It's a testament to Pettit's ability that, as players entered the league who were at once more skilled and more physically gifted than he was, the Hawks forward remained a marquee talent. Even before Pettit got his title in 1958, players would find ways to further destabilize time and space. And to think, only a few decades earlier, it would have been an uneven backboard having all the fun. —*B.S.*

OTHER EARLY NBA NOTABLES:

GEORGE YARDLEY: Despite his gangly physique and premature baldness, "The Bird" was an accomplished dunker and a precursor to leaping white boys like Billy Cunningham and Bobby Jones. The first player to score 2,000 points in a season, Yardley played only seven seasons in the NBA, becoming the first player to retire after posting a 20-point average in his final season.

DOLPH SCHAYES: Schayes couldn't jump but he averaged 12.3 rebounds a game and, although he stood 6′8″, had a deadly outside game—often hitting two-handed set shots from 25–30 feet. A twelve-time All-Star in fifteen seasons, the indefatigable Schayes played 764 straight games, including nearly an entire season with his shooting arm in a cast, during which he developed excellent off-hand skills.

WATARU "WAT" MISAKA: Although Misaka appeared in only three games for the Knicks in 1947, he earned his place in the history books for being the first non-white person to play in the NBA (then known as the BAA). A 5′7″ Japanese American from Utah, he predated the first African American players in the NBA by three years.

	1957	1958	1959	1960	1961
NBA FINALS CHAMPION	BOSTON CELTICS	ST. LOUIS HAWKS	BOSTON CELTICS		
FINALS LOSER	HAWKS	CELTICS	LAKERS	HAWKS	
MOST VALUABLE PLAYER	BOB COUSY	BILL RUSSELL	BOB PETTIT	W. CHAMBERLAIN	BILL RUSSELL
POINTS per game leader	Paul Arizin **25.6**	George Yardley **27.8**	Bob Pettit **29.2**	W. Chamberlain **37.6**	W. Chamberlain **38.4**
REBOUNDS per game leader	Bill Russell **19.6**	Bill Russell **22.7**	Bill Russell **23.0**	W. Chamberlain **27.0**	W. Chamberlain **27.2**
ASSISTS per game leader	Bob Cousy **7.5**	Bob Cousy **7.1**	Bob Cousy **8.6**	Bob Cousy **9.5**	O. Robertson **9.7**

THEY WALKED THIS EARTH

1957–1969

The history of the NBA breaks down neatly into decades with one notable exception: This thirteen-year stretch, when the Boston Celtics tromped the planet without mercy. With Red Auerbach in command and Bill Russell prowling the lane, the Celtics won eleven championships; others could push, but in the end Boston almost inevitably came out on top. That made for a whole generation of players whose careers were thwarted, or frustrated, by this run of success. Wilt Chamberlain, Elgin Baylor, Jerry West, and Oscar Robertson, among others, had to content themselves with being some of the greatest and most influential players to ever lace up sneakers. What's more, with Russell, Wilt, Baylor, and the ill-fated Maurice Stokes, African Americans were given a chance to contribute meaningfully—the other big story of this period, and not so separate from that of the Celtics. All this from a group that was barred from play, then suppressed, until they could be denied no longer.

1962	1963	1964	1965	1966	1967	1968	1969
		BOSTON CELTICS			PHILA. 76ERS	BOSTON CELTICS	
LAKERS		WARRIORS	LAKERS		WARRIORS	LAKERS	
BILL RUSSELL	**BILL RUSSELL**	**O. ROBERTSON**	**BILL RUSSELL**	**W. CHAMBERLAIN**	**W. CHAMBERLAIN**	**W. CHAMBERLAIN**	**WES UNSELD**
W. Chamberlain **50.4**	W. Chamberlain **44.8**	W. Chamberlain **36.9**	W. Chamberlain **34.7**	W. Chamberlain **33.5**	Rick Barry **35.6**	O. Robertson **29.2**	Elvin Hayes **28.4**
W. Chamberlain **25.6**	W. Chamberlain **24.3**	Bill Russell **24.7**	Bill Russell **24.1**	W. Chamberlain **24.6**	W. Chamberlain **24.2**	W. Chamberlain **23.8**	W. Chamberlain **21.1**
O. Robertson **11.4**	Guy Rodgers **10.4**	O. Robertson **11.0**	O. Robertson **11.5**	O. Robertson **11.1**	Guy Rodgers **11.2**	O. Robertson **9.7**	O. Robertson **9.8**

GREEN AND BLACK AND RED ALL OVER

The Mind and Spirit of Auerbach's Über-Dynasty

STOGIES: Cousy called Auerbach's victory-cigar ritual "the single most arrogant act in sports." During his career Red smoked, in chronological order, Robert Burns, Antonio y Cleopatra, Hoyo de Monterrey, and Dutch Masters cigars.

RED VS. PURE AESTHETICS: In the seventies, Auerbach created a series of *Red on Roundball* instructional films for the NBA, featuring various stars from the league. For the most part, these clips cover useful subjects like how to set a solid pick. The lone exception came when Pete Maravich dropped by. Maravich engages in such spectacular feats as dribbling two balls between his legs very close to the ground and dropping and catching a ball behind his back with a clap in between. Red struggles valiantly to explain how these drills have any practical application.

Between 1957 and 1969, the Boston Celtics won eleven NBA championships, including eight straight from 1959–66. Usually, when we confront this kind of sustained, bone-pulping dominance, there's cause for uneasiness. At some point along the path to perpetual victory, souls are sold, man becomes machine. This is the banner of the twentieth century.

Yet while these Boston teams were ruthlessly efficient, they never forfeited their humanity. They reveled in it, in fact. The dynasty's architect, the loudmouthed, cigar-chomping Red Auerbach, might have come across as the unlikely hybrid of Mel Brooks and George C. Scott's Patton. Cinematically speaking, however, the best comparison is John Cassavetes. A film like *Husbands* may feel improvised, but Cassavetes never stopped clutching his script, and worked closely with his actors so they could approximate just the right kind of naturalism. Likewise, Auerbach put his players in chains so that they might really be free, limiting their roles so they might truly flourish.

When Auerbach came to the Celtics in 1950, basketball was unsophisticated, its teams made up of undifferentiated forwards and guards and a de facto center. Lakers coach John Kundla had started the league down the path toward specialization by designating one stronger forward and a principal ball handler. Having George Mikan, the NBA's first true anything (big man or otherwise), likely encouraged Kundla to move in this direction. But Auerbach made an art of role playing. Hot-shit guard Bob Cousy, who had learned his evasive dribbling and no-look distributing on integrated New York City courts, dominated the ball. This freed up Bill Sharman to pay attention to what he did best: get open shots and knock them down with a minimum of fuss. That makes Sharman the first pure shooting guard. Forward Frank Ramsey was undersized, perimeter-oriented, and preferred to come in off the bench as instant offense. He now holds the dual distinction of being both the NBA's first small forward and its first sixth man. Tommy Heinsohn's loopy inside-outside game makes him the forerunner of both tweener forwards and coach-sanctioned gunners. Defensive wizard Bill Russell has claimed that he himself could have scored more, but didn't deserve the touches.

Auerbach's philosophy allowed individualism and collective order not only to coexist amicably but to fuse into one. By pinpointing which individuals could contribute and making them better at it, Red fashioned himself a tool kit to work with. It was then his job to figure out exactly how all these finished products fit together and how best to employ them. Today these roles are part of basketball's vocabulary, but at the time they were just Auerbach's way of letting his players' strengths dictate the division of labor.

RED'S PUNCHING BAG: Auerbach never yelled at his two relatively introverted stars, Russell and Cousy, and he was loath to discipline Bill Sharman or Frank Ramsey, neither of whom responded well to criticism. He was also very sensitive about possibly demeaning black players. That left the perennially out-of-shape Tommy Heinsohn and his pack-a-day cigarette habit to bear the brunt of Auerbach's abuse.

That's not to say Red had no ideas of his own. Before coming to the Celtics, any team he'd coached, from D.C.-area high school up through his tenure with the BAA's Washington Capitols, had run the fast-break offense Auerbach learned from George Washington University's Bill Reinhart. However, in what one might sentimentally regard as his breakthrough as a coach, Auerbach had to learn to live with Bob Cousy. Auerbach's first seasons with Boston saw him grudgingly accept a star he did not want and then use this rare talent to defile his beloved fast break—all without violating his philosophy, and all because circumstance demanded it. Circumstance, in fact, was at the heart of his philosophy—a great American pragmatist if ever there was one.

When owner Walter Brown brought on Auerbach in time for the 1950 draft, Red had no interest in Holy Cross standout Cousy. The Celtics had been stockpiling regional college players in a largely futile ploy to boost attendance; Red wanted to win, not pander to fans, and thus angrily dismissed Cousy as yet another "local yokel." There were also questions as to whether Cousy's circuitous way with the rock wasn't just a little too fancy, or foreign, for the hard-nosed pro context. Auerbach got his way but would soon find himself stuck with Cousy anyway. The Tri-Cities Blackhawks drafted Cousy, then traded him to the Chicago Stags when contract negotiations stalled—Cousy was insisting on additional money for his dream business, a Massachusetts driving school. The Stags subsequently folded, and in a dispersal draft, the Celts drew Cousy's name from a hat.

Owner Walter Brown was elated, Red peevish. It didn't take

START
01
CELTICS
6
21

4
15
65
64
63

THE JAZZ-O-METER

1960s RATING: Very jazzy (90/100)

NAPTOWN NATIVES: Oscar Robertson was a big jazz fan and attended Crispus Attucks High School in Indianapolis with jazz musicians Freddie Hubbard, James Spaulding, and Larry Ridley. In recent years, Ridley has held a number of "Jazz & Basketball" motivational workshops with former Globetrotter Hallie Bryant, who also attended Crispus Attucks. Hubbard, in particular, had a reputation as a formidable basketball player, and, when asked about it in the immortal book *Notes and Tones*, he responds by name-dropping Kareem and boasting, "He knows it because I grew up with Oscar Robertson, and he's the baddest!"

GREEN NOTES: On the racially diverse Celtics teams of the era, almost all of the players loved jazz. The night after they won their tenth championship in 1968, the team went out to a jazz club to see Cannonball Adderley.

BIG SMALL'S: In 1961, Wilt Chamberlain bought the legendary jazz club Small's Paradise and gave it the awkward and oxymoronic name Big Wilt's Small's Paradise. One of the central nightclubs of the Harlem Renaissance, during Wilt's reign its performers were more likely to be soul acts such as James Brown or comedians such as Redd Foxx.

long for Auerbach to swallow his pride and acknowledge that, in fact, Bob Cousy was more than a native son with a crowd-pleasing game and a love of three-point turns. Had Red been less shrewd, he would have immediately turned Cousy loose on the break and ignited an entirely new style of play—except the shot clock was still four years away, which meant that stalling, the antithesis of what one would have expected from Auerbach and Cousy, was still the surest means of victory. Thus Auerbach employed Cousy's speed and vision to keep anything else from ever happening.

Mercifully, the shot clock was unveiled in 1954, and Auerbach promptly pushed the new rule to its logical (and quite sensible) extremes. More possessions meant more chances to score, and getting up the court before the defense could set up increased field goal percentage. With Cousy, Sharman, and Ed Macauley leading the way, the Celtics turned into a one-way bonanza—until, so the story goes, Auerbach got religion and procured the services of Russell, who would provide the defense (today, proverbially) needed to win championships. Except Russell's version of defense didn't slow down the game or stop the ball. It continuously looked to trigger the offense or shave transition down to an instant.

Red had never seen Russell play when, in 1956, he dealt the Hawks' Macauley and the rights to Cliff Hagan, a dreamy Kentucky standout then with the military, for Russell's draft rights. Reinhart had watched Russell as a junior at the University of San Francisco and convinced Red that this unconventional big man was the latest development in fast-break research. Russell's teammates funneled opposing players toward the rapacious center, and Russell got the ball back to them as fast as possible, sometimes not even bothering to make it past half-court himself. He could be seamlessly integrated into everything the team was already doing, thus creating a basketball Möbius strip as his defense led to more offense, which led to more defense. The Celtics could remain a free-flowing orgy of scoring, using only a handful of set plays and expecting their shooters to jack up attempts as soon as they saw the basket clearly.

Making Bill Russell the most important player on the Celtics was, to say the least, brazen. But, true to form, Auerbach either didn't bother to note the racial implications of the move or just wasn't particularly interested in them—even given Russell's strong political convictions and willingness to share them with others. In 1950, Auerbach backed Walter Brown's pick of Duquense's Chuck

Cooper, the first African American drafted into the NBA, because Coop could play. Now he was willing to give up two white future Hall of Famers for a young black player who would first gut and then renovate fully the edifice Red had built. What's more, while Russell needed some refining, he didn't need Auerbach to tell him who he was. Russell already understood how his skill set could most dramatically affect a game, and in Red he found the one coach who grasped how revolutionary he could be. Call them mentor and muse—there's no separating Auerbach from Russell. Russell was the totalizing factor that allowed Red's game plan to encompass both ends of the court.

Auerbach won his first championship in 1957, Russell's first year. The following season, Russell was the MVP, but due to an injury to the second-year center, Boston lost in the Finals to the Hawks and ex-Celtics Macauley and Hagan. They wouldn't cede the title again until 1967; after that, they tacked on two more for good measure.

Red's approach to sustaining the Celtics dynasty was no less distinctive. With a few notable exceptions, Auerbach was a firm, almost arrogant believer in "best available." He didn't attempt to clone players or turn specialization into standardization. In fact, as teams around the league were starting to process the lessons of Celtics 1.0, Auerbach was grooming a second wave that revamped the original team's division of labor. By the time Cousy retired in 1963, the Celtics had taken on more of Russell's personality—in both game and temperment. Sam Jones, K. C. Jones, John Havlicek, and Satch Sanders were all relentless defenders, exceptional athletes, and extremely capable scorers who sought balance above all else. Gone were all traces of the early NBA that had sometimes infected the Celtics, the egotism and lust for buckets that had reigned when contracts were based on scoring and when financial security was scarce. Sam Jones could take over games but preferred to do so only when necessary. This almost dismissive attitude toward individual glory was about as abrasive as well-balanced basketball gets. Playing a role was a form of professionalism and a point of pride, not an exercise in self-abnegation. And, just as important, the team's self-sacrifice was, as Nietzsche suggests, its own kind of pent-up swagger.

Celts 2.0 emerged gradually, propping up the Cousy/Heinsohn/Sharman teams while at the same time phasing out their style of play. The championships continued unabated, the vets wore down

DOUBLE-DIPPING: A number of Boston Celtics played other sports professionally.

BILL SHARMAN played in the Brooklyn Dodgers minor-league system from 1950 to 1955.

GENE CONLEY pitched in the majors for eleven seasons, posting a 91–86 record and a 3.82 ERA over his career.

K. C. JONES was drafted by the Los Angeles Rams despite not even playing college football.

JOHN HAVLICEK was drafted by both the Boston Celtics and the Cleveland Browns in 1962.

THE REAL MR. CLUTCH: Jerry West is Mr. Clutch, but among the Celtics, Sam Jones held the nickname. Using his patented bank shot, Jones averaged at least 23 points per game in five consecutive playoffs, including a 28.6 mark in 1965, when the Celtics defeated West's Lakers in a five-game Finals.

KICKIN' IT WITH KENNEDY: After the Celtics won their fifth straight NBA championship in 1963, the team was invited to the White House to meet the president. At the time, such visits had not yet become a tradition, and they were invited only because John F. Kennedy, being from Boston, was a huge Celtics fan. The players got to hang out in the Cabinet Room, pretending they were government officials and joking with the president. When Kennedy and the team said their good-byes, Tom "Satch" Sanders famously told JFK, "Take it easy, baby."

more slowly than they would have otherwise (and sometimes hung on longer than they should have), and the players who would define the team's future had to content themselves with supporting parts well into their primes. It was not until the retirement of the irreplaceable Russell, in 1969, that the team's regenerative process ground to a halt. But these extended apprenticeships were a key element of the Celtics culture. In 1964–65, the New Celtics became the first NBA team to field an all-black starting five when Willie Naulls stepped in for the injured, and aged, Heinsohn. The team played better with this lineup, and while it's tempting to claim that racism kept Naulls from retaining his starting spot, this analysis ignores precisely what kept this diverse bunch so tight: Heinsohn was taking his curtain call, and no matter who got the most minutes, he'd start as long as he was able. No one objected because no one questioned the value of respect.

Today Red Auerbach is a hero to those who espouse a conservative, coach-centric version of the game. That makes a certain amount of sense; he casts such a long shadow over the NBA's history that his name is synonymous with tradition, and nostalgia dictates that the game under Auerbach's watch was in some sense prelapsarian. Plus, the man shouted, cursed, stomped, and won like crazy. It's this perception of Auerbach and his teams that has led those who see coaches as subordinate to—or at least only as good as—their players to conclude that Celtics hegemony was just one big fucking drag.

However, now anyone with an Internet connection can readily watch footage of these teams racing down the floor, whipping the ball past defenders, and then knocking down a split-second jumper or finishing with brio—tough and focused, sure, but a hell of a lot of fun. Red's way speaks directly to the sphinxlike riddle of basketball: How do individual and team coexist in a way that makes the most of both? Auerbach's intermingling of player and team identity is perhaps his greatest insight. And, at the same, it's a nonanswer. That might explain why, to this day, no team has managed to replicate either Red's methods or the run of success they yielded. *—B.S.*

PRIDE OF THE CELTICS

Bill Russell and the Price of Winning

Bill Russell wasn't the NBA's first African American player, but he was its Jackie Robinson. When Robinson joined the Dodgers in 1947, he was allowed to bring more than his skin to the game. He got the chance to star, even forcing the sport to bend to his whim as a base runner. Robinson's entry into the major leagues had been so hard-fought, he practically had to back it up with jaw-dropping play.

By contrast, the integration of pro basketball came easier but was far less conclusive. Chuck Cooper (first drafted), Earl Lloyd (first to play in an NBA game), Nat "Sweetwater" Clifton (first to sign a contract), and Don Barksdale (first in the All-Star Game) broke the barriers. Their experiences weren't anywhere near as harrowing as what Robinson faced. NCAA hoops was mixed; the color barrier had already been broken in baseball; most pros came from major cities and attended college; and with the exception of St. Louis, all NBA cities were above the Mason-Dixon. Nevertheless, these athletes endured taunts, slurs, indignity, and, perhaps worst of all, neglect. Black players were supposedly valued for their defense yet were assigned to guard only each other—knowing the ball likely wasn't coming their way. Letting African Americans into the NBA was no problem; it was what happened next that left the likes of Cooper and Barksdale feeling they had been wasted.

Maybe basketball's less virulent attitudes about race were a mixed blessing; it's also possible that this was an object lesson in urban versus rural forms of prejudice. It was only with Bill Russell's rookie year that a black player would, like Robinson, be given a chance to really justify his presence. Red Auerbach handpicked Russell to complete his team. Russell answered the call by redefining stardom, upending the league's offense-first mentality, and delivering a championship to the Celtics. African Americans had been consigned to the game's dirty work, practically ensuring that none would grab the spotlight

THE ART OF THE PSYCH-OUT: In a 1965 article for *Sports Illustrated*, Russell declared that psyching out the opponent was the difference between winning and losing. His primary tactics involved attacking rookies early, generally forcing players out of their established habits as often as possible, and knowing how to "steer" players into specific areas of the court. Russell also hit on the tenets of advanced statistical work, noting that the difference between a 6-point and a 10-point lead is relatively minimal—the real difference is in the mind.

FREE RADICAL: As a student at USF, Russell enjoyed going to coffeehouses in the city's North Beach district and visiting clubs to see Mort Sahl and Pete Seeger: "Those coffeehouses opened up a new way of thinking for me, because I saw that at least some white people got the blues, were irreverent, and weren't tight-assed. Most of the white folks at USF walked like moving fence posts, while the beatniks looked more like sloping question marks."

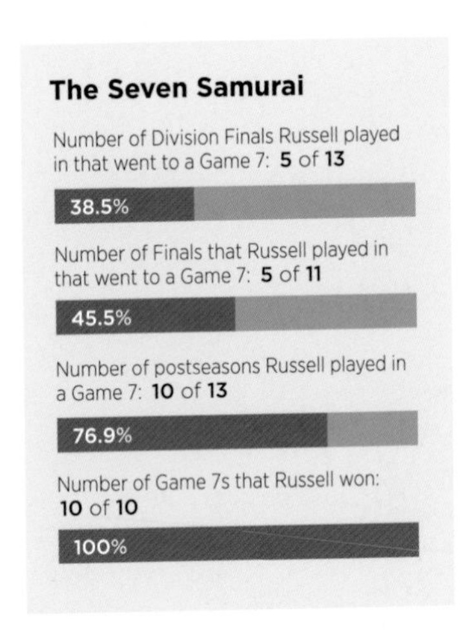

STARS OF TRACK AND FIELD: The seven-foot barrier was the last frontier for high jumpers in the mid-twentieth century, and Bill Russell came very close to being the first one to break it. While at USF, he won the event at the 1956 West Coast Relays with a jump of 6 feet 9 1/4 inches, even though he rarely practiced and had an unorthodox style ("I wore a silk scarf, basketball shoes, and black glasses"). That year, *Track and Field News* ranked Russell as the seventh-best high jumper in the world. Wilt Chamberlain was also an accomplished all-around track-and-field athlete. At Kansas, he won the high jump at the Big Eight championships in 1958, and also competed in the shot put and 100-yard dash.

as Robinson had. Russell subverted this stereotype by taking a highly cerebral approach to what had formerly been considered unskilled labor—the fifties-NBA equivalent of reappropriating the n-word.

The Great Nicknameless One was a late bloomer whose entire career rested on a single breakthrough before his senior year of high school. Then an afterthought as a player, Russell had been invited on a barnstorming tour because of his height. Daydreaming on the bus, Russell began visualizing his teammates' moves on offense. He then saw the faint outlines of himself alongside them, going after the ball instead of looking to put it into the hoop. Coupling this intuition with his height and leaping ability, Russell devised a new form of virtuosity to replace the relatively static raised arm. His teammates soon referred to his blocked shots as "Russell moves" the way the automobile was once called the Model-T.

His sole scholarship offer came from the University of San Francisco, where he and fellow Celtics teammate K. C. Jones led the Dons to titles in 1955 and 1956. The Dons harnessed defense, jumping, and creativity in ways that all-white teams had barely begun to imagine, elements of "Negro basketball" that, at the time, were hardly standard NCAA praxis. In particular, Russell's dunks, sometimes off alley-oops, stupefied opponents. Coach Phil Woolpert insisted the team exercise some discipline, but Russell was already intent on refining his game. For all the exultation of the Dandy Dons, Russell understood that unfettered athleticism would never be enough. Russell and Jones spent endless hours in the gym working out the geometry of rebounds, concluding that it was the horizontal axis that mattered most. Sometimes Russell would alter a shot without even making a play on the ball, toying with opponents in the same way that Robinson did on the base paths.

Two titles in college, and then the seemingly endless run as a Celtic. You can say Russell did all the little things, was the consummate unselfish basketball player, or knew the game inside and out. You can cite "intangibles" or observe that Russell was far more skilled than he's usually given credit for. To wit: Every year he was on the Celtics, Russell finished second on the team in assists. Russell's most impressive play, the blocked shot, wouldn't even be recorded officially until 1973–74. And even then the numbers wouldn't have meant a thing. While anecdotal numbers kept by the center and others suggest that Russell had his fair share of triple-doubles, what mattered was his ability to keep the ball in play. If the Celtics lost possession, Russell hadn't done his job.

Mostly, though, he just won, shaping an entire decade while only sporadically dropping more than 20 points. His ability to influence outcomes bordered on mystical. Yet Russell himself, while not lacking confidence, was a skeptic by nature. The label of "winner" had so thoroughly wormed its way into Russell's brain that each pregame was a tribulation. When he first came into the league, he would enter an anxious, trancelike state and vomit before each game. This practice didn't spring from cowardice or self-doubt but anxiety in the German sense (thrown out into utter meaninglessness and uncertainty) or the French (urge to jump off a bridge with thick glasses on). In those moments, Russell stood on the precipice, undefined. To him, "winner" wasn't a compliment, it was an existential bind. Eventually, Russ managed to suppress his meditative gag reflex in all but the really momentous contests; this only amplified the significance of the ritual.

Contrast this solemnity with Red's extroverted, almost farcical, victory cigar. The puking and the cigar were total opposites: Russell purifying, negating, and expunging in preparation for the unknown; Red marking a fait accompli with pollution, celebration, and materialism.

Russell was the first African American MVP, the first to be without question the most important player on his team, a member of the first all-black starting five, the league's first black coach, and the first black coach to win a title. Yet despite his all-business exterior on the court, Russell was hardly a model employee. He was moody, stubborn, and had practice habits that would make Allen Iverson blush. When he was named Red's successor in 1967, it was in large part because no one else wanted to deal with him—and he wouldn't take orders from anyone but Auerbach. Russell was simply unquestioned when it came to making a case for himself as a professional athlete.

This wasn't his struggle, though. Russell was after a different kind of recognition, and herein lies his dilemma. Unflinchingly progressive and an avid reader, music lover, and art collector, Russell was a renaissance man when it was inconceivable to many that athletes, least of all black athletes, came outfitted with brains. Russell insisted on being viewed as much more than a dumb jock,

PURGE OR SPLURGE: Bill Russell's habit of vomiting before each game is unique, as it involves the expulsion of matter; most other players' pregame rituals involve some sort of ingestion:

BILL SHARMAN: Religiously drank a cup of tea with honey to give him energy before each game.

DARRELL ARMSTRONG: Taking a more vigorous approach, Armstrong drank at least six cups of coffee with almost a pound of sugar before each match.

RAY ALLEN: Self-described as borderline OCD, Allen would eat chicken and white rice at precisely 2:30 P.M. each and every game day.

ROD STRICKLAND: Was notorious for gorging on hot dogs from the press room before each game. In an inadvertent tribute to Russell, he scarfed down so many frankfurters before a March 1998 contest in New Jersey he vomited on the court.

THE COLLECTOR: Bill Russell was the first African American player to seriously collect art—he owns numerous African sculptures as well as work by artists such as Phoebe Beasley—making him a precursor to these other modern-day athletic aesthetes:

CHRIS WEBBER: His collection of African American artifacts spans four centuries and features pieces related to African American icons like Phillis Wheatley and Booker T. Washington. A representative example: Frederick Douglass's cane, which has illustrations from his autobiography carved into it.

RAY ALLEN: Primarily focused on blue-chip twentieth-century artists, Allen owns pieces by Joan Miró, Andy Warhol, and Marc Chagall.

GRANT HILL: Owns a substantial collection of African American art, with a focus on Romare Bearden, John Biggers, and Elizabeth Catlett.

SHAQUILLE O'NEAL: Curated a gallery show titled Size DOES Matter featuring art-world heavyweights like Andreas Gursky, Cindy Sherman, and Maurizio Cattelan. Has stated that he plans on commissioning an oversized sculpture of himself from hyperrealist sculptor Ron Mueck. Shaq said, "I would like him to make it two stories high . . . put it in the middle of a residential neighborhood . . . and in the head I'd have my office."

scary specimen, or hapless bouncing body. What speaks of the real Bill Russell, though, is the fact that he did so when it was both impossibly bold and almost certain to backfire.

In this sense, he was the anti–Jackie Robinson. Sports was never enough; Russell wanted to be seen as more, wanted those who praised his play to also confront everything else he stood for. Instead he was dismissed or ignored, much as Cooper, Barksdale, and others had been on the court—even when he went on record as opposing the Vietnam War in 1963, or used his government-sponsored goodwill trips to hang around the favorite haunts of African revolutionaries. White athletes at least had the option of being whole people; apparently, when the athlete was black, he had to fight for every inch. Muhammad Ali made people acknowledge him by converting to an exotic religion, changing his name, dodging the draft, and shooting his mouth off with abandon. Russell was just deliberate enough for everyone to look the other way.

And then there was Boston, which Russell called "a flea market of racism." You could not have picked a less hospitable place for Russell's "I am somebody" expectations of stardom. Russell had grown up in rural Louisiana and then in Oakland, giving him experience with the Deep South climate that would give rise to international outrage and the same streets that spawned the Black Panthers. By the time he joined the Celtics, Russell was among the athletes called on by Dr. King to make appearances at movement events. Back in Beantown, the city to which he would eventually bring eleven titles, his suburban home was broken into and smeared with shit. Most black Celtics drew a sharp distinction between the city and the franchise, and with good reason. Teammate K. C. Jones had a cross burned on his lawn, African American Celtics couldn't join the city's country clubs, and their white teammates received endorsement deals galore while even Russell received no local offers. To keep themselves motivated, the Celtics dedicated each new stab at a championship to some new cause or other. Cousy's last season, Red's farewell, Heinsohn's curtain call . . . there was camaraderie at stake, but it almost seemed redundant. There was something almost satirical here, or, more depressing, an admission that the Celtics were a world unto themselves, and that "doing it for the fans"—fans who in a second would turn on African American players, whose interest in hockey tickets topped their interest in the Celtics even as the team piled up trophies—simply wasn't an option. Boston, and the nation as a whole, needed Bill Russell to be the ultimate winner on the court. Anything beyond that was an inconvenience, and any problems Russell had with that arrangement were his own damn fault. On principle, Russell refused to sign autographs, and at one point took to sending out a glossy photograph of himself emblazoned with a favorite observation of his: "We learn to make a shell for ourselves when we are young and then spend the rest of our lives hoping for someone to reach inside and touch us. Just touch us—anything more than that would be too much for us to bear." Instead of engaging in a simple transaction, Russell held forth on the human condition and, perhaps, his own limitations as a public figure—all of which, to many fans, just made him look like more of an asshole.

After leaving basketball, Russell split with his wife and took off for Los Angeles with little more than his Lamborghini to his name. There, he wandered around dressed, in his own words, "exactly like the official composite description of your typical hijacker." He had a popular drive-time radio show, was a draw on the college speaking circuit, and played a lot of golf with Jim Brown. Russell remained opinionated, though he had mellowed to some degree. He was no longer fighting against the gag order of athletic stardom; now he was just another famous name, from somewhere, hanging out in southern California. When he returned to the NBA as coach of the Sonics, he didn't expect his players to match him or the Celtics; he wanted only to share his knowledge of the game with the kids. Instead it was Boston all over again, but with the generation gap standing in for race.

Then again, Russell may very well have been dissatisfied with a roster full of eager pupils. He just didn't care about making people accept him if it was too easy or if he knew they'd never understand. Russell wanted so badly to really reach out and touch others, but if others remained content with simply marveling at his NBA résumé, something was missing. That's why it's possible that Russell's dynastic years may have also been, in a sense, the man's greatest disappointment. His career is a marvel, the closest sports gets to utter triumph. Yet this presumes that, for Russell, basketball was the only thing at stake. *—B.S.*

RUBBER MEETS THE ROAD: In 1963, at the height of the civil rights movement, Russell became interested in the idea of moving to Africa. After visiting twice, he and a friend bought 200,000 acres of land in Liberia, on which they built a rubber plantation. Russell later spent part of the off-season in Liberia, managing the plantation and hunting in the jungle. Although he talked about retiring in Liberia and invested a total of $250,000 in the plantation, it eventually went bankrupt.

THE SOUND SALVATION: The most impressive player-DJ was Don Barksdale, the league's first African American All-Star. Before integration, Barksdale was the Bay Area's first black DJ and hosted a late-night love-line program in Oakland. Hall of Fame football coach Bill Walsh remembered Barksdale's "deep mellow voice" on KDIA: "His voice used to make me fall in love with my date. I'd try the deep voice, but all I got was the steamed-up windows and the dead battery."

13
PHILA

THE NUCLEAR OPTION

Wilt Chamberlain, the Man Who Went Too Far

We're used to thinking of history as both bigger and smaller than the present: bigger in that it often takes on the glare of mythology; smaller as it's seen in the rearview, giving the impression that we've surpassed it. Then there are figures like Wilt Chamberlain, whose body of work is most staggering when we drag it, kicking and screaming, into the harsh light of the present. Wilt dropped 100 in a single contest, averaged 50 for a season, and obliterated the NBA record book during the first leg of his career. We're all too used to explaining away this kind of freak occurrence. But Chamberlain didn't simply dominate basketball or alter its course. Like no one before or since, he threatened to outmode it.

WILT DESTROYED MY LIFE: B. H. Born was the Most Valuable Player of the 1953 NCAA Finals. He played Chamberlain one-on-one when Wilt was still a teenager and lost 25–10. Born was so dejected that he gave up a promising NBA career and became a tractor engineer ("If there were high school kids that good, I figured I wasn't going to make it to the pros").

Writing during Chamberlain's time at the University of Kansas, Jimmy Breslin titled a *Saturday Evening Post* column "Can Basketball Survive Wilt Chamberlain?" Given the climate of the times, it's hard not to view Chamberlain as a dramatization of some larger cultural anxieties. Americans lived in constant fear of nuclear annihilation, their might as a nation suddenly irrelevant in the face of a single fissile weapon; tromping through college and then the pros, Chamberlain was that dread in basketball form. The NBA was, in Wilt's own words, a "bush league," but he brought out fans in droves and attracted an unprecedented amount of media attention. It was as if Wilt not only imperiled basketball but reminded spectators that the whole world likewise hung by a thread. This was bigger than basketball—at bottom, it was sports as cold war performance art.

Yet despite his massive numbers, wealth, and jet-setting lifestyle, Wilt was fundamentally ill at ease. He was an exceptionally sensitive man who wanted nothing more than to love and be loved. Early on, he had to be reassured by Eddie Gottlieb, owner of the Philadelphia Warriors, that his public image was endlessly good for business. Chamberlain's famous utterance "Nobody roots for Goliath" is widely misunderstood as a commentary on being

THE CHAMBERLAIN ARGUMENT: Wilt Chamberlain even penetrated the lofty world of political theory. In his 1974 work *Anarchy, State, and Utopia,* libertarian political philosopher Robert Nozick invoked Wilt to show that the concept of just distribution advocated by liberal theorist John Rawls was incompatible with liberty. In the Wilt Chamberlain Argument, Nozick argues that if every person in a society of one million people gave Wilt a quarter, thus creating a huge disparity between Wilt and everyone else, it would still be a just society because each person freely gave him that quarter. Basically, Wilt was such an exceptional human being that when Nozick wanted to argue that not all men are created equal, he turned to Chamberlain as the most obvious example.

tall. But Wilt knew full well what he was doing to the sport, that as a player he was both riveting and reviled, a prodigious athlete painted as a rampaging freak. Don't forget, it took a miracle for David to slay Goliath; we take his side as much out of relief as out of respect for the Judeo-Christian hero. Chamberlain took public opinion personally, and as his career wound on, he was increasingly guided by a need to prove others wrong or to get out from under misperceptions about him. Wilt also had a remarkably ambivalent relationship with his own strength. He refused to go full bore around the basket for fear he might maim an opponent. That's how he came to develop a fadeaway jumper that, for a seven-footer, was decidedly ahead of its time. Some fearful white people interpreted this quality as sinister and, yes, probably nefariously Soviet; David Wolf wrote that, for black fans, this approach was the epitome of badness that needed not show its hand.

At every turn, Wilt found himself creating a new kind of spectacle—whether or not he wanted to. We're now accustomed to seeing high schoolers hyped up as the Next Big Thing, treated like All-Stars, and given their choice of big-ticket college programs. At Overbrook High School in Philly, Chamberlain was the first. Recruited by over two hundred schools, Chamberlain finally chose Kansas because Phog Allen was a disciple of Naismith, a link back to the game's origin that's touching, humble, and, given the apocalyptic pall Wilt would soon cast over the sport, faintly Oedipal. While Wilt bided his time with the JV squad, the NCAA set about altering its rules to lessen his eventual impact. Based on his performances in exhibition games, the governing body of college hoops preemptively outlawed offensive goaltending and in-bounds passes over the backboard, another Chamberlain favorite. Throughout his career, Wilt struggled with his foul shooting (he found his greatest success shooting granny style in 1960, but gave it up, worried it made him look "like a sissy"). In practice that season, he decided to just dunk them in, taking off from the line. The NCAA caught wind of these experiments and immediately passed a rule against breaking the plane on free-throw attempts.

Chamberlain joined the varsity in 1956. In his first game, he went for 52 points and 31 rebounds, breaking two college records to announce his arrival. However, he never delivered a title to Lawrence. In 1957, an overmatched Jayhawks team lost the championship to UNC in a triple-overtime threnody that launched the "great individual player, but a loser" meme. As a junior, Chamberlain faced ceaseless triple teams and got little help from his teammates, so he bolted a year early to chase tail with the Globetrotters in Europe. For some reason, Wilt saw fit to continue this tradition even after he became the biggest thing going in the NBA, which says a lot about both his feelings for the game and how totally weird Wilt could be. Bill Russell and Oscar Robertson bristled at the thought of playing for Abe Saperstein, but Chamberlain saw it as a nice vacation and a chance to make people happy. His critics wanted a villain, death's head with a finger roll. Instead they were often left shaking their heads or pulling at their hair.

In 1959 he joined the Philadelphia Warriors, who had diabolically employed the league's territorial draft to snag Chamberlain as a high school junior. He immediately became the most overwhelming offensive force the league had ever seen. The numbers can leave you punch-drunk: For 1959–60, he averaged 37.6 points and 27 rebounds, a natural disaster bearing down on what had previously been a nice, friendly hamlet adjusting to black players and faster play. Goliath, though, was more than a mere giant. Watching him in his prime, you're immediately struck by the squiggly moves and flashes of velocity in Wilt's game. One especially telling photo, from 1964, captures a taut, rippling Chamberlain on the verge of a dunk against St. Louis. He hoists the ball high over his head in one hand, about to throw down the "dipper dunk" that gave him his nickname of choice (he found "The Stilt" objectifying). His head is nearly up at the rim, his lower body battering with the shoulders of hapless Hawk center Zelmo Beaty. Wilt looks every bit the former high jumper, as well as the ogre who could snap off limbs if he didn't take care, even in midair. The three other Hawks in the frame have distanced themselves from the action, leaning away as if to spare themselves from a sonic boom. Their eyes bug out in amazement, even though we know they have seen this all before.

If Wilt could be terrifying, outrageous, transcendent, and even profane, there was always the counterweight of Russell, the gold standard for nobility in basketball. In fact, Chamberlain seemed capable of anything but being Russell. The Russell/Wilt binaries have since become staples of NBA discourse: team/individual; unselfish/selfish; defense/offense; effort/natural talent; absolute devotion to the game/wavering interest; results/stats; and, most

THE MEN WHO LOVED ONLY NUMBERS: In his 1991 memoir *View from Above*, Chamberlain infamously claimed to have bedded more than 20,000 women in his lifetime, including Kim Novak and Dixie Carter of *Designing Women*. This puts him in competition with these other great lovers from history:

GEORGES SIMENON: The prolific Belgian writer claims to have slept with more than 10,000 women, including Josephine Baker.

MOULAY ISMAIL IBN SHARIF: The ruler of the Moroccan empire during the seventeenth and eighteenth centuries is alleged to have fathered 888 children with a harem of 500 women.

WARREN BEATTY: Hollywood's most notorious bachelor had approximately 12,775 sex partners, according to Peter Biskind's biography *Star: How Warren Beatty Seduced America*.

viciously, winner/loser. Russell's greatness is enhanced by keeping the superhuman Wilt at bay. Wilt, for all his grand doings, later said he felt he had to win two championships to truly prove himself. In 1979, Russell himself wrote, "I can't think of any two players in a team sport who have been cast as antagonists and as personifications of various theories more than Wilt and I were. Almost any argument people wanted to have could be carried on in the Russell vs. Chamberlain debate, and almost any virtue and sin was imagined to be at stake."

Between 1959 and Russell's retirement in 1969, the two played against each other 142 times, an average of 14 games a year. They almost always met in the playoffs, either in the Eastern Finals or for the title, depending on what team Wilt was with. In 1961–62 alone, the Celtics and Wilt's Warriors faced each other 19 times. It should come as no surprise that Chamberlain's 1966–67 Sixers were the team that broke Boston's eight-year championship streak. In addition to Wilt, the team had stars Billy Cunningham, Chet Walker, and Hal Greer on its roster, making for a squad that could match any of the Celtics teams. They got the ring and set what was then the all-time record for team wins, with 68, providing the ultimate vindication for Wilt as winner and teammate. Yet, as if unaware of the significance of this season, in 1967–68 he still made a churlish point of leading the league in assists in the hope that it would inoculate him once and for all against criticisms of selfishness. It's a macho journalistic cliché to write that some athletes "don't get it," but sometimes you have to wonder if the game came too easily to Wilt for him to ever inhabit it naturally.

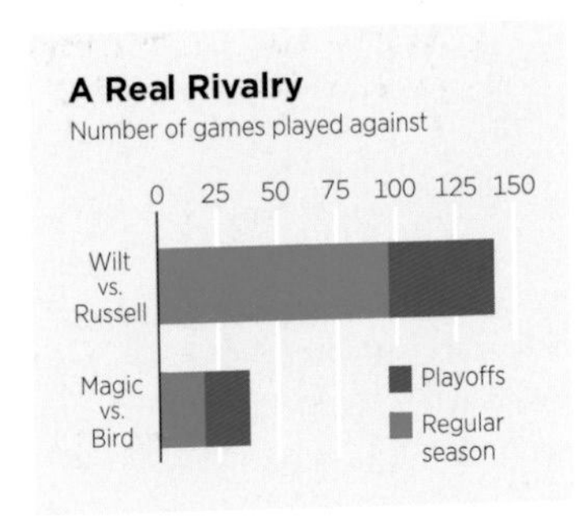

THE WEIRD WARRIORS: The 68-win, title-winning 1966–67 Philadelphia 76ers are rightfully considered the best team Wilt ever played on, but don't discount the ingenuity and all-around charm of the 1959–60 Philadelphia Warriors, his first team. In addition to Chamberlain, the Warriors had Guy Rodgers, a high school opponent of Wilt's and an early innovator of the alley-oop who regularly threw passes off the backboard for Wilt to send home; Woody Sauldsberry, the Rookie of the Year in 1958 and the first prototype for the point forward position; and an aging Paul Arizin. Naturally, the Warriors finished second in the East at 49–26 and lost to the Celtics in the Conference Finals.

In Game 7 of the 1969 Finals—Russell's last, Wilt's first with the Lakers—Chamberlain removed himself with six minutes remaining in the fourth to briefly recover from a banged shin. When he asked to reenter the game, coach Butch van Breda Kolff, who had spent the entire season feuding with his star center, refused. The Celtics won, again, and questions swirled about the severity of the injury and whose decision it had been to keep Chamberlain out. Russell retired and went on a tour of campuses, where he responded to a question about the game with, "Any injury short of a broken leg or a broken back is not enough," making national news and leading to a rift between the two giants that neither seemed inclined to sort out. It certainly didn't help matters that Chamberlain had campaigned for Nixon in 1968. Wilt could be stubborn and defensive when it came to matters of race;

politically, he was a libertarian who resented the notion that he was automatically property of the Democrats. It's also possible Wilt saw some of his own agitated melancholy in Tricky Dick.

Wilt got his second title in 1972, along with a 69-win season that topped the single-season mark he'd help set with the Sixers. Yet he seemed more distant from the NBA than ever. He took up residence in the hills of Bel Air, hosting parties in a Frank Lloyd Wright–inspired home he had helped design. His two enormous white Great Danes were his constant companions, and Wilt would descend, Zarathustra-like, from his fortress to do his job with the Lakers or play some beach volleyball—his real passion. For 1972–73, his final season, Wilt averaged a career-low 13.2 points per game but managed a league-best 18.6 rebounds each night and an absurd field goal average of .727, still a record. He was thirty-six years old and would entertain thoughts of a return to the NBA as late as fifty, when the Nets and Cavs both approached him about a comeback. Chamberlain likely would have given it a shot if anyone, including himself, had doubted for a second that Wilt could contribute. Even in retirement, this was part of being Wilt Chamberlain: Proving a point was less important than knowing he never had to prove a thing.

Wilt died of a heart attack in 1999, at the age of sixty-three. By then, the 20,000 women he claimed to have bedded rivaled the 100-point game as the number that summarized his life; the Berlin Wall had fallen, the Red Scare was over, and with Chamberlain, too, the looming menace of the past had given way to garish consumption. Appropriately, Russell delivered one of the most moving tributes of all at the funeral. The public couldn't know, but Chamberlain and Russell had actually been close friends through most of their playing days. As they became aware of the historic significance of their rivalry, there was a thaw. The grudge that had built up over time gave way to warm, spirited images of the pair—Russell graying and magisterial, Wilt balding and outlandishly fit despite the heart trouble he kept secret—that are nearly as powerful as the ones of them locked in combat under the basket.

Standing next to a gigantic casket and a photo of a middle-aged Chamberlain, Russell was handed the microphone, paused, and then, looking at the ground, uttered a single line: "Today, I am unspeakably injured." —*B.S.*

THE THIRD MAN: Chamberlain and Russell lorded over the big men of their era, but don't discount Nate Thurmond. In fourteen seasons, from 1963 to 1977, Big Nate made seven All Star Games, scored at least 20 points per game in five seasons, topped 16 rebounds per game eight times, and earned five All-Defensive honors. In 1974, Thurmond registered the league's first recorded quadruple-double, and he is one of only four players to grab 40 rebounds in one game.

THE TRANQUILLITY OF TRAINS: Contrary to the public perception of their on-court rivalry, for most of their careers Russell and Chamberlain were good friends off the court, and affectionately called each other by their middle names, Felton and Norman. Russell had Thanksgiving dinner at Chamberlain's house for six consecutive years while they were players, and when their teams faced off in Boston, Chamberlain would stay at Russell's home, where the duo would spend hours watching and playing with the model-train universe Russell had set up in his basement.

THREE ON A MATCH

Elgin Baylor, Jerry West, and Oscar Robertson

So the Celtics weren't exactly a repudiation of the individual. But as hive-minds go, they were damn close to perfection, dispensing with the rest of the league and flipping a giant middle finger to teams built around more salient stars. Wilt at least was in the frame. He broke Boston's streak, at any given time was their chief competition, and provided the only possible counterargument to their way of doing business. That left Elgin Baylor, Jerry West, and Oscar Robertson, the three greatest casualties of Boston's scorched-earth decade, to make do with something between bad luck and outright tragedy.

Baylor took the Minneapolis Lakers to the Finals in 1959, his rookie year, only to be swept by Boston. West joined him on the team in 1960; the pair lost to Boston in the Finals six times between 1962 and 1969. In the early going of 1971–72, the thirty-seven-year-old Baylor gave up his roster spot to improve L.A.'s chances, after which they promptly embarked upon an NBA-record 33-game win streak. West finally got his title that season; Baylor was given a ring as a tribute to his years of service, but he likely saw it as a show of pity. As for Robertson, his Cincinnati Royals prospered early on before falling into disarray, due in no small part to a benighted, at times openly negligent, ownership. He demanded a trade to Milwaukee, then played sidekick to Lew Alcindor as the Bucks went all the way in 1971.

For a bunch of losers, Baylor, West, and Robertson have had no problem achieving immortality. Each of them forged a template for superstardom that has persisted to this day. Baylor is recognized as the father of all high fliers. West is Mr. Clutch despite his inability to win the big one, and it's his silhouette, not Russell's or Cousy's, that's on the NBA logo. Robertson was prickly and demanding, but he's synonymous with the all-around excellence of the triple-double. That Baylor only sort of got a title, and West and Robertson had to wait for theirs, only underscores how important their individual contributions were to the sport.

GREEN ESTEEM: Though neither Baylor, West, nor Robertson was ever able to halt Boston's reign of terror, there were no three players the Celtics had more respect for:

BAYLOR: "I say without reservation that Elgin Baylor is the greatest corner-man who ever played pro basketball." *—Bill Sharman, speaking at Baylor's retirement in 1971*

WEST: "Jerry, you are, in every sense of the word, truly a champion. If I could have one wish granted, it would be that you would always be happy." *—Bill Russell, speaking at the Forum before West's last game in 1974*

OSCAR: "I told my players to hold their hands as high as possible and spread their fingers wider apart to get more reach. So Oscar shot between their fingers."*—Red Auerbach, explaining why the Celtics were unable to stop Robertson in 1964*

FIRST IN FLIGHT

Elgin Baylor was named after his father's watch. Four decades later, Elgin Baylor Lumpkin, who went on to become the raunchy, space-age R&B vocalist Ginuwine, was named after him. Baylor, the 6′5″, 225-pound forward who spent his entire career with the Lakers, is basketball's stylistic bridge between gentlemanly timekeeping and stuttering syncopation. He's generally credited with breaking the game's vertical plane. However, like the Wright Brothers', his accomplishments should not be measured in feet. Don't watch newsreels of Baylor expecting to see him kissing the rim or cradling the ball way up above a sea of defenders. Compared to those who followed in his footsteps, Baylor played a more subtle game, a series of broken dribbles, lateral glides, and exploratory parries that resolved into either a bounding drive or high jumper. Cat-quick and muscular, Baylor scrambled opponents' expectations instead of trampling them.

GOD'S HEAD FAKE: Baylor had an advantage beyond his basketball skills: a facial tic that freaked out and confused defenders.

Academic troubles nearly kept Baylor out of college. He ended up at the College of Idaho, initially there on a football scholarship despite his lack of any organized gridiron experience. Baylor got in one season before transferring to Seattle University, lured by fond memories of the 5′9″ post-playing twins John and Ed O'Brien. The O'Briens had led Seattle to a victory over a still-legit Globetrotters team in 1952. In 1956–57, his first year with SU, Baylor just missed averaging 30 points and 20 rebounds per game.

A first-team All-American the following year, Baylor decided to skip his final year of eligibility and enter the 1958 NBA draft—not exactly early entry, but it was the first time a player would assert that he'd exhausted what college ball held for him by leaving before he had to. Coach Van Sweet of the College of the Pacific was happy to see him go, calling Baylor "too far advanced for the college game." The abject Minneapolis Lakers took him first overall, expecting him to turn the team around and improve their gate receipts. Baylor did both. He averaged 24.9 points per game, including a 55-point performance that, at the time, was the third best in league history. If Russell's impact had been lost on some, Baylor left no doubt as to where things were headed.

GREATEST SHOW ON EARTH: The Lakers were in such dire straits before Baylor's arrival that team president Bob Short pulled out all the stops to market the team in 1958. Before the first game of the season, he had the team paraded through the streets in a series of National Guard jeeps, with coach John Kundla out front in a tank.

Then, in 1959, Wilt Chamberlain touched down in the league and suddenly Baylor's overall shock value dwindled. Wilt had the bigger numbers, and in an era when national telecasts were rare, this earned him the headlines. Never mind that Baylor himself averaged 34.8, 38.3, and 34 points per game from 1960–61 to

STARS RECOGNIZE STARS: The success of Baylor and the Lakers in Los Angeles helped make the Memorial Sports Arena a hot spot for Hollywood talent. Some of the most frequent attendees were Dean Martin, Bing Crosby, and Doris Day.

1962–63, set an NBA record with 71 points in a game on November 15, 1960, and put up a Finals-record 61 in 1962's Game 5. Wilt captured the public's imagination to such an extent that he overshadowed Baylor. In retrospect, it's strange to think that the big man could have been more fascinating than a rippling acrobat. Baylor was certainly the more artful player, dwarfing guards as he danced around them like a boxer, sailing into centers, and making it all look easy without rubbing it in. Perhaps Wilt, the grotesque depositing ball in basket at will, provided a more accessible (not to mention more lurid) narrative. He fit better with the conventions of the early-sixties game, as well as the day's assumptions about race.

Thus Baylor seems to recede almost as soon as he arrives. He never led the league in scoring. Fittingly, his most impressive performances came during the 1961–62 season, when he was stationed in Fort Lewis, Washington, as a member of the Army Reserves. Joining the team only for weekend games and practices, he was an apparition who blew into town, threw up his 38 points a night, and then went back to life as a private in the military. It's both an incomplete campaign and an extraordinary one, as well as a career high that didn't even count—the perfect metaphor for today's version of Baylor.

A LITERAL LOCKOUT: At the 1964 All-Star Game, Baylor helped organize a players' revolt, protesting their lack of a pension plan and locking themselves in the locker room. Bob Short banged on the door and called for Baylor and West to come out, but they would not relent. The players eventually got their pension, albeit a relatively shoddy one, and recognition for the union Bob Cousy had begun to organize ten years earlier.

Soon thereafter, injuries set in. Baylor's knees would first trouble him in 1963–64; in the 1965 postseason, the top eighth of his left kneecap was ripped off, and he had surgery to remove calcium deposits, followed by a summer of calisthenics developed by the doctor entrusted with Sandy Koufax's arm. It saved Baylor's career but made him less omnidirectional, as he never again topped 30 points per game. Baylor continued to make All-Star teams and strive for that ring, even as his deteriorating joints measured the remainder of his career like an hourglass.

Baylor could in theory be docked for his fruitless Finals trips, and the martyrdom of 1972 could easily turn his story into a melancholic one. We want to see him as a visionary, if only to save him from this story. However, doing so miscasts his game, thus leaving us with a player who is neither of his day nor wholly prescient. Elgin Baylor doesn't need your sympathy or spin. As Oscar Robertson put it, "Animal, vegetable, or glowing green radioactive minerals couldn't stop him." It's high time we consider, free of prejudice or fantasy, just how truly great Baylor was on his own terms.

THE CLOSER

If Chamberlain obscured Baylor, then Laker teammate Jerry West just plain shrieked louder. Baylor was a missive from another planet, West the unalloyed need to win. When the Lakers drafted West, who had been a star at West Virginia, in 1960, they put together a one-two combo for the ages. They were dubbed Mr. Inside (Baylor) and Mr. Outside (West) after their favorite places to operate on the floor. Tonally, though, it was Baylor—elusive and unpredictable—who was the "outside" one, while West went for the gut every time. West was a proficient scorer, a fiend for steals, a deft shooter, a gifted passer, and a tough-as-nails SOB who soldiered through pain. His long, lanky frame gave him all the advantages of wingspan that drive scouts wild today; his broad shoulders, ballast. He didn't exactly play with swagger, but there was an insistence to him that could chill your blood. But Jerry West's approach to the game is best summed up by Chick Hearn's nickname for him, Mr. Clutch, a strange one for a player who spent so many years coming in second. West so routinely hit key shots that this moniker was more a statement of fact than a compliment. When West heaved in a sixty-footer to send Game 3 of the 1970 Finals into overtime, it was one of the least surprising miracles sports has ever seen.

A hell-bent perfectionist, West lived in a basketball universe where there was no such thing as chance, only tasks at hand he was duty-bound to carry out. Never was this more apparent than when the final buzzer was already hanging in the air. West said in interviews that he "found it easier to play the game late," a logic that was a total reversal of how almost any other athlete thought about the often chaotic closing minutes of a game. Then again, some people lose their minds when the moon is full, while others sprout fur and go on the hunt. A product of small-town West Virginia who grew up dreaming of his very own Mountaineers jersey, West was sometimes portrayed as a hick and mocked for his high-pitched voice and heavy Appalachian accent. He abhorred the "Zeke from Cabin Creek" persona the media attempted to stick him with early on. He may have been easygoing and well liked, but as a player he was morbidly intense and ruthlessly self-conscious. His humility was unsettling, searing, not folksy or familiar.

The frustration of the 1960s Lakers weighed on his teammate Baylor, but for West it was nothing short of torture, a

NO LOGO: The NBA logo is famously based on the silhouette of Jerry West. The only other athlete known to have inspired his league's logo is Jim Ferree, a former golfer on the Senior PGA Tour. Commissioner Deane Beman chose Ferree as the model for his distinctive knickers, which gave the Senior Tour logo a different yet similar look to the PGA Tour's brand.

RIVALRIES NEVER SLEEP: West's own dislike of the Celtics as a team extended well past his retirement. In fact, he claims to not own a single piece of green clothing.

cataclysmic marriage of nature and nurture. In his mind, there were no contingencies, flukes, or moments of grace; heroic play fell somewhere between duty and predetermination, while every bad shot or turnover was a failure that should have been otherwise. All of this was recorded on some balance sheet he kept in his brain. He wound up believing in a strange brand of basketball Calvinism. As his wife, Jane, once told a reporter, "Jerry never thinks he's fated to lose. He believes he's going to win. He has so much confidence. It would be easy when he lost if he felt he was fated. But he is sure he's going to win. You see, that's exactly what makes it so hard afterwards."

The losses didn't just hurt West, or the Lakers, but upset the natural order of the cosmos. This explains why he'd often disappear for days on end after a big loss. It was something akin to a spiritual crisis.

What made West's absolutism all the more remarkable was the laundry list of injuries he dealt with. He took on the burden of infallibility with a body that was rarely, if ever, on his side. Sitting out was, for West, a defilement of the way things should be. He was supposed to be present and in place to deliver the win,

The Many Kinds of Mr. Clutch

Jerry West is heralded as one of the most clutch players in NBA history, but given the primitive state of basketball statistics during his era (the NBA didn't even record blocks and steals until West's final season, much less keep track of detailed play-by-play data), it is difficult to get a complete picture of his clutch performances. What we do know is that over his fourteen seasons in the league, West played in 189 games that were decided by 2 points or less. By using the historical newspaper accounts for each of these 189 games, we were able to piece together a rough portrait of his clutch career. What stood out was not just the buzzer-beaters but the sheer variety of ways West came through when it mattered most, often making multiple clutch plays at both ends of the court, especially late in the playoffs.

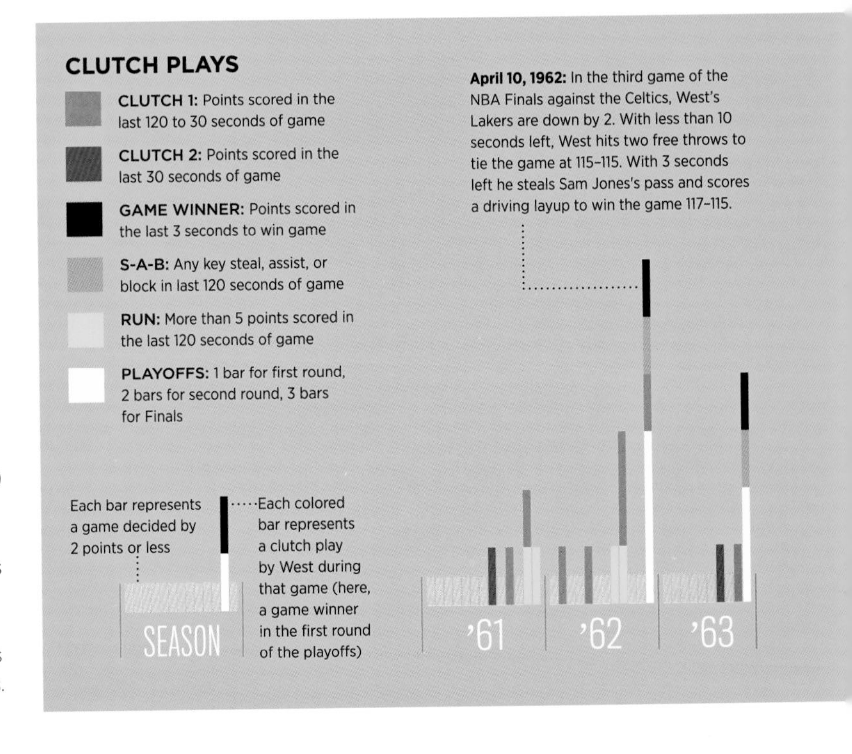

because that's what stars did. Drunk on adrenaline and worry, he mostly just ignored his injuries, dragging himself through the season lest something go wrong in his absence. He broke his nose nine times, tore his MCL, and pulled muscles galore. Game 7 of the 1970 Finals is famous for Willis Reed's triumphant limp out of the tunnel as he overcame a thigh injury long enough to score twice and play several ineffectual minutes. West, meanwhile, had been playing since Game 3 with a badly jammed thumb on his shooting hand. He needed injections straight into it, still going 9 for 19 from the floor in a losing effort and having nothing to show for it but his own self-recriminations. Chamberlain would at one point complain that West was praised for his valor while his black teammates caught hell if they dared miss a game. Yet if anything, West showed the world the difference between injury-prone and soft.

West retired in 1974 at age thirty-six, still an elite player but dreading the day his body finally gave out on him as Baylor's had. He coached the Lakers for three years, making the Conference Finals in 1977, switched to scouting, and was promoted to general manager for 1982–83. By the time he left the organization in 2002,

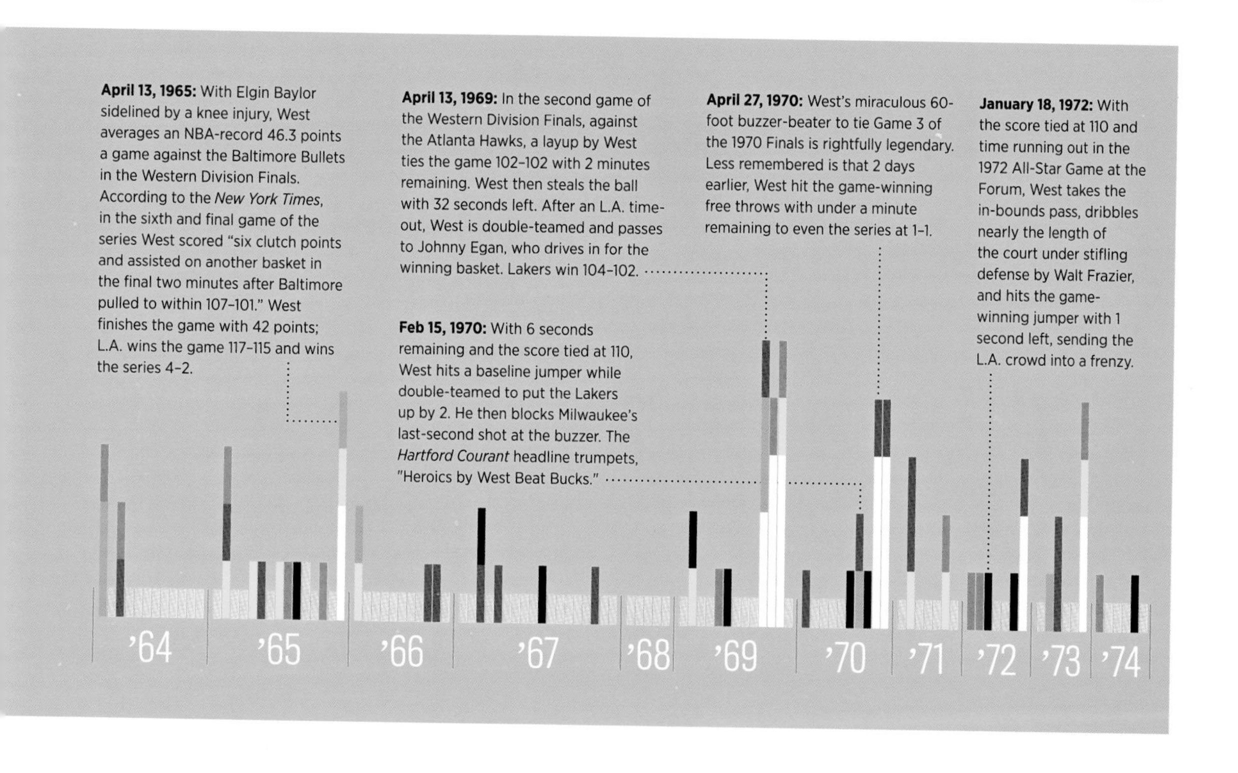

he was the proud owner of seven more championship rings, perhaps the only seven seasons of his twenty that he could bear to reflect on. During the Shaq-Kobe three-peat, West would set his VCR and go take in a movie, watching the games only after the fact. His anxiety level was just too high, especially as he had less and less power to affect what he still saw as the inevitable. There was one more go-round, as savior of the Memphis Grizzlies, which he transformed from laughingstock to playoff team, before leaving in 2007.

In 2009, he announced that he'd suffered from atrial fibrillation throughout his playing days and attributed his persistent restlessness and keyed-up sense of purpose to this disease. While this news heightened the myth of West as the consummate gnarled, grotesque angel of battle, it also took some of the air out of the room with a very common sadness. Let us now praise famous men, indeed.

THE TRIPLE THREAT

THE ANTI-HOOSIERS: When Oscar was a sophomore, Crispus Attucks High School lost to tiny Milan High School in the 1954 state playoffs. That game would provide the inspiration for the movie *Hoosiers* (featuring Crispus Attucks coach Ray Crowe in a small role), but the Crispus Attucks squad would go on to become one of the best high school teams in history.

We can spend days debating what hurts more: spending a decade falling just shy of your grandest hopes and dreams, or clawing and thrashing just to get a peek through the keyhole. Baylor and West felt it slip through their fingers every summer. But they could safely assume they'd be back next year. By comparison, Oscar Robertson spent his peak seasons playing as much basketball as is mortally possible, and yet he found himself wandering around the mall at closing time, just like everyone else shopping on Saturday. During Oscar's ten years in Cincy, the Royals were a combined 421–385, pretty much the same as the Lakers. Finishing second or third in the conference from 1962 to 1967, they put in an appearance in the playoffs those seasons, getting as far as the Conference Finals twice. However, these numbers don't quite capture the total clusterfuck of Robertson's time as a Royal. They were in the West for two years, then the East, where they were caught in the Wilt-Celtics crossfire. Taking Boston to a seventh game in the 1963 East Finals, they were poised to open up a second front for the Celtics or at least become the division's resident gadfly.

But their peak formation of Robertson and Jack Twyman in the back court and forwards Jerry Lucas and Bob Boozer up front was gradually broken up, for no good reason. Even then, the Royals continued to rise up and show what a Robertson team could do, pushing Boston to a full five-game series in 1966's first round.

But the new ownership had other concerns, such as scheduling neutral-arena games that would grant concessions contracts to its hot dog business. Bad deals were made left and right, things fell to pieces, and in 1969, Bob Cousy was brought in as head coach. Cousy—who later admitted he came back only for the money—wanted the team to run, while Oscar wanted to play his pitiless, grind-it-out game. These two strains of basketball engaged in a standoff with positively Darwinian implications. On top of that, each man demanded more respect than the other was willing to give. When Cousy went so far as to come out of retirement for a few dismal games while Robertson supposedly faked an injury, things turned hostile, with the press backing Cousy. The Royals continued to slide; the playoffs became a distant memory. Eventually, Robertson engineered that fateful trade to Milwaukee.

Robertson's legacy, though, is not what his teams did but how he played the game. For most of the decade, Robertson was responsible for what's widely regarded as the most complete basketball ever committed to hardwood. Just as Wilt's greatness is often summed up by 100, so Oscar's rep has been passed down in epithetical form: He *averaged* a triple-double for 1961–62. Robertson wasn't on Chamberlain's or Baylor's level as a scorer (who was?), and both topped him in rebounding. But Oscar was a big guard who also had to contend with running an offense, even taking it upon himself to coach from the floor. The triple-double was more than pure numbers, it was indicative of a man who was everywhere at once on the court. Over the course of his basketball education, Robertson had played every position. He had the strength and rebounding instincts of a forward; as a scorer, his shooting touch and ability to work his way inside off the dribble made guarding him a cynical, stingy chess match; he attracted enough attention to produce plenty of open looks for others; and he was always looking to exploit the mismatches he created, whether for himself or through the chaos they engendered elsewhere on the floor.

Recent advances in statistics have shown that if every season had been as gonzo as 1961–62, Oscar's triple-double might not be such a singular achievement. The likes of Magic Johnson (who made the feat significant simply because it was a benchmark to be reached, not a matter of course), Jason Kidd, and LeBron James would've pulled it off themselves. Yet Robertson himself has been quick to point out that if you lump together his first five seasons, the average is a triple-double. To take it a step further, in his 2003

Triple-Doubles Till Death

Ages at which players would pass Oscar's 181 triple-doubles, at their yearly rate through 2009, or had they never retired and continued to play, at their yearly rate

	Career total	Yearly rate	
O. Robertson	181	12.9	
	Career total	**Yearly rate**	**Age he would pass Oscar**
Magic Johnson	138	10.6	36
Jason Kidd	105	6.6	48
W. Chamberlain	78	5.6	46
Larry Bird	59	4.5	62
Fat Lever	43	3.9	68
John Havlicek	30	1.9	117
Grant Hill	29	1.9	117
Michael Jordan	28	1.9	121
LeBron James	28	4	63

THE MOTHER OF INVENTION: Unable to afford a real basketball as a child, Robertson made do with a ball of rags tied together with rubber bands. Some other players' unique practice habits born out of necessity:

MARQUES HAYNES: This Globetrotter credits his legendary skills to countless hours dribbling a tennis ball on the cross ties of a local railroad track.

BOB COUSY: Fell out of a tree and broke his right arm as a child, forcing him to dribble left until he healed; thus he became nearly ambidextrous.

PETE MARAVICH: Practiced dribbling two miles a day as he jogged back and forth to the nearest playground. Later, he learned to dribble the ball while riding his bicycle to the courts. His father, an overbearing basketball coach, also made him dribble blindfolded, wearing gloves, and outside the window of a moving car.

BILL BRADLEY: During one summer vacation, Bradley was forced to practice his dribbling on the narrow corridors of the Queen Elizabeth cruise ship, using fellow passengers as moving obstacles. He did this while also wearing ten-pound lead slivers stuck in each sneaker and special homemade glasses with cardboard taped to the sides to limit his vision.

memoir, Robertson points to a quote from Willie Mays about Jose Canseco's becoming the charter member of the 40/40 club: "If I'd have known that was such a big deal, I would've done it a few times myself," the implication being that, had Robertson cared, he could've easily grabbed a few more boards, as if the other team didn't even figure in the equation. Oscar scoffed at stats not out of modesty but because he had too many columns to keep track of. He knew that his game brought with it an avalanche of numbers. Today he dismisses the idea that a single rebound or assist here or there could really have mattered that much.

The note of bitterness there is perhaps the most misunderstood aspect of Robertson. Even during those first few upbeat seasons, Robertson was known as a loyal but volatile teammate; the Cincy media was fond of painting him as moody, imperious. There was a grain of truth to all of this—Robertson had grown up in Indianapolis when that state was Klan Central, and he absorbed an inordinate amount of psychic pain that, out of necessity, he kept bottled up. Robertson spent most of his time at the "Dust Bowl," outdoor courts in his neighborhood where he'd learn that on the court, taking punishment was a rite of passage, not a sign of weakness, and dishing it out was the right of those who had proven themselves. It was a just version of the world that had nothing to do with his everyday reality, and so Robertson put his heart and soul there.

There could be slurs from whites in games, on the court or in the stands, but Robertson could silence them with jump shots. When his Crispus Attucks Tigers became the nation's first all-black state champions in 1954, that faith in the game as not only an escape but a kind of utopia was affirmed—even though the city wouldn't let the Tigers and their fans celebrate their title downtown, rerouting the parade back into the black section of town. Robertson was one of five athletes who integrated the University of Cincinnati after being convinced that life there would be different. But while he didn't face active hostility on campus, he was very much alone. Much of the city was still segregated. He had several prominent black families serving as his lifeline, and yet Robertson continued to struggle with shyness and, when the team went on the road, anger that he continued to suppress. He was double-crossed by a *Sports Illustrated* reporter who had gained his trust during an interview, and from that point on Robertson regarded the media with suspicion, if not with outright animosity.

By the time he began his pro career, Robertson was a bundle of contradictions: polite and easy around those he trusted, stone-faced to the public, and on the verge of blowing up around those who failed to respect his boundaries. He steamrolled all comers on the court, and yet apart from barking at teammates who didn't meet his expectations, Robertson let very little of himself show on the court. All of which might explain why the media learned to take Robertson for granted, resorting to open mockery toward the end of his time in Cincy. Maybe they wished he was more voluble or more leading-man-esque or at least showed a spark that belied his all-business demeanor. It probably didn't help that, in addition to not taking shit from management, Robertson was heavily involved with the Players Association from its inception and eventually lent his name to the lawsuit that would bring about free agency. Maybe the city would've liked Robertson to provide enough ups and downs to make being a fan, you know, exciting. Instead all they got was the stolid Robertson, night in and night out reaching the logical limit of how much one man could do on a basketball court—and of how much one man could contribute to helping his team win.

Robertson supposedly found some sort of redemption (or, if you insist, humility) with the Bucks. When camera crews caught up with Oscar immediately following a four-game sweep of the Baltimore Bullets, he was grinning broadly, his whole face for once relaxed. But his eyes remained unchanged, as if to wrench the hypocrisy out of an audience who suddenly felt compelled to acknowledge this diminished version of a master. That's the paradox of this era, and it's only become more pronounced with time. The Celtics owned the NBA title, making fools of these big-named prima donnas and leaving them scrambling for a single ring. Looking back across four decades, though, all those titles become a blur, and the yearly reckoning handed out by Russell and friends is reduced to one gigantic trophy. At the same time, Baylor, West, and Robertson have survived as both folk heroes and the forerunners of most major talents who have come since. These were the days of the greatest team effort ever, but it was also the age when, as they say in the pictures, a star really was a star. —*B.S.*

THE SCOURGE OF TEAMMATES: The season before Robertson arrived in Cincinnati, sixth-year swingman Jack Twyman became the first NBA player to average 30 points per game. With Oscar in town, Twyman never again averaged better than 25.3 and topped 20 just two more times in his career, proving once and for all that the Big O had a negative effect on his teammates. Or that's the story that fits Oscar's reputation, at least. In reality, Twyman's seasons with Oscar roughly mirrored his production before the two teamed up, suggesting that the 30-ppg season was an outlier.

BUSHELS AND BASKETS

Examining the NBA's Statistical Explosion

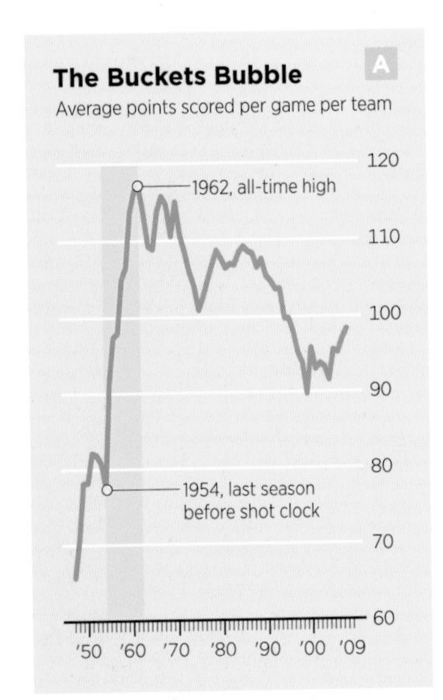

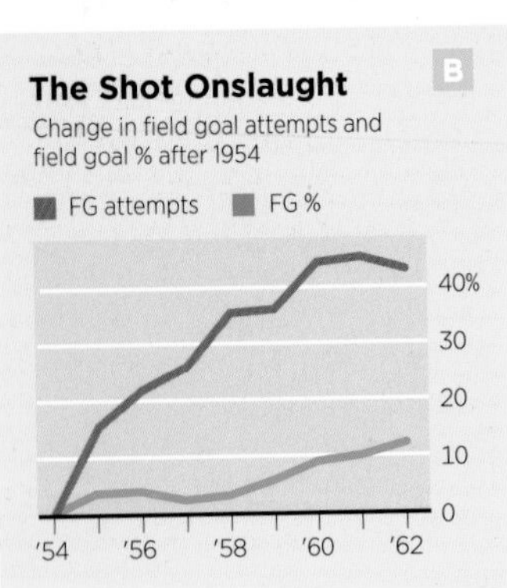

In 1962, team scoring in the NBA reached an all-time high of nearly 120 points per game (see chart A). That same year, Wilt averaged 50 points and Oscar averaged a triple-double for an entire season. Five different players averaged over 30 points a game (actually six, if we count the 38.8 points Baylor averaged during the 48 games he played that season). Walt Bellamy, a rookie, averaged 32 and 19. Clearly something was in the water.

Countless scholars have burned the midnight oil trying to explain the roots of this great leap forward in offensive production. Originally, the spike in scoring was attributed to the virtuosity of the individual performers (Wilt, Oscar, Baylor, et al.). But in recent years, the game's wise men and number crunchers have argued that the scoring boom was actually due to the accelerated pace of games during this era: The introduction of the shot clock in 1955 had sped up games, faster games meant more possessions, and with more possessions came more opportunities to score.

So even though shooters were becoming somewhat more efficient—exploiting fast breaks and off-ball screens for easy points and replacing antiquated techniques like the set shot with more accurate, newfangled weapons like the jumper—the overall rise in shooting efficiency, as measured by field goal percentage, was dwarfed by the increase in pace, as measured by field goal attempts (see chart B). In other words, it wasn't that players got better at making shots; they were just taking a lot more of them.

But if the equation were really this simple, if more possessions simply meant more points, why did it take ten years after the introduction of the shot clock for scoring to reach its peak, and why aren't today's teams still dropping 120 points a night?

Of Fields and Field Goals

To fully explore the nuances of the NBA's statistical explosion, let us now turn to an era of comparable numeric and social upheaval: the English agricultural revolution. Between 1720 and 1840, wheat production in England jumped from a mere 19 bushels per acre to roughly 30 bushels per acre—a colossal increase in food production. As with the NBA's scoring boom, this growth was due to both an increase in efficiency and resources. On the one hand, farmers were getting better at tilling their fields, but more important, because of a new subdivision of land known as enclosure, all of a sudden there were a lot more fields to till.

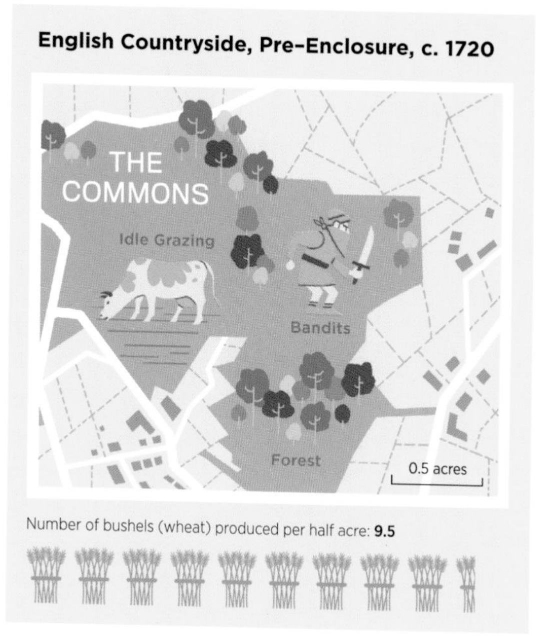

In the early eighteenth century, about one quarter of the English countryside consisted of large tracts of wild, untamed land known as the commons. These unfenced meadows, marshes, and forests were collectively owned and collectively farmed by the local peasants. But as anyone who has ever joined a food co-op knows, collective ownership can be a pain in the ass. Because no one person owned the land, no one person had the incentive to improve it. Thus the commons remained largely undeveloped, used for subsistence farming, idle grazing, and just plain hanging out. Additionally, because there were no fences or property lines, nobody really knew who owned what, leading to frequent instances of trespass and theft. Though later idealized by Marxists, hippies, and Wikipedia users for their collectivism and crunchy romance, the commons were in reality places of waste and chaos—generating vagrancy and crime, but ultimately very little wheat.

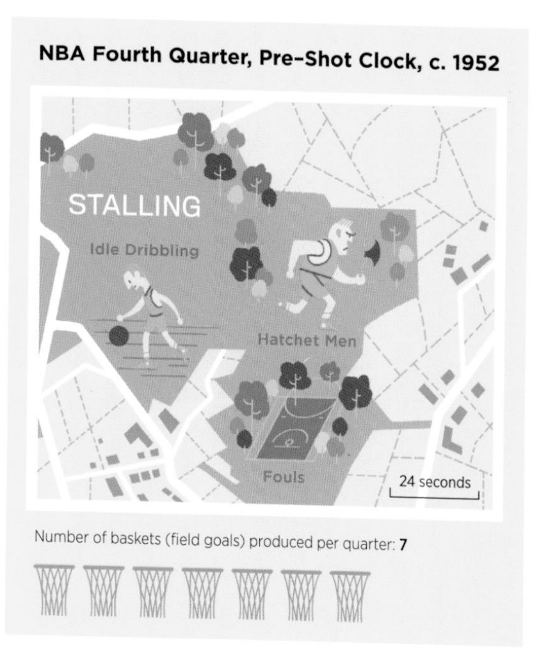

If one were to map an early 1950s NBA game, one would find a similar situation, with most fourth quarters dominated by large swaths of alternating idle and violent play known as stalling. Since there was no shot clock, when one team got a lead late in the game, their best ball handler would dribble around aimlessly in an attempt to kill time. The only way the opposing team could get the ball back was to foul, so unskilled big men—known as goons and hatchet men—proceeded to clobber each other. These "freeze and foul" tactics repulsed the fans and the media. During the 1954 playoffs, the Knicks and Celtics played a game so slow-paced and foul-plagued that the TV execs cut away before it was even over. Thus, like the English commons, the game of basketball was left wild and underdeveloped, and the fourth quarter was viewed as a place of waste and chaos—generating inane playmaking and brutal fouls, but ultimately very few points.

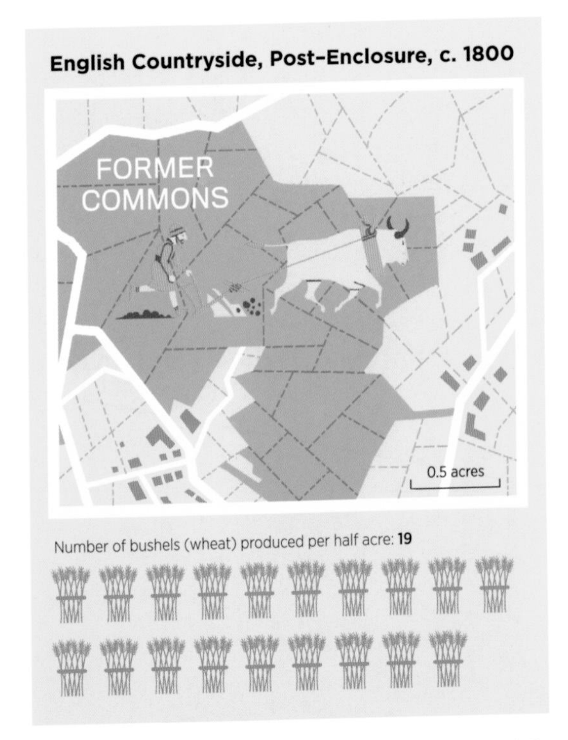

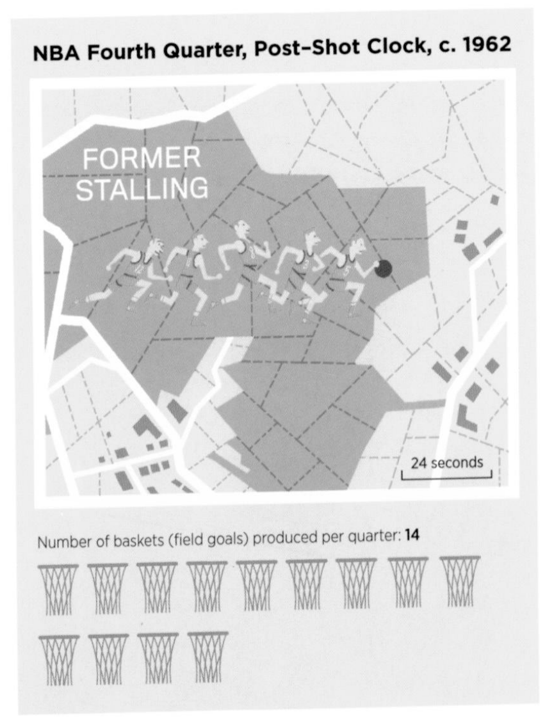

Starting with the Enclosure Acts of 1755, all of this changed. By parliamentary decree, the peasant farmers were evicted from the commons and the land was subdivided into tidy, privately owned parcels enclosed by fences and hedgerows. Having redrawn the boundaries of land ownership, the capitalist farmers set about maximizing the yield of their crops, producing nearly twice as much wheat as they had before.

Similarly, in 1954 the NBA owners introduced the shot clock, which effectively destroyed stalling by chopping up every possession into uniform units of no more than 24 seconds. With teams now forced to shoot at a steady clip and a higher premium placed on offense, scores went ballistic, with teams throwing up nearly twice as many field goals per quarter as they had before the shot clock.

Free Your Mind and Your Wheat Will Follow

These changes didn't happen overnight. For England, it took nearly a century to adapt to the new land enclosures and really start pumping out the wheat. In the NBA, it took almost a decade for teams to acclimate to the shot clock and really start racking up the points. This was because the shot clock, like the process of enclosure in England, did more than simply divvy up the game into tidy little possessions: It transformed the players' very orientation to offensive production, requiring them to learn a whole new way of thinking about the game. In the pre-shot-clock era, teams viewed possessions much like subsistence-level crops: Once one team took the lead, they had what they needed and looked to score only as much as necessary to survive; the rest of the time, they would simply stall. After the shot clock, however, offensive strategy became more like modern capitalist agriculture, aimed at maximizing the number of points scored, irrespective of the margin. The goal was no longer subsistence and survival: Producing points, like producing wheat, became an end in itself. And as incentives increased, so did innovation of new offensive strategies.

This shift in mentality was reflected by more consistent scores throughout the league. Before the shot clock, teams were almost schizophrenic on offense; in 1951, the Bullets scored more than 100 points in ten games and less than 60 in another ten. That same season, the Celtics scored 118 points one game, then 65 points three days later. With the shot clock, this variance in offensive production steadily declined (see chart C). Teams now simply tried to score as much as possible all the time. And the fans loved it. Attendance figures, which had flatlined in the 1950s, were soon growing neck and neck with point totals (see chart D).

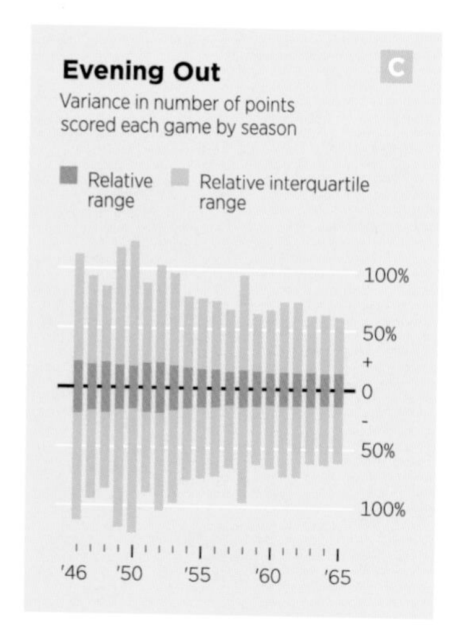

The End of an Explosion

So why did the stats boom peak in 1962 and then eventually peter out? The answer is defense, or rather, the prior lack thereof. Red Auerbach once noted, "Basketball is like war in that the offensive weapons are developed first, and it always takes a while for the defense to catch up." And in 1962, the offense was still winning the war. In fact, offenses might have gotten too good. In 1961, Detroit coach Dick McGuire said, "The kids are making shots we wouldn't even dare take. The science is going out of the game and it's becoming dull. Who wants to watch Wilt stuff them in?"

But ten years later the defense had finally caught up and scores had dropped to 112 points per game. Before the 1972 season, Jerry West noted the shift in the way the game was played, stating, "Defenses all around the league are more sophisticated. This has necessitated a change in all players. The days of four or five guys averaging 30 points are gone." Players were no less offensively skilled, but with coaches now introducing complex, zone-like defenses, making defense-specific substitutions at the end of quarters, and tinkering with lineups to orchestrate mismatches at either end, the point totals were gently falling back to earth.

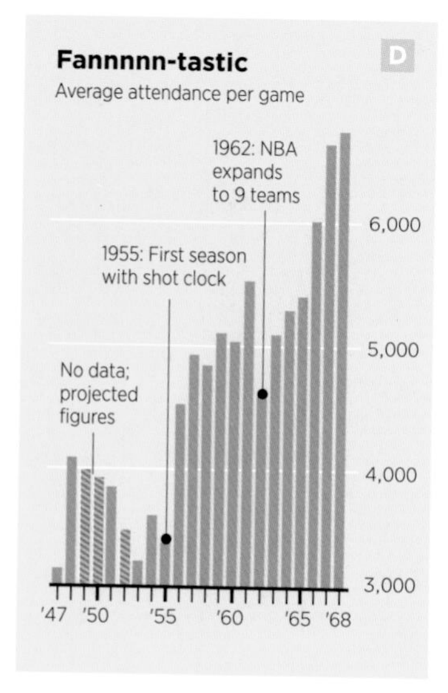

If there is a final lesson to be gleaned from the NBA's statistical explosion, it won't be found in the divine mathematics of pace and possession, nor the Herculean accomplishments of that era's individual stars, but rather in the sheer degree to which the game itself was able to morph and mutate. In this particular era, we see the manipulation of the sport at each level: Management institutes the shot clock to boost attendance; the players adapt, reorienting their games around new priorities—creativity, speed, and efficiency; and finally, the coaches react with new defensive schemes of their own. The game of basketball has always been malleable, and each instance of tweaking or tinkering with the rules sets off a chain reaction of adaptations, adjustments, and countermoves, all headed ineluctably back to the center.

MISSING IN ACTION

Stokes, Hawkins, and Careers That Never Were

READY-MADE: Maurice Stokes came into the NBA fully formed. In his first game, he put up 30 points, 20 rebounds, and 8 assists.

RUNNING SCARED: Stokes was so dominant as a collegian that St. Francis had a difficult time scheduling opponents once he proved his talent. When Stokes was a freshman, St. Francis played 30 games, but the next season they were able to nail down only 18 dates. Seton Hall coach Honey Russell made it clear why: "We won't play you until you lose Stokes."

All ghosts are not created equal. With a career cut short, what we make of it becomes the second half of the story, if not a story unto itself. Maurice Stokes played three rip-roaring seasons for the Rochester/Cincinnati Royals before a mishandled head injury left him paralyzed just shy of his twenty-fourth birthday. Connie Hawkins starred at basketball stronghold Boys High in the late fifties and then, for all intents and purposes, disappeared until he was allowed into the NBA as a twenty-seven-year-old rookie. Stokes had been a first-round pick in 1955, but only after gaining national exposure at the NIT with Division II St. Francis College; he came and went in five years, gone to all except the fraternity of players. Hawkins started young and lingered in the imagination for a decade, long after the world probably should have given up on him. He was a fog who never materalized or lifted.

While NBA old-timers speak of Maurice Stokes with reverence—Chet Walker calls him "a player who combined the moves of Oscar Robertson *and* Elgin Baylor, who could do everything every night"—he's largely forgotten today. Those who have heard of him most likely know him as a treacly footnote. In the last game of the 1958 regular season, the third-year Cincinnati Royals pro knocked his skull against the hardwood but kept playing. Stokes suited up for the first playoff contest and held himself together. However, on the flight back, he fell gravely ill, sweating uncontrollably and suffering a seizure before lapsing into a coma. Stokes woke up paralyzed, unable to speak, and without any safety net—as teammate Jack Twyman put it, "He was a guy lying there without a team. There was no insurance. No compensation."

Twyman and his wife, Carole, who already lived in Cincinnati from college, were Stokes's only option. That's how the white couple became his caretakers, a story immortalized in the 1973 film *Maurie*, which featured Frank Sinatra's rousing theme song, "Winners." This human-interest aspect of Stokes's career has overshadowed the basketball part, and that's its own kind of injustice. Stokes could have altered the sixties' competitive landscape and perhaps the evolution of the sport itself. Yet he has been reduced to a valiant cripple, his story flecked with civil rights–era poignancy for good measure.

Maurice Stokes is very likely the best, and most important, NBA player no one's ever heard of. Before Russell or Baylor, he was turning the sport on its head as the league's first game-changing African American. The Royals passed on Russell because they had Stokes, who at that point was the hardiest rebounder the league had ever seen; while officially listed at 6′7″, 232 pounds, Stokes was such a punishing presence inside that his peers recall him weighing 275. He had an eye for fine details to rival Russell's and enough twists and turns in his game to match Baylor at his best. Stokes was a point center, a contradiction in terms that represents the most improbable of hybrids—the spectrum of positionality chewing on its own bright-colored tail. It was considered a modern miracle when, in Game 6 of the 1980 Finals, rookie Magic Johnson started at center, but Stokes pulled it off on a nightly basis, overpowering all comers in the paint and then streaking downcourt to lead the break. As the 1956 Rookie of the Year, he set a single-season mark for rebounding average; he was the league's third-best assist man in 1957 and 1958. For his swan song as a pro, Stokes, a whirlwind of size, strength, and speed brimming with on-court IQ and a devotion to unselfish acts, averaged 16.9 points, 18.1 rebounds, and 6.4 assists.

With Oscar Robertson lighting it up at the University of Cincinnati, the Royals were poised to nab him in the territorial draft and form a one-two tandem that would've put them on a level with the era's elite. Factor in Twyman and Jerry Lucas, headed over from Ohio State, and this team might have seriously challenged the Celtics. But Stokes shouldn't have to rely on hypotheticals. His time in the NBA, however brief, certainly speaks for itself.

After his accident, Stokes lived another twelve years, tirelessly fighting to take back his body. Eventually, he got back some use of his hands and arms, improved his speech, and could take a few steps at a time down the hospital hallway. Stokes busied himself with books (poetry and his still-unpublished memoirs) and pottery and kept up with politics (from the moment he regained consciousness, Stokes never missed a single chance to vote). He

MIDAIR SACRAMENT: Stokes became so fearful on the fateful flight back to Cincinnati that he requested to be baptized so that he might die a Catholic. Religious teammate Richie Regan performed the ceremony—albeit quite informally.

THE SAFETY OF CRASH: The Stokes ordeal has forever changed teams' safety precautions regarding airplanes and illness. Most recently, Bobcats forward Gerald Wallace was forced to travel cross-country in a tour bus to Charlotte after suffering a broken rib and collapsed lung against the Lakers in January 2009. Wallace rode more than 2,400 miles, spending most of his time watching cartoons and movies with his wife and daughter. He told ESPN.com that "it was kind of like being at home in your house, except we were moving."

THE CULTURAL CENTER: From 1958 on, Kutsher's Country Club in the Catskills was the site of a star-studded benefit game for Stokes. Stokes was not the only star athlete with connections to Kutsher's. Wilt Chamberlain worked there as a bellhop while an amateur and bragged about his efficient bag-moving system in his first autobiography. Kutsher's served as a training space for boxers Muhammad Ali, Leon Spinks, and Floyd Patterson; was the inspiration for the resort in *Dirty Dancing*; and hosted the All Tomorrow's Parties festival in 2008 and 2009.

THE HAWK IN CONGRESS: In his 2009 confirmation hearings, Attorney General Eric Holder solemnly intoned Hawkins's name in the Senate when Wisconsin senator and Milwaukee Bucks owner Herb Kohl asked Holder about his basketball skills. Holder answered: "I've got a New York City game. I come from the city that produced Connie Hawkins, Kareem Abdul-Jabbar, Nate 'Tiny' Archibald. I learned how to play ball at P.S. 127 in Queens."

continued to follow the NBA, engaged while never pining. For Maurice Stokes, the mind-set of the athlete was as rewarding as the kinesis.

Stokes became part martyr, part oracle, all good-natured Buddha sitting in his hospital room. Players from all around the league stopped by for what was nearly a pilgrimage. He also entertained famous fans like Bill Cosby—who much to Stokes's amusement insisted on calling him Fat Albert—and had a visit from Roy Campanella, a scene that practically begs dramatic treatment. In most of the photos and home movies from that time, Stokes is laughing heartily, often with Twyman by his side looking equally beatific.

Stokes gave us indelible proof of his greatness. By contrast, Hawkins protruded from the sixties like a phantom limb as he wandered the decade in exile. And this persisted. An older, faded version of the Hawk was an All-Star in the seventies. But it's the Hawkins of memory, the Brooklyn schoolyard legend, whose cult appeal has persisted. Stokes's résumé, however abbreviated, is concrete proof that the Association was robbed of a major figure; questions remain whether Hawkins could have lived up to the hype. But they still talk about Connie Hawkins.

Hawkins grew up in Bed-Stuy at a time when the Brooklyn neighborhood was beginning to register the consequences of white flight. A shy, spacey kid wandering through life in ill-fitting, threadbare hand-me-downs, Connie slept a lot, ate little, stared ahead blankly in school, and showed the most enthusiasm for his collection of comic books. Taller than his peers and long-limbed as they come, Hawkins soon found his way to basketball at the local YMCA, then to the junior high team. He still wasn't sure how much he cared about sports. Yet when he found himself ushered into the A-list world of late-fifties playground ball, Hawkins's boundless athleticism, loping moves, seemingly limitless reach, and esoteric court vision were already taking on the contours of a blacktop signature. They also landed him a spot at Boys High, the social status that came with it, and, for the first time in his life, a sense of self-worth.

In his teens, Hawkins became a cornerstone of New York hoops lore, a marvel for his slo-mo hops, fluid body control, and ability to outmaneuver anyone remotely approaching his size. He was the Hawk, with a game and nickname that ensured a certain kind of immortality—not to mention the built-in advantage of competing

JOE'S

CONNIE'S DOPPELGÄNGER: Sherman White was considered one of the best schoolyard players in New York during the 1950s. A 6′10″ monster capable of mixing it up inside, White also had an impressive handle and a deadly outside jumper. While at Long Island University in 1951, White led the nation in scoring with 27.7 points per game and was in line to become the Knicks' first-round draft pick. He then became mired in the 1951 college point-shaving scandal, spent nine months in prison, and was barred from the NBA.

MOE BETTER BLUES: Hawkins was only one of many players to get railroaded by a major investigation because of tenuous ties to Molinas. Running buddy Roger Brown was banned from the NCAA and NBA. Like Hawkins, Brown eventually made his way to the ABA, where he was a four-time All-Star and three-time champion before retiring in 1975. Also, while many white, actually guilty players escaped the wrath of the NCAA and NBA, North Carolina standout and future Nuggets coach Doug Moe did not, despite never doing more than accepting $75 for a flight to meet with the fixers, whose offers he explicitly turned down.

in Madison Square Garden on occasion. Still, Hawkins remained remarkably unworldly, naïve, and, yes, poor. During this period, Hawkins befriended Jack Molinas, who had been banned from the NBA for gambling as a rookie in 1950 and was now the criminal mastermind behind a far-reaching point-shaving ring. Hawkins innocently accepted free meals, petty-cash handouts, and use of Jack's red Caddy but was never a part of the operation.

Iowa won the backroom bidding war for Connie's services. He spent his freshman year slipping in and out of melancholy, waiting for his chance to play the next year, and mesmerizing the campus with his play in exhibition games. Then law enforcement took down Molinas, Connie's name cropped up in an interview, and he was spirited back to New York, where he was detained in a hotel for days and grilled by detectives who could smell fear. Hawkins ended up signing a garbled, contradictory statement that, while it was never enough to bring charges against him, still lumped him in with the scandal. He was expelled from Iowa, received no offers to play elsewhere, and was hastily banned from the NBA.

Hawkins returned to Brooklyn, his life ruined by a combination of hysteria, Kafkaesque peril, and the fundamental callousness of the powers that be. At first too devastated to even play, eventually Hawkins started to take his game out in public again. But it became dismally clear that Hawkins was too good to play out his best years in semipro leagues or blacktop courts. This effect was only heightened, and given pathos, when Hawkins matched up with current college players and pros, especially in citywide tournaments like the Rucker. He similarly outclassed the entire American Basketball League when he spent a season with the Pittsburgh Rens, and he tore himself up inside weathering three years with the farce the Globetrotters had become.

The ABA was founded in 1967–68 as little more than a get-rich scheme in which many owners cared little for hoops itself. Against this sunken, tawdry backdrop, Hawkins led the Pittsburgh Pipers to the inaugural championship. After Connie's searing 41-point outburst on a gimpy knee forced a Game 7, Bill Sharman, scouting the terrain as he readied himself to jump leagues, gushed, "He was moving on sheer desire . . . I've never seen a performance like that. He made some moves I've never seen before. Hawkins belongs in the same class with Jerry West, Elgin Baylor, and John Havlicek." Based on eyewitness accounts and what scant footage exists from this period, Sharman's ravings jibe with most views of Hawkins in his prime: a swooping, slashing wraith whose instincts for the coarse and the fantastic were equally heightened.

In early 1969, the knee got worse; Hawkins received less than optimal care for it and then never got a chance to properly recover from surgery. Anyone who saw the young Hawk will tell you he was never the same after that. Then again, they practically have to. That's the kind of story it is.

Late in 1966, David and Roslyn Litman, Pittsburgh lawyers who had been affiliated with the Rens, filed an antitrust suit against the NBA. They argued that Hawkins was being unfairly denied employment and that Hawkins had never received anything resembling due process during the point-shaving investigation. Miraculously, in 1969 the league decided to settle, agreeing to give Hawkins a financial settlement and a place on the expansion Phoenix Suns. Hawkins got several years to show the league the tail end of what it had missed, saw some playoff and All-Star action, slowed down, and retired in 1975–76. Maybe this was a happy ending; maybe it wasn't. It certainly follows the classic arc of redemption or, to be more fair about it, release. And yet Hawkins's career, such as it is, also inspires disgust. It was such a colossal waste, for nothing whatsoever. Stokes was gone too soon as an athlete but became a different kind of hero and discovered another form of contentment. Connie Hawkins shed tears when he got that call and certainly made the most of his time in the Association. Still, wasn't every minute he played there a stinging reminder of all those he hadn't?

Today, both Stokes and Hawkins are enshrined in the Basketball Hall of Fame. Hawkins went in with the class of 1992, Stokes in 2004. Hawkins benefited from name recognition, as well as the ecumenical nature of the Hall, which pretty much acknowledges any organized basketball competition; Stokes's election came as a result of tireless lobbying from Twyman. Stokes is a curiosity, an incredible man who just happened to have once played ball. Hawkins, whatever the particulars of his career, is a cipher not only for city hoops at its finest but also for all those players we're left wondering about. That Stokes's career really needs no such enchantment is, in the end, the real point of his story. —*B.S.*

I'M CONNIE HAWKINS, AND YOU'RE NOT: In 1975, *Saturday Night Live* debuted on NBC. In the show's second episode, Hawkins played one-on-one in a sketch against Paul Simon, a strange choice unless you consider Simon's immersion in the culture of his native New York. Giving up a 16-inch advantage to Hawkins, Simon managed to prevail in what announcer Marv Albert called an "incredible upset."

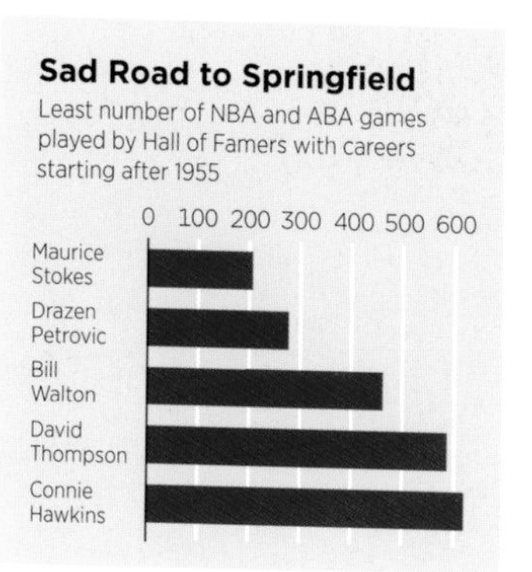

	1970	1971	1972	1973
NBA FINALS CHAMPION	NEW YORK KNICKS	MILWAUKEE BUCKS	LOS ANGELES LAKERS	NEW YORK KNICKS
FINALS LOSER	LAKERS	BULLETS	KNICKS	LAKERS
MOST VALUABLE PLAYER	WILLIS REED	K. ABDUL-JABBAR	K. ABDUL-JABBAR	DAVE COWENS
POINTS per game leader	Jerry West **31.2**	K. Abdul-Jabbar **31.7**	K. Abdul-Jabbar **34.8**	Tiny Archibald **34.0**
REBOUNDS per game leader	Elvin Hayes **16.9**	W. Chamberlain **18.2**	W. Chamberlain **19.2**	W. Chamberlain **18.6**
ASSISTS per game leader	Lenny Wilkens **9.1**	Norm Van Lier **10.1**	Jerry West **9.7**	Tiny Archibald **11.4**

THE BIG PAYBACK

1970–1979

The NBA of the seventies can be split up into two, maybe even three, distinct phases. Early on, the Knicks won a pair of championships, Wilt and West finally got a chance to live without the Celtics suffocating them, and a young center named Lew Alcindor looked ready to follow in the footsteps of Russell. At the same time, the rebellious ABA was cooking up its own potent, snarling form of hoops, one in which style was inseparable from substance. But soon, war broke out between the two leagues, salaries skyrocketed, players' Afrocentric leanings changed the game's image, and legal cases started influencing the direction of the sport. The NBA got rid of the pesky ABA in 1976, absorbing four of the strongest teams and, most important, getting dynamic performers like Julius Erving and David Thompson. The decade ended with image problems for the league, an identity crisis, and concerns about an alienated public. But, these uneasy years also produced distinctive players like Bob McAdoo and Bobby Dandridge, who are well worth remembering.

1974	1975	1976	1977	1978	1979
BOSTON CELTICS	GOLDEN STATE WARRIORS	BOSTON CELTICS	PORTLAND TRAIL BLAZERS	WASHINGTON BULLETS	SEATTLE SUPERSONICS
BUCKS	BULLETS	SUNS	76ERS	SONICS	BULLETS
K. ABDUL-JABBAR	BOB McADOO	K. ABDUL-JABBAR	K. ABDUL JABBAR	BILL WALTON	MOSES MALONE
Bob McAdoo **30.6**	Bob McAdoo **34.5**	Bob McAdoo **31.1**	Pete Maravich **31.1**	George Gervin **27.2**	George Gervin **29.6**
Elvin Hayes **18.1**	Wes Unseld **14.8**	K. Abdul-Jabbar **16.9**	Bill Walton **14.4**	Truck Robinson **15.7**	Moses Malone **17.6**
Ernie DiGregorio **8.2**	Kevin Porter **8.0**	Slick Watts **8.1**	Don Buse **8.5**	Kevin Porter **10.2**	Kevin Porter **13.4**

THE GET ALONG GANG

Why Everybody Loves the New York Knicks

BASKETBALL'S HAJJ: Just how much did New Yorkers love basketball in the first few decades of the NBA? The Knicks led the league in attendance in nineteen of the twenty-five seasons from 1952–53 to 1976–77 despite missing out on the playoffs in nine of them. The Knicks haven't ranked higher than third since, due to the preponderance of large arenas and all those weirdo hipster punks taking over the city.

FOUND SOUND: Walt Frazier has claimed that the now-ubiquitous "DE-FENSE" chant was created for the Knicks.

Just as Red Auerbach laid claim to the sixties, another red-headed New York Jew would become the chief basketball auteur of the seventies. Red Holzman's Knicks played a precise, team-oriented ball that relied on something akin to neural networking. There was a system, but it was fleshed out by discovery, as open-ended truisms like "hit the open man" and "see the ball" provided guidelines. On offense, the team gave itself over to nonstop cutting and ball movement, what guard Walt Frazier called "making a poem." However, at the other end, they were more like one of Wittgenstein's language games, introducing the league to the coordinated, interlocking defensive schemes that expected players to observe parameters while thinking for themselves.

If Auerbach was Cassavetes, then Holzman would be Robert Altman, whose highly stylized films nevertheless depend on a certain amount of actor independence. The overlapping dialogue in *Nashville* or offbeat languor of *The Long Goodbye* are as much a product of the cast's inventiveness as the director's strict vision. By exerting control, Auerbach created the illusion of spontaneity; Holzman, like Altman, set syntax and cues for his troops and then counted on them to complete the picture.

When the Knicks won their first title, it offered the NBA its first glimpse at life after Russell and, for the first time since the NCAA's 1951 point-shaving scandal, once again made hoops-mad New York the center of the basketball universe. The Brooklyn-born Holzman had spent two years with the varsity of Nat Holman's illustrious City College program before going on to a fine career in the NBL and fledgling NBA, and then he landed coaching gigs in Puerto Rico and in the NBA. In fact, Holzman's model was a direct descendant of the ball that had been played in New York colleges during the first half of the century. It harked back to the city's past and resonated with generations of fans from the New York disapora (and not just Jews).

But while these Knicks echoed this bygone era, they were also very much of the present. By 1970, the nation's racial, cultural, generational, and socioeconomic divisions were deeper than ever. The Knicks reflected this cultural landscape; they seemed to have a player representing every demographic, a diverse cast of characters that few pro sports teams achieve. And while this alone gave them broad-based appeal, it was their style of play that made them into something bigger, a metaphor for a post-sixties community that wasn't bitter and broken. With Nixon in office and Vietnam still raging, such optimism was perhaps naïve, but it was enough to transport an NBA team beyond sports and into the pop-culture consciousness at a time when the league still ran a distant third behind baseball and football. When it comes to feel-good stories, everyone loves the one about the pimp, the nerd, the black Southern gentleman, the white workingman, the hippie, and the street urchin they picked up along the way. The Knicks were America's Team for a country trying to make sense of itself—and wondering what coexistence might look like.

As the team's point guard and the Knick with the greatest appetite for the limelight, Walt Frazier was the front man. Known for his dandy's wardrobe and scene-making presence, he had a taste for spectacle that inspired him to ride the subway to the Garden in full minked-out regalia. His nickname Clyde was a reference to his fondness for wide-brimmed hats, much like those worn by Warren Beatty in 1967's *Bonnie and Clyde*. But underneath all the pageantry, Frazier was shy, serious, and introspective; on the court, he was direct, even blunt. His actual play offered little in the way of tangible thrills: Signifying on the public's expectations, Frazier was a solid, ergonomic guard who put up matter-of-fact buckets and saved his flair for game-changing steals. A consummate professional, he assiduously watched his diet and fitness and maintained his general peace of mind. This disconnect between style and persona worked to Frazier's advantage; his all-business game couldn't distract anyone from the expensive threads and custom Rolls-Royce, but it insulated him from bias.

PROLIX AND LOQUACIOUS: Frazier has had a successful career as a color commentator on Knicks broadcasts on both TV and radio, alongside Marv Albert and Mike Breen. Walt is famous for his rhyming phrases, love of SAT-level vocabulary words, and a perpetually bemused tone of voice that would suggest copious nitrous oxide intake if encountered in a stranger. In a 1975 profile of the Knicks for *The New Yorker*, esteemed sportswriter Herbert Warren Wind noted that Frazier read *Bartlett's Familiar Quotations* and a pocket dictionary on team flights, a bit of information that should surprise absolutely no one.

Willis Reed may be the only player to have overshadowed himself: Today, Reed is most famous for a single heightened moment. In Game 5 of the 1970 Finals, he had suffered a torn thigh muscle. He sat out Game 6 and wasn't expected to return that postseason. But miraculously, Reed dragged himself out onto

Knicks-Celtics
KNICKS VANQUISH PISTONS, 115-106
Lucas Notches 24 as Knicks Solidify Playoff Berth
WEEKEND SPORTS
Knicks Belt Celts, Move Into Final
24-YEAR DROUGHT ENDS FOR KNIC
NEW YORK K
NO. NAME POINTS
6 Tom Riker
7 Dean Meminger
10 Walt Frazier
12 Dick Barnett
15 Earl Monroe
16 Charlie Paulk
17 Henry Bibby
18 Phil Jackson
19 Willis Re
Rackley
Bradley
Milt Williams
26 Eddie Mast
32 Jerry Lucas
COACH: WILLIAM (Red) HOLZMAN
TRAINER: DAN WHELAN
NEW YORK 10
Reed Injur
Frazier Guides N
To 3-2 Series Lea
Pro Basketball
and Under Pres
ick Champio
1970 WORLD CHAMPIONS
Basketba
Frazier's Steal and Shot Win Uphill Battle
s Take First Title,
ng Lakers, 113 to 99
KNICKS IN PLAYOFFS
CITY NEWS
NEW YORK'S PICTURE NEWSPAPER
LONG ISLAND FINAL
8¢
KNICKS WIN IT!
Willis And Knicks No. 1
JOURNAL RTS
Knicks Once Ag
the Bi ey Come
nship Blend: Teamwork a

Knicks win
KNICKS WIN TITLE; TOP LAKERS, 102-93
York Triumphs in Five for 2d Crown in 3
—Reed Is Star
Goes to Seventh Ga
KNICKS DO IT, 10
Monroe Ignites Knicks
Basketball
Mighty Knicks:
1973
WORLD CHAMPS
e Game Away
NewYork's Newest Sports
Lakers
Defense sparks Knicks' win
SQUARE GARDEN
rally mo
away
NEW YORK 2
NEW YORK 24
NEW YORK 15

THE FORGOTTEN KNICK: The collegiate National Player of the Year at Michigan, forward Cazzie Russell came to the Knicks in 1966 with a big contract and equally sizable expectations. As a rookie, he averaged 11.3 points per game, and as a sub, Russell was a key scorer for their first championship team. Unfortunately, his lack of a defining personality or quirks led to his being traded for crazy Jerry Lucas.

KNICKERBOCKER KNICKNAMES: The Knicks took their name from Diedrich Knickerbocker, the occasional pen name of Washington Irving and eventually a slang term for New Yorkers. Madison Square Garden, the game's most hallowed arena, is the Mecca of Basketball. But this nickname had little to do with devotion to the sport; it was borrowed from the Shriners' Mecca Temple, a venue that hosted boxing and wrestling matches in the '20s and '30s.

the floor for Game 7, scoring the first two buckets before taking a seat—but giving the Knicks the emotional lift they needed to get past the Lakers. Reed's entrance would be employed to shape and sculpt all memory of this contest. Frazier, in fact, remains to this day somewhat annoyed that no one remembers the game he played subsequently. It also cast Reed forever as a brave but empty John Henry, overlooking the fact that he was an undersized double-double machine and an excellent passer who had won the league's MVP in that first title season. Polite and generous off the court—no one was more likely to loan you his Cadillac than Willis—he was nevertheless willing to step into the role of enforcer when necessary, playing the intimidating black man without letting it rub off on his amicable reputation.

Veteran power forward Dave DeBusschere had come over from Detroit, his hometown and the city he repped endlessly in spirit. DeBusschere was an acolyte of blue-collar basketball, grating on opposing forwards, raking in rebounds and going after loose balls even if it cost him his teeth, and setting screens like they were *his* flashy drive to the hole. This made him a beacon for the silent majority, a hard worker who showed there was intelligence to be found in the trenches—a man of the people who doubled as an aspirational ideal. Yet DeBusschere had all-around game and as much basketball IQ as anyone in the league. The Pistons had even at one point experimented with DeBusschere as head coach.

Future U.S. senator Bill Bradley was a highly skilled small forward who, as a clean-cut All-American at Princeton, had been one of basketball's first Great White Hopes. Before joining the Knicks, Bradley spent two years as a Rhodes scholar overseas, where he realized not only that he'd been cast in a self-limiting role but that the new Bill Bradley needed basketball as badly as others had needed Bill Bradley to be the Golden Boy. Bradley gladly cast aside the superstar trappings of his college career to become one of the Knicks' most unobtrusive, and heady, players. If the mature Bradley had decided he needed basketball, this was the basketball he needed. The neon-bright Dollar Bill nickname, a leftover from the high expectations and huge contract of his rookie year, became almost wry as Bradley carved out a niche for himself as the team's scruffy intellectual. He was refined but unpretentious, geeky but not without his own dry, acerbic wit. In a way, Bradley's playing days prefigured his political career to come.

Today, holy-fool role-player Phil Jackson is the best known of all these Knicks. A longhair who smoked a pipe (always tobacco!), Jackson had starred at the University of North Dakota, where, in true Zen fashion, his comically imperfect game, with its flapping arms, dogged intensity, and deceptively astute timing became its own kind of crooked perfection. Jackson actually missed the entire 1970 season after undergoing spinal-fusion surgery; he has since said that, while it was torture to be away from the action, watching alongside Holzman was the beginning of his own coaching aspirations. Certainly, the triangle offense that has won Jackson ten rings is in keeping with Holzman's philosophy.

The Knicks didn't repeat in 1971; the Baltimore Bullets eliminated them in the Conference Finals. Anvil-headed big man Wes Unseld equaled New York's toughness down low, but Baltimore's real catalyst was guard Earl Monroe. Monroe was the most beguiling scorer of his generation. His tightly calibrated spins and Rube Goldberg–like sequences of fakes and shimmies had made him notorious on the East Coast since he'd been a teen in Philly. Monroe had the uncanny ability to find an open look where there was none, his twists and turns reconfiguring the space around him until he suddenly materialized in the open. Most players get one nickname, and if they're lucky, it's good. Monroe's collection seemed to express the inability of language to capture his game: He was Black Jesus, the Pearl, Black Magic, and Thomas Edison. Supernatural figure, thing of beauty, malicious trickster, technical provocateur, and, through all of it, from the people and for the people.

Kept from big-conference college ball by a combination of bias, poor scouting, and general recruiting noise, Monroe played for Clarence "Big House" Gaines at Winston-Salem State. His exploits made their way to the sports pages, and Baltimore picked him second in 1967. Monroe remained a shadowy, if now semi-legendary, figure, materializing for the All-Star Game or a few playoff contests; in his classic essay "A Fan's Notes on Earl Monroe," Woody Allen recalls the young Monroe as going "beyond the realm of sports as sports to the realm of sports as art," differing from his peers on account of "the indescribable heat of genius that burns deep inside him." In the fall of 1971, Monroe was feuding with Baltimore's management over money and threatening to jump to the ABA—a move that, had it happened, would've been either a coup for the ABA or the ultimate

WHATSOEVER ADAM CALLED EVERY LIVING CREATURE:
Long before he came to New York, Earl Monroe was given the nickname Black Jesus for his revelatory moves. The trend of biblical nicknames never caught on, but several other stars of the '70s had their own holy precursors:

BLACK JOSEPH: *Walt Frazier*. Both men were snappy dressers with the gift of gab, suave enough for everyone to assume they slept with the boss's wife, yet smooth enough to talk their way out of it.

BLACK ELISHA: *Julius Erving*. Apprentice to the prophet Elijah, Elisha took up his master's mantle when Elijah was brought up to heaven in a whirlwind. Elgin Baylor retired the season before Erving entered professional basketball, leaving Dr. J to point the way forward for a new brand of athleticism in the sport.

BLACK SAUL: *Spencer Haywood*. An atypically tall boy, Saul was anointed the first king of the Israelites by the prophet Samuel, only to suffer from crippling paranoia as an old man. Big man Haywood was a phenom from a young age, a four-time All-Star who nevertheless failed to achieve his full potential due to a series of alienating actions, including an antitrust lawsuit against the league to enter early and an attempt to hire a hit man to kill Paul Westhead, his coach, as a member of the champion Lakers in 1980.

WHITE CAIN: *Rick Barry*. Cain, the first villain of the Bible, murdered his brother in cold blood and generally demonstrated poor impulse-control and anger-management skills. Barry was a notorious asshole who was almost universally disliked.

OUT IN THE STREETS: In the late '60s, Harthorne Wingo left tiny Friendship Junior College in his native North Carolina to head to New York and make himself a basketball player. Wingo played for several years on city playgrounds, gaining such a reputation that the Knicks signed him in 1973 as the first player to go directly from street ball to the NBA. After four seasons with New York, Wingo went on to a very successful career in Europe. He reentered the public consciousness in the mid-'90s as the namesake of the father in the children's show *C Bear and Jamal,* a cartoon about a boy and his cool hip-hop teddy bear (voiced by Tone Loc). Unfortunately, the creators spelled it *Hawthorne* Wingo, a common mistake that also wormed its way into the Beastie Boys track "Lay It on Me," off the *Paul's Boutique* album.

ghettoization of Monroe. Instead he went to the Knicks, still only a year removed from a title.

There were concerns that Monroe would disrupt the Knicks. On a team that stressed ball movement, economy, and poise, Monroe's contortive one-on-one play could in theory gum up the works. There were also concerns that Monroe couldn't coexist with Frazier, but these were unfounded. Nor did Monroe, whose game and similarly loud sartorial sense belied his low-key personality, bring any baggage to the so-called Rolls-Royce Back Court. Those who insinuated that the two superstars would clash on the court didn't know their basketball, either. Frazier was a pure point, while Monroe excelled at seat-of-the-pants scoring, making them partners in crime.

After a shaky and injury-plagued 1971–72, Monroe responded by inserting himself into the Knicks' logic, subduing himself to match the tone, picking up his defense, and yet still playing ball the only way he knew—being himself within the parameters of Holzman's system. The rest of the team adapted to his presence accordingly: The Knicks won their second championship in 1973 (if you're counting, that's the sum total of the banners hanging in the Garden). Greil Marcus wrote of Sly Stone that he was "less interested in crossing racial and musical lines than in tearing them up"; Earl Monroe could be a Knick not because the team embraced his every single nickname but because it didn't matter as long as he saw the ball and hit the open man.

Holzman was at once more and less concrete than Auerbach; if Auerbach wanted to essentialize his players, Holzman was an essentialist about the game itself. As willing as he was to trust his players, he also insisted on a version of basketball in which certain principles were not only acknowledged but revered. At the same time, Holzman knew that basketball had moved past the days of City College. If the Knicks offered hope for the country, they did so while acknowledging that things would never be the same again. For America, these teams were not an attempt to deny the trauma of the sixties but a reality that offered a way forward. They continue to resonate because, in the end, the Knicks are about the possibility of shared values even after the whole world seems to have broken wide open. A "New York in the Seventies" episode of *Scooby-Doo* directed by Altman—that's why everybody loves the Knicks. —*B.S.*

The Knickerbookers

From Hard Court to Hard Cover

Athletes love talking, and books are filled with words. It's natural, then, that athletes would want to write books, since books make talking permanent. The trouble, of course, is that while idiotic ejaculations at press conferences and lockerside chats at least dissolve into air, tomes penned by athletes, most of which are dumb, banal, and filled with useless reflections on life, are indeed permanent and often become blockbusters. We all become a little bit stupider, and public library shelves become crammed with this garbage. The New York Knicks of the early 1970s have produced more published volumes than any sports team in history; it's no accident that the team who elevated off-court fame into an art form made a grand foray into publishing. But what truly distinguishes them from other athletes-turned-authors is the high quality of the work produced by these Knicks. Fittingly, their books boast the same mixture of style and smarts that made them champs. *—J.G.B.*

DAVE DeBUSSCHERE

★★★ The Open Man: A Championship Diary
with Dick Schaap (Random House, 1970)

The first book-length dispatch to come howling from the locker room of the cham-peen Knicks, this memoir came courtesy of reserved, relatable, and remarkably unboring Dave DeBusschere. DeBusschere worked alongside writer Dick Schaap, who was at the time on a roll of coauthoring sports books, fresh off 1968's immensely popular *Instant Replay*, which profiled NFLer Jerry Kramer. *The Open Man* chronicles every day of the 1969–70 season, from training camp through Game 7, with wits, smarts, and the occasional roarer (sometimes inadvertent, as DeBusschere explains for rube readers what precisely this weird New York delicacy called a bagel might be). DeBusschere is tough on himself, but this allows for levity; he ends up having a blast at it all, offering self-deprecating asides even while hanging out at Robert Redford's proto-Sundance ski resort after a game in Salt Lake City. DeBusschere was the Knick least at home with celebrity, but this quality often works to his advantage in this eminently readable chronicle of the NBA.

WILLIS REED

★★ A View from the Rim: Willis Reed on Basketball
with Phil Pepe (Lippincott, 1971)

Another co-scribed account, this one helped along by Phil Pepe. Pepe interviewed Reed at length—often interminable length, it appears, as he seems to transcribe Willis's every meandering mumble. Example: "My height has been listed as anywhere from 6-8 to 6-11. I've even read that I'm probably shorter than 6-8. Well, this is the truth—I'm 6-10. Actually, I'm not quite 6-10, but I'm not 6-9 either. I'm somewhere between 6-9 and 6-10, but I'm closer to 6-10 than I am to 6-9. I was always taught that when something is more than half, you go to the next whole number. So I consider myself 6-10." It goes on like that. The book is a jumble of inspiring life lessons and tips on how to rule at basketball, often within the same chapter. So it is that a four-page illustrated guide to jump shooting, featuring Reed in full uniform in the middle of a photogenic field, interrupts advice on what the aspiring young athlete should eat. All the same, a lovable mess.

BY THE SAME AUTHOR:

A WILL TO WIN: THE COMEBACK YEAR (Prentice-Hall, 1973)

WALT FRAZIER

★★★ Rockin' Steady: A Guide to Basketball & Cool

with Ira Berkow (Prentice-Hall, 1974)

An ode to egotism, this is really just a guide to how to be Walt Frazier. From chapter one, titled "Cool," readers are asked to take a magic Clyde-ride through Frazier's world view, most of which involves basketball, the supremacy of style, or his supremacy at being stylish. "Cool" explains how to look cool, act cool, and wear deodorant; "Defense" explains guarding Dave Bing; "Offense" covers everything, right down to tips for when the ball is headed out of bounds. For some reason, the two-page chapter "Statistics" comes next; it includes the box scores from Frazier's four favorite games as a pro. "Rockin' Steady: Game Day" goes from hanging out at home ("My living room. I like to keep it dark, like a night club") to meeting fans. "A General Guide to Looking Good and Other Matters" details the cost of clothing, proper diet ("No way you can be cool and be fat"), and how to catch a fly in midair (no, really).

BY THE SAME AUTHOR:

CLYDE (Rutledge Books, 1970)

BILL BRADLEY

★★★★ Life on the Run

(Bantam Books, 1976)

Bradley is, of course, the most lettered of the 1969–70 Knicks, so it is no surprise the smart-ass smartyslacks needed no meddling coauthor. The book switches between thoughtful profiles of each of his teammates and equally detailed accounts of specific game days. Written after the championship seasons have ended and his former cohort of Reed, DeBusschere, and Lucas have all retired, Bradley clings to the game despite the evident call of other lives. As such, his account gives a distinctly unromanticized vision of the league, replete with the exquisite boredom and enchantment of life on the road. The only thing lacking here is much evidence of Bradley's signature zaniness during these years (his roommate DeBusschere more than compensates with ridiculous tales in *The Open Man*).

BY THE SAME AUTHOR:

VALUES OF THE GAME (Artisan, 1998)
THE JOURNEY FROM HERE (Artisan, 2000)
THE NEW AMERICAN STORY (Random House, 2007)

PHIL JACKSON

★★★ Take It All!

with George Kalinsky (Macmillan, 1970)

Jackson, who admits he felt challenged by his teammates' logorrhea to come up with something unique, contributed photos and captions to this oversized photo book chronicling the 1969–70 season. Featuring creative cropping and daft design, the book was called "a new art form" by *The Wall Street Journal*. Kalinsky recalls Jackson lying on his floor with a notepad, ready to rock and roll on the text, and saying, "Let's do it." "This on Saturday afternoon," Kalinsky notes. "By Sunday night, we had the book finished." In addition to all else he has accomplished in life, Phil is also apparently capable of hatching a new art form in only 24 hours. What's most revealing is how the future NBA über-coach felt more like an observer of his own team than a member.

BY THE SAME AUTHOR:

MAVERICK (Playboy Press, 1975)
SACRED HOOPS (Hyperion, 1995)
MORE THAN A GAME (Stories Press, 2001)
THE LAST SEASON (Penguin Press, 2004)

JERRY LUCAS

★ The Memory Book

with Harry Lorayne (Stein and Day, 1974)

All-around oddball Lucas contributed the strangest yet most successful Knickbook (a #1 bestseller), despite its having nothing to do with the game of basketball. Lucas was blessed with a photographic memory and cursed with the obsessive-compulsive habit of counting everything. He and coauthor Harry Lorayne, a magician and card specialist, outline numerous memorization tactics, written in the form of a peculiar Socratic dialogue. The book promises to turn readers into total-recall machines, though it's unclear whether the reader has a better chance of becoming a Hall of Fame forward or an obscure magician.

BY THE SAME AUTHOR:

REMEMBER THE WORD (Acton House, 1975)
READY, SET, BELIEVE (Jerry Lucas Memory Training Inc, 1980)
BECOMING A MENTAL MATH WIZARD (Shoe Tree Press, 1991)
READY, SET, REMEMBER (Lucas Educational Systems, 1998)
NAMES & FACES MADE EASY (Lucas Educational Systems, 2000)
LEARNING HOW TO LEARN (Lucas Educational Systems, 2001)

NOTES FROM THE UNDERGROUND

What the Hell Was the ABA?

In 1966, the National Football League agreed to a complicated and cautious merger with its upstart rival, the American Football League—an out-of-nowhere operation that, if nothing else, had proven the country had a bottomless lust for football. Inspired by that fairy-tale union, the following year a ragtag group of business owners founded the American Basketball Association, which sought to similarly cash in by forcing the already-established NBA to swallow its competition alive and pay for the privilege of doing so.

The ABA was a professional sports league in the same way that a lump of viral matter counts as a life-form. Without taking anything away from the years Julius Erving or anyone else spent there, it's probably best not to think of it as a league, at least not in the sense the NBA was. Thirty years later, we still don't really know what to make of the phrases "ABA All-Star" or "ABA Championship." The ABA was the staging area for a new style of play, one that would eventually kick in the doors to the establishment. At the same time, it was an opportunistic jumble of renegade finance; teams that changed locations, names, or owners on a moment's notice; and marketing ideas that ranged from ingenious branding to ham-fisted gimmicks.

The NBA already had the household stars, the major basketball markets, and the national airtime. The ABA had none of the above. Unable to compete with the NBA's material power, the ABA countered with classic guerrilla tactics: changing the terms of engagement.

Like most professional sports leagues, the NBA was a collection of individual teams competing against each other for a title. It tried to attract fans and media on the basis of those teams' success and the quality of their play. The ABA simplified the equation: All it wanted was to distract eyeballs, dollars, and new markets away from the more established league—figuring out what to do with them (if indeed it ever got them) was a secondary concern at best.

PICTURES AT AN EXHIBITION: Starting in 1971, the ABA and NBA played combative exhibition games pitting various teams from both leagues against each other. Even though the games didn't count toward any official records, players regularly earned technicals and were often ejected. The first few years, NBA teams typically won, but in the last three series of exhibitions before the merger, the ABA gained the upper hand with series wins of 15–10, 16–7, and 31–17. The ABA won all games played between the champions of each league.

BEST NAMES IN THE ABA: Red Robbins, Trooper Washington, Levern Tart, Cincinnatus Powell, Goose Ligon, Willie Wise

ANYTHING FOR LAUGHS: ABA halftime performances and marketing gimmicks included Halter Top Night and John Brisker Intimidation Night (Brisker was a role player on the visiting team prone to fighting, so the host Utah Stars arranged for a platoon of local boxers to line the court). But perhaps the most outrageous was a haftime show put on by the Indiana Pacers featuring Victor the Wrestling Bear, an actual bear who wrestled several local TV personalities.

Its weapons were far from conventional. In addition to its raw, frenetic play and ceaseless efforts to poach high-profile players from the NBA, the ABA came up with seemingly random publicity stunts; invented the three-point shot and the dunk contest; and staged surreal halftime performances (which included everything from *Playboy* bunnies to live bears, though never, unfortunately, at the same time). The league used an iconic red-white-and-blue ball that was a master stroke of branding and especially popular on inner-city courts. In theory, each of these PR microvictories brought the league that much closer to the macroparadise promised by the would-be merger.

When it came to stocking their roster, the ABA had to resort to all sorts of tricks. The original owners had deluded themselves into thinking the NBA's stars would happily jump ship, but in fact the only known commodity they were able to lure over during the first season was the ever-contrarian Rick Barry. So the ABA rewrote the rule book.

From the start, the league took a chance on pariahs like Connie Hawkins and Doug Moe. In 1969 it invented the "hardship rule," which gave a college underclassman permission to join the ABA if he and his family needed the money. While this decision was to have far-reaching implications, at the time its aim was painfully specific: allowing nineteen-year-old Spencer Haywood to join the Denver Rockets after his sophomore year at the University of Detroit. By 1976, the ABA had pushed its altruism to the limit, allowing high schooler Moses Malone to enter its draft. The league also instituted the dreaded Dolgoff Plan, which visited a form of economic terror on the NBA's owners. The Dolgoff Plan enabled ABA teams to offer enormous contracts by spreading the money out over time, bundling it into deferred payments and annuities. This sparked a period of vertiginous salary inflation in which the NBA was forced to match the ABA's almost imaginary contracts with cold, hard cash. The NBA, in it for the long haul, had to consider reality when structuring its payrolls. The ABA just made a down payment and promised players the rest later.

THE FIRST HIGH SCHOOLER: Contrary to popular belief, Moses Malone was not the first player to go from high school to the pros without playing in college. Seven-foot Detroit-area center Reggie Harding was selected by the Pistons straight out of Eastern High School in both 1962 and 1963. Harding would go on to play five seasons in the NBA and ABA, spend time in jail, have several drug problems, and threaten to shoot Pacers GM Mike Storen in the middle of a television interview. After his retirement in 1968 Harding held up a liquor store, only for the clerk to recognize him and ask, "What are you doing, Reggie?" His response: "It ain't me, man." He was murdered on the streets of Detroit in 1972, at age thirty.

There was no "I" in ABA. It didn't matter which team in particular stole a player or cultivated something resembling a fan base, so long as it brought attention to the league. Like that little virus staring out at the world from its petri dish, the league's daily activity consisted of mutating wildly, exchanging bits of genetic material at random, and compounding itself at a dizzying rate. The

ABA's teams bore little resemblance to their NBA counterparts. Like our friends the llama or the buffalo, NBA teams stayed alive in terrible isolation and often in direct competition for each other's resources—in the buffalo's case, grass and shrubs, in the NBA teams' case, wins and draft picks. In 1968, Lew Alcindor (later Kareem Abdul-Jabbar) was seriously considering joining the upstart league after college. The NBA's shot at Alcindor came via the Milwaukee Bucks, the team that had drafted him, and Alcindor negotiated solely with them. The ABA owners, on the other hand, negotiated as a committee, sending Commissioner George Mikan himself—armed with a million-dollar check and a mink coat—in an attempt to woo Alcindor. Any individual team might die tomorrow, but as long as enough teams persisted for the league to carry on, it could be reborn through self-sacrifice. Thus, in the ABA, franchises rose, fell, changed hands, changed locales, and changed names with comic abandon, to the point where their individual identities became meaningless: Between 1967 and 1976, the New Orleans Buccaneers became the Memphis Pros, became the Memphis Tams, became the Memphis Sounds, became the Baltimore Hustlers, only to play their final three games as the Baltimore Claws.

By 1970, the ABA had established enough of a presence—and become enough of a nuisance—that the NBA owners voted 13–4 in favor of a merger. However, for better or worse, the league was given the opportunity to mutate further and mature into something worth remembering. That spring, NBA Players Association president Oscar Robertson filed a far-reaching antitrust suit that, among other things, claimed that getting rid of the ABA would give the NBA a monopoly. The merger was blocked, and the ABA lasted six more seasons.

In the fall of 1971, Julius Erving came to the Virginia Squires as a free agent. Erving would radically alter the dynamic between the ABA and the NBA. Before Erving, the NBA was worried only about losing its rightful player-property to the ABA; it had never considered that the ABA might also be discovering and developing talent it had missed. The incentive for a merger had largely been to move on untapped markets (especially the Southern ones that it had hitherto ignored) and to tamp down salary inflation. With Dr. J, however, it became clear that the ABA might have something to say about the direction of the game. Along with David Thompson and George Gervin, Erving was the kind of player who benefited

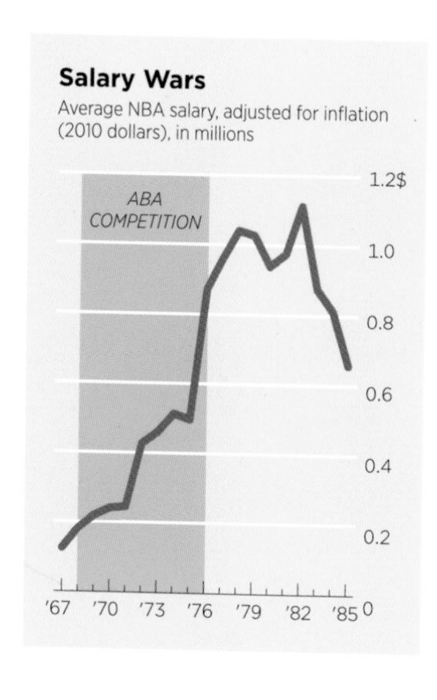

FIT TO PRINT: When the New Orleans Buccaneers moved to Memphis in 1970, ownership settled on Pros as the team's new name, a choice that was widely mocked for its lack of ingenuity. It was chosen because management didn't want to spend money on new uniforms and needed a name that would fit in the same space as "Bucs." When Oakland Athletics owner Charlie Finley bought the franchise in 1972, he changed the name to another four-letter word: Tams, an acronym for Tennessee, Alabama, and Mississippi, the states in the franchise's regional market.

Bucs
25
SPURS
44
VIRGINIA
35
MEMPHIS
11
NETS
32
31
STARS
22

THOMPSON
33
"FLY"
35
Indiana
25
OAKS
Colone
53
CONDOR
Sounds
2

from being given the chance to cut loose in the ABA—as opposed to a pro who had just turned down the wrong dark alley.

At the University of Massachusetts, Erving twice averaged 20 points and 20 rebounds for the season but went undrafted by either league. Before long, he would become the ABA's signature player—though he was more frequently whispered about than actually seen in action, owing to the ABA's lack of television coverage and comically low attendance in most arenas. Standing 6′8″, with impossibly long arms, power to spare, and the ability to rise skyward without any clear point of liftoff, Erving dominated through sheer force of style. He was far from polished, but when he went up with the ball, palming it in one huge hand as his 'fro stood at attention, there was a sense that basketball itself was changing. Like man in outer space, it was at once inspiring and unsettling.

Erving had his antecedents, other players who had placed a premium on artful intimidation. Elgin Baylor was the obvious reference point. Earl Monroe shed defenders by telling them false tales. Connie Hawkins's game was strung out on effortless control. The bombastic Gus Johnson had already introduced the pros to the concept of dunking on fools' heads. Dr. J brought these strains together, bifurcating the lane, surveying the floor from above, and then either throwing down with fury and panache or laying it in with a flick of the wrist.

If Erving was the ABA's hood ornament and the guy coveted by the NBA (for a change), the Nuggets' Thompson was that headlong rush into the unknown, into the positively limitless, that once and for all made the ABA player a valuable commodity. There was real violence in the way Thompson sent himself flying into and over traffic, hanging there an extra beat as if to add insult to injury. Some players wow us by doing things on the court that our brains can only begin to formulate. What made Thompson so intoxicating was that, like the superheroes who earn a beleaguered city's trust, he took a basic human urge and amplified it beyond recognition. We all want to fly; we all know the feeling of jumping skyward, however fleetingly aloft. In Thompson, dreams became realized; ideas, reified; the ordinary, transmuted into something profound.

Even by the ABA's spring-loaded standards, the young Skywalker was all but unstoppable. He was already familiar to fans as a frequent recipient of alley-oops at NC State (except

GUS STORIES: Gus "Honeycomb" Johnson came to the ABA after a ten-year NBA career and played only 50 games for the Virginia Squires, but he was an outsized personality worthy of the league's reputation for oddballs. Here are just a few stories:

LUCAS ENVY: In 1963–64, Johnson finished second in NBA Rookie of the Year voting to college teammate Jerry Lucas. He resented the higher-profile Lucas so much that he used to stare at pictures of him in his hotel room to get psyched for games against the Cincinnati Royals.

TOOTH . . . : Anticipating popular style by several decades, Johnson had a gold star drilled into one of his front teeth.

. . . AND NAIL: As a collegian at Idaho University, Johnson once touched a spot 11.5 feet high on a beam at a local bar from a standing start. The bar's owner put a nail in the spot, named it "Gus Johnson's Nail," and challenged anyone to duplicate the feat. In the twenty-three years before the spot's demolition, Dennis Johnson came closest from a standstill and actually touched the nail with a running start.

that, since the dunk was then illegal in college ball, Thompson was careful to lay the ball in—until his final home game). In the Final Four of his senior year, he swatted Bill Walton's shot in the paint; that summer he was number one in both the NBA's and ABA's drafts. Thompson's game was at once filthy and ethereal in a way that remains irresistible to this day. It was no accident that MJ picked Thompson to do his Hall of Fame introduction; Bill Simmons has called Thompson "the Intellivision to Jordan's PlayStation." Unfortunately, he would struggle to pull together a pro career worthy of his gifts, while his young admirer would take this modality and turn it into basketball scripture.

Plagued by drug problems, knee injuries, and knee injuries caused by drug problems (he fell down a flight of stairs at Studio 54 in 1984, well after both Thompson and that scene were played out), Thompson flamed out not long after the merger finally came to pass in 1976. He did, however, stick around long enough to sign a then-record contract with the Nuggets in 1978, for $4 million over five years. This came after a season when, in a last-ditch effort to win the scoring title, he'd put up 73 points in the final game of the regular season. Fellow ABA alum George Gervin poured in 63 to maintain his lead.

OLD SKYWALKER: David Thompson couldn't escape freak injuries even in retirement. At the 1992 All-Star weekend in Orlando, he blew out his knee in the NBA Legends Game. After the 1993 contest, the league ditched the Legends Game for the Rookie Game, in large part because of injuries like the one sustained by Thompson.

That was typical of Gervin, the spindly pride of the ABA's San Antonio Spurs, who did for downcourt drift what Erving and Thompson did for upward velocity. Gervin slid through softer air than the rest of us and had the kind of touch that made the ball look as if it wanted to go through the hoop. His trademark finger roll was perhaps the world's only soft-focus kill shot, devastatingly effective and yet insidiously intimate. Nicknamed the Iceman, Gervin wasn't regal like Doc or off-the-charts exuberant like Thompson. He was a massacre in pastel; conventional wisdom holds that he was simply a "quiet" scorer who hung huge point totals on opponents without their even noticing. But that underestimates the sneaky, even creepy, quality of Gervin. Gervin's ability to put teams away had more in common with a well-dressed hit man who never speaks, or a sleek, aerodynamic zombie, or the Angel of Death, or the zombie Angel of Death that the Almighty would love to hire if his fee weren't so high. The discovery that Gervin, like Thompson, had spent his peak years coked to the gills makes him even more unsettling, in retrospect. He was a survivor, but only because he conserved his pulse to begin with.

In 1976 the merger finally came true, and the NBA let in four

ABA teams: Denver (Thompson), Indiana, New York (Erving), and San Antonio (Gervin). Among the players and coaches, there had always been concerns that they had been trapped in an elaborate hoax, squandering their best years while the owners had had their sights on selling out all along. But this had given rise to a certain underdog pride among them, with the world at large ignoring them, their own league more interested in self-immolating business than basketball, and the NBA pretending for as long as it possibly could that they were second-class citizens. It wasn't just that they wanted to stick up for themselves as credible basketball players; they also embraced the style they'd helped create, and indeed the whole ABA experience, as their own, a cohesive whole that had value in itself. Out of necessity, they maintained a sense of irony, even gallows humor, about the league as an operation. That didn't mean, though, that players didn't feel like they were a part of something bigger, no matter how crazy, broke, or drugged-out some among them may have been. They were also the least surprised when the message of the ABA followed the few teams, and more than a few players, who made it into the NBA after the merger.

NO NEWS IS BAD NEWS: The ABA was littered with players who could've been among the greats had they the power to overcome their demons, but no one had more potential than Marvin "Bad News" Barnes. Barnes, or "News," as he liked to refer to himself, was a 6′9″ forward who could do everything. Steve "Snapper" Jones told David Halberstam that Barnes was the most talented player he had ever seen: "As quick as Walter Davis. The rebounding instincts, timing, and strength of Moses Malone. Could shoot like Marques Johnson."

In 1989, Terry Pluto published *Loose Balls*, an oral history of the ABA that helped spark a renewal of interest in the league. Several years later, the Beastie Boys' tour shirt incorporated the red-white-and-blue ball, cementing the league as a signifier of the funky, overstated seventies. That was the ABA on display in a 2002 Nike spot in which Vince Carter, Paul Pierce, and others suited up for the long-suffering Roswell Rayguns. Inserted into old game footage the same way Fred Astaire dances with a vacuum cleaner, with Bootsy Collins prancing across center court, this is the slick, romanticized version of the ABA. It's basketball revivalism's answer to blaxploitation.

WHAT HAPPENED TO THAT BOY? At the time of the merger, there were six ABA teams still afloat. The NBA was letting only four franchises in. Something had to be done about the Spirits of St. Louis and the Kentucky Colonels. Colonels owner John Y. Brown—founder of KFC—was bought out for $3.3 million, which he used to buy half of the Buffalo Braves in 1976. He was elected governor of Kentucky in 1979. Ozzie and Dan Silna, the brothers who owned the Spirits, opted for a percentage of the television money garnered by the Nuggets, Pacers, Nets, and Spurs—in all perpetuity. They are interviewed every few years for having made what might be the shrewdest business move ever.

Except the ABA was also incomplete and frequently incoherent. It certainly wasn't a viable alternative, and its only clear objectives had little to do with reinventing the game. Yet it's possible to conceive of it as a workshop or laboratory—more Kool Herc's rec room than a Parliament concert. As unsatisfying a description as this may be, it's also the league's most lasting legacy. —*B.S.*

LEFT OF CENTER

Kareem Abdul-Jabbar and Bill Walton

The two most important centers of the seventies were a grave black Muslim no one liked and a campus radical whose career was over in a blip. By the time Kareem Abdul-Jabbar hung up his protective goggles in 1989, he had played twenty seasons, won six titles, been named MVP six times, and appeared in an astounding nineteen All-Star Games; he was the league's all-time leading scorer and the proud owner of a second act that nearly eclipsed his first. In aggregate, Bill Walton got in about three seasons' worth of All-Timer play before foot problems did him in; his reputation depends almost entirely on the style and symbolism of the 1977 Trail Blazers. Gale Sayers, who played a sport premised on violent collision, managed about five seasons and is thought of as an incomplete. Walton, however, is no grandiose fragment but a near-messianic figure who appeared to the league in its most gnarled hour.

Each man was, in his own way, inseparable from the landscape of 1970s America: serious, talented, plagued by ideology. In 1971, Kareem, then Milwaukee's stoic savior Lew Alcindor, helped the aged Oscar Robertson win his sole title, allowing the surly vet to be seen in a charitable light. But immediately thereafter, Kareem went public with his conversion to Islam and adopted his new name, shrouding the pensive giant in suspicion—especially once he made it clear that religion defined him every bit as much as basketball. Walton, on the other hand, was the classic campus actvitist. His antiwar, pro-vegetable convictions were dismissed as something between youthful indiscretion and mere eccentricity rather than ever being thought of as a hole in the bottom of an immense basketball talent. If Kareem was seen as a threat, inseparable from what he represented in society, then Walton, like so many other white kids, was bound to get over it all.

But there was an added dimension to all this. When Walton arrived in the league in 1974, the league badly needed the Big Redhead to resuscitate good, honest basketball (played by folks

OPERATION KINGFISH: The ABA was so intent on wooing Kareem (then Lew Alcindor) that, in the months before the 1969 draft, it undertook a bizarre research campaign dubbed Operation Kingfish. The league hired professional psychiatrists to analyze Alcindor, interviewed his friends and family, and even hired a private detective to trail him around UCLA—all to figure out what made the inscrutable big man tick.

THE OTHER ONE: Walton was the first inductee into the Grateful Dead's Hall of Honor, a distinction he received in recognition of his dogged devotion to the principles of love and harmony espoused in the band's music. In the press release announcing his induction, Walton compares the Dead to basketball greats such as Michael Jordan and Magic Johnson.

KAREEM ON THE SCREEN:
Kareem was not the first player to enter Hollywood. Wilt played to type as a warrior in *Conan the Destroyer* and Russell inhabited a butler in an episode of *It Takes a Thief*. But he embraced the role like no one before, in sharp contrast to his aloof persona.

ROGER MURDOCK: *Airplane!* In his most famous role, Kareem plays an airline pilot in this spoof of Hollywood disaster films. In his most famous scene, a little boy identifies him as Kareem, which he denies until the kid starts noting a lack of effort on defense. Kareem briefly breaks character for the money quote: "Tell your old man to drag Walton and Lanier up and down the court for forty-eight minutes."

HAKIM: *Game of Death*. This kung fu story finds Kareem fighting Bruce Lee as the final villain, Hakim, in the hero's quest for vengeance. The imposing Hakim is defeated only when Lee realizes he has an unusually strong aversion to sunlight.

THE ARCHANGEL OF BASKETBALL: *Slam Dunk Ernest*. Kareem bestows a pair of magical basketball shoes on a dimwitted Southerner in the eighth film featuring Jim Varney's character. Ernest finds that the shoes give him great basketball gifts, but he eventually discards them for the sake of friendship and leads his team to victory over the NBA's Charlotte Hornets.

HIMSELF: *Full House*. In one of the most memorable episodes of the popular series, Kareem helps notoriously horrible player Jesse find his "sweet spot" so he won't embarrass himself in a three-on-three tournament.

with normal names). As much as the cocaine scourge, salary upheaval, or in-game fisticuffs, having Kareem Abdul-Jabbar lord over the NBA was indicative of this most ambivalent of eras. Walton, who had followed Kareem at UCLA and admired the older center's intellectual independence, became his antidote.

Fans didn't connect with Kareem, and he didn't seem particularly concerned with appealing to them. His Los Angeles predecessor Chamberlain threatened to destroy the game; Kareem played it so well, and with such a sense of detachment, that it trivialized his achievements. But this notion presumes that there is no inherent value, or meaning, in mastery through ritual and repetition. It draws a loaded distinction between greatness and going through the motions of greatness. The sky hook, Kareem's signature move, was absolutely unstoppable but relied on a wonderfully simple—and to some degree, drab—premise: The ball was kept just beyond the earthly peril of defenders, and all that was left was for Kareem to calculate the proper trajectory. That Kareem relied more on laconic geometry than pure size or strength made him all the more remote and vexing as a player. It was that easy for him, and yet there wasn't even a spectacle for the price of admission. As players all around him sought greater individual expressiveness, Kareem seemed intent on giving himself over to the shot he knew to be true.

In the seventies, basketball supposedly got too black, as evidenced by a slew of conversions to Islam and crazy hairdos. But Kareem was his own enigma, a strange, implacable creature who took this trend a step further. His personality seemed a natural fit for this new faith and for his game, which was seemingly premised on stone-faced devotion. It was virtually impossible for Middle America—he was, after all, in Milwaukee—not to view Kareem, and by extension, his game, as alien. This unspoken public discomfort became outright scandal in 1973, when the Black Mafia, a Philadelphia-based crime syndicate with ties to the Nation of Islam, massacred seven people in Kareem's D.C. townhouse—including five children. The target was Hamaas Abdul Khaalis, leader of the Hanafi sect that Kareem belonged to; once a member of the Nation, now Khaalis had denounced Elijah Muhammad in a letter. This theological dispute led to swift, crazed retribution that had more in common with the Tate murders than a mob hit.

Kareem had been on the road at the time. Yet even before the killers were identified, the incident gave the impression that on the planet Kareem inhabited, this kind of thing could happen. He entered a strange limbo where he was acknowledged as the league's best player and yet was widely held in suspicion or just plain disliked. In 1975 Kareem was traded to the Lakers, which at least provided him with more cosmopolitan stomping grounds. But it would take the arrival of the ebullient Magic Johnson for the nation to get past his now sinister cast—much as Kareem had done for Oscar Robertson a decade earlier.

By then, Walton was on the rise. Both Kareem and Walton had played for Westwood's bromide-spewing legend John Wooden. Wooden, for all his Midwestern rectitude, never clashed with Kareem, instead guiding him with a practical hand and believing in his powerful relationship with the sport. It's not hard to imagine that, despite their cultural differences, Wooden respected Kareem for both his serious, studious temperament and his austere lifestyle. With Walton, things were different. To Wooden, this was an earnest young man who had decided to flout convention and was, in the coach's words, "easily distracted by fringe ideas." Kareem, on the other hand, was on a solemn quest for knowledge of self. He would later say, "My choosing Islam was not a political statement; it was a spiritual statement." Walton couldn't claim this kind of calling, so his life away from basketball suffered from a lack of focus. However, as much as he delighted purists with his play, Walton caused the biggest stir by letting his red hair grow long, getting arrested at an antiwar demonstration, and taking on two-bit activist Jack Scott as his personal guru. He was an improbable hybrid of classic hoops and yippie agitation.

THE BIG REDHEAD, SILENCED: Walton stuttered terribly for the first twenty-eight years of his life, covering up his lack of social confidence by taking refuge in basketball. Then, after randomly meeting announcer Marty Glickman at a social function, everything changed. Glickman told Walton that speech was a skill like any other, something that must be practiced every day in order to develop. He gave Walton several tips, including reading out loud daily, chewing sugarless gum to strengthen jaw muscles, and identifying troublesome sounds and working on them. In time, Walton overcame his impediment and has become a powerful advocate for stutterers. He's worked often with the Stuttering Foundation of America, as has Denver Nuggets forward Kenyon Martin.

In *Drive, He Said,* Jack Nicholson's 1971 directorial debut, protagonist Hector Bloom confronts the Walton-like predicament of a big-time college athlete–cum–campus radical. An adaptation of Jeremy Larner's 1964 novel of the same name, it was advertised as "The Disenchantment of an All-American Jock." Superficially, it captures the predicament you would expect of a Walton-like character, or perhaps of Walton as he appeared to Wooden. Bloom feels the game in his bones, and Nicholson wants us to understand this; the wide-angle, classical-scored rendering of a layup drill is as gorgeous as hoops-as-cinema gets. At the same time, Bloom finds himself sucked into midgame protests and badgered by his draft-dodging roommate to spend more time fighting the system. The All-American Jock finds himself torn between his beliefs and a silly little sport that offers mainstream acceptance

THAT'S TERRIBLE: You either loved or hated Bill Walton as an announcer, but all can agree that his bizarre style set him apart from the cliché-spouting likes of Mark Jackson and Jon Barry. His greatest hits:

1. "And when I think of Boris Diaw, I think of Beethoven and the age of the Romantics."

2. "You look at Vladimir Radmanovic, this guy is cut from stone. It's as if Michelangelo were reading and a lightning bolt flashed before him."

3. "Yesterday we celebrated Sir Isaac Newton's discovery of gravity. Today, Fabricio Oberto is defying it."

4. During the 2007 FIBA Tournament of the Americas, Walton praised dictatorial leader Hugo Chávez for the way he has empowered and educated poor Venezuelans.

5. "The only man who can stop Cliff Robinson is Cliff Robinson. The man is unstoppable, even at thirty-eight."

6. "If Eric Piatkowski continues playing at this level, he's going to replace Jerry West on the NBA logo."

7. "If Anthony Johnson ever gets a jumper, who's going to stop him?"

8. "Atlanta needs all thirteen lottery picks."

9. "Where would the L.A. Clippers franchise be without Sean Rooks?"

10. "Robert Horry is the greatest inbounds passer in the history of the NBA."

11. On Larry Johnson during the '99 Finals: "What a pathetic play from a pathetic human being."

12. On Penny Hardaway's decline: "He had everything. He had . . . a doll."

13. "John Stockton is one of the true marvels, not just in basketball, or in America, but in the history of Western civilization!"

and presumably a career; in Larner's novel, the main character decides to burn the campus to the ground. The film ends up with Bloom neither here nor there: Suspended from the team, he then watches his deranged (via sleep deprivation, meant to fool army psychiatrists) roomie being carried off by police.

But Hector Bloom isn't nearly the phenom that Walton was, nor as cybernetically in tune with the rhythms of the game. Walton actually offered hope for resolution between these two aspects of himself rather than continued dissonance. Walton was such a peculiar character not because of how good he was at basketball but because of how compatible basketball seemed to be with his personality. On the court he never demonstrated anything short of total immersion in the game, a quality that to the untrained eye contrasted sharply with Kareem. There was something refreshing about Walton, who dominated by inhabiting the game fully, not by imposing himself on it. This suggested that Walton might not be as schizoid as was often assumed, raising the possibility that, unexpectedly, sport contained within it the possibility of transcendence; the mind-set needed to internalize the flow of the game as Walton did lent itself to all sorts of hippie cant. The inconclusive ending to Nicholson's movie leaves the door open to this overlap and hints at it in certain exchanges. Perhaps Jack departed from his source material because, secretly, he too would like to see sport and the counterculture find common ground.

The meaning of Walton's game became more pronounced when he got to Portland, where he was surrounded by players closer to his level and, with coach Jack Ramsay, found himself in a system that catered to his strengths. Walton's passing skills were unmatched among big men, and he got off on the interplay of teamwork, nonstop motion, and fine details like cuts and far-off screens. With Ramsay's offense alternately radiating from and flowing through Walton, the big man was the enlightened opposite of the traditional pound-it-in approach to using seven-footers, and all because he had the ability and awareness to justify this Copernican shift.

Walton's brief moment at the top and the team that was both an extension of him and his ideal band of travelers are still treated as objects of reverence. The Blazers' 1977 title run was not just an assertion of Walton's greatness but of the value he represented during this troubled period of the NBA. Walton's generational angst mattered far less than what his Blazers stood in opposition to: namely ego, individual flash, and, whether they liked it or not, the importance of African Americans to the game. It's worth noting, though, that despite this team's reputation as the antithesis of the big, bad, black NBA, Walton played his best ball when working off the brawny ABA refugee Maurice Lucas, and the two of them bonded over their interest in Communism. Maybe Lucas, like Walton, saw in this all-for-one philosophy a mirror for the ideology he favored. The Blazers topped the badder-than-thou Sixers 4–2 in the Finals; Philly's roster was a bundle of speed, power, ups, and bravado that boasted the likes of Dr. J, George McGinnis, Darryl Dawkins, and World B. Free. They were very nearly an All-Star team, but they couldn't match Portland's utopian model.

The downfall of those Blazers came swiftly. The following year, Walton was coaxed into playing on a fractured foot during the playoffs after having missed the preceding twenty-two games; he never recovered fully and would go on to blame the team doctor, Coach Ramsay, his teammates, the front office, and even Jack Scott for his problems. He demanded a trade, ended up with the San Diego Clippers, and then was barely serviceable for what should have been his prime. Walton finally salvaged his career as a veteran retread in Boston, winning Sixth Man of the Year as a member of the 1986 Celtics championship team. Fittingly, he would go on to become a highly entertaining broadcaster, while Kareem wrote volumes of amateur history and wondered why no team seemed interested in offering him a head coaching position.

In the end, though, Kareem and Walton are more alike than they are different. As the rest of the league was busy reaping the benefits of the salary boom, each embodied a different kind of purism. In the stately Kareem and the playful Walton, there was a wholly original perspective on how to approach the game, philosophically speaking. It's a bit strange to say that such dominant athletes are as significant as thinkers. Yet, without taking anything away from their off-court pursuits, their most influential thinking had to do with basketball—rooted in concerns of their era but as an outlook on hoops, timeless. Each lived by his own version of the philosophy expressed in this statement by Kareem: "You have to be able to center yourself, to let all of your emotions go . . . Don't ever forget that you play with your soul as well as your body." *—B.S.*

THE JAZZ-O-METER

1970s RATING: Pretty jazzy (80/100)

KAREEM ABDUL-JABBAR: Kareem grew up with jazz, since his father was a Juilliard-trained trombonist and singer who used to hang out with Dizzy Gillespie at nightspots like the legendary Minton's Playhouse. When Kareem converted to Islam, his mentor was Hammas Abdul Khaalis, a former jazz drummer. After Kareem lost his beloved jazz record collection in a 1983 house fire, many fans sent him records in the mail or stopped by the locker room after games to give him albums. Kareem also started his own jazz record label, Cranberry Records.

SPENCER HAYWOOD: Was a jazz aficionado as far back as his high school days: "Detroit was in the midst of the Motown revolution; everyone was listening to Stevie Wonder, and the Temptations, and the Supremes, and here we were groovin' to a higher order of music, preparing our minds for battle. Then we'd go out, cool as Miles Davis, and annihilate the other team." Haywood owns over 10,000 jazz albums and DJed weekly at jazz radio station WRVR-FM when he played for the Knicks.

A FAMILY AFFAIR: Haywood's high school teammate Ralph Simpson (an ABA All-Star with the Nuggets) shared his love for jazz, which he passed on to his daughter, the Grammy Award-winning singer India.Arie. She grew up listening to her father's John Coltrane, Miles Davis, and Ella Fitzgerald records.

The Hair Up There

The history of basketball players and hair is long and contentious. In his autobiography, *Second Wind*, Bill Russell claims that NBA owners were so horrified that he and Wilt Chamberlain had grown small beards shortly after entering the league that they called a secret meeting in 1959 to vote on whether to institute a rule banning facial hair on the court. "The league was faced with the first two hairy athletes in modern professional sports," writes Russell, "and the reaction couldn't have been any worse if we had taken up arson as a hobby."

Thankfully, the vote never passed, and in part due to Russell and Wilt's fearless beard-blazing, by the 1970s hair was more than just dead cells that grew out of your head. It was a statement of identity, with longhairs, conscious brothers, and a Broadway musical all swearing by its symbolic powers. In the NBA, how you wore yours said as much about you as your game.

But how much hair was there? To find the answer, we analyzed 1,522 basketball cards issued from 1969 through 1979. We coded player hair for length and volume by assigning four levels to head hair (while controlling for balding), and two levels each for mustaches, sideburns, chin hair, and beards. The answer: a lot of hair.

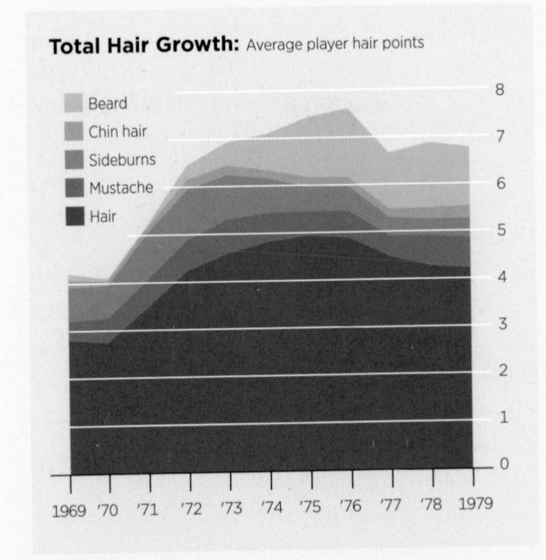

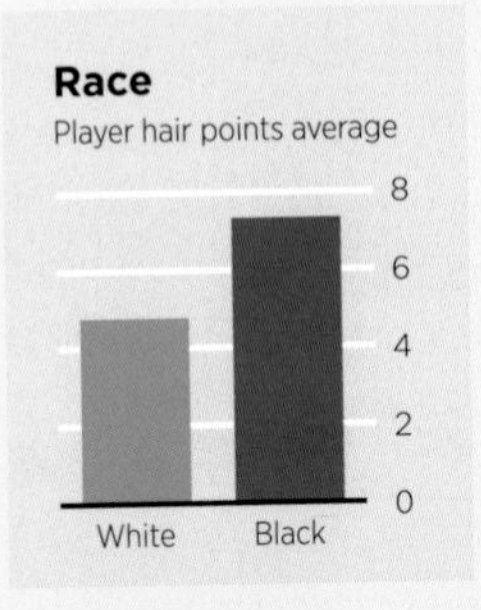

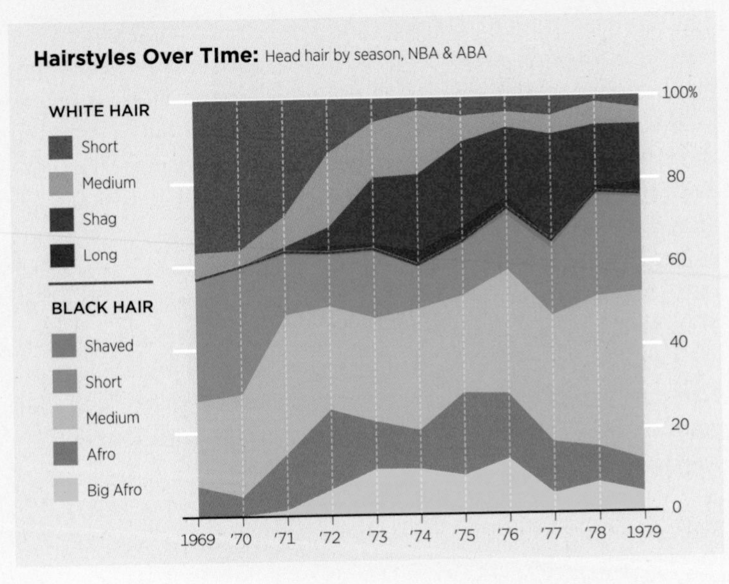

HEAD HAIR KEY

SLICK WATTS, 1976
TOTAL HAIR PTS: **0** (head 0 + facial 0)

TINY ARCHIBALD, 1973
TOTAL HAIR PTS: **3** (head 2 + facial 1)

BOB McADOO, 1975
TOTAL HAIR PTS: **8** (head 4 + facial 4)

WES UNSELD, 1974
TOTAL HAIR PTS: **6** (head 6 + facial 0)

ARTIS GILMORE, 1977
TOTAL HAIR PTS: **14** (head 8 + facial 6)

JERRY WEST, 1970
TOTAL HAIR PTS: **3** (head 2 + facial 1)

PHIL JACKSON, 1974
TOTAL HAIR PTS: **8** (head 4 + facial 4)

PETE MARAVICH, 1974
TOTAL HAIR PTS: **8** (head 6 + facial 2)

BILL WALTON, 1976
TOTAL HAIR PTS: **10** (head 8 + facial 2)

HAIR CHAMPIONS

GAR HEARD

DARNELL HILLMAN

JOE CALDWELL

HAIRIEST TEAM: THE 1975–76 LOS ANGELES LAKERS

K. ABDUL-JABBAR

GAIL GOODRICH

CORKY CALHOUN

LUCIUS ALLEN

STU LANTZ

CAZZIE RUSSELL

PAT RILEY

KERMIT WASHINGTON

PUNCH-DUNK LOVETRON

The NBA's Lost Years Reconsidered

To acknowledge Michael Jordan is human; to appreciate Elvin Hayes, divine. The late 1970s have gained near-universal scorn as the Dark Ages of the NBA, the days in which basketball as we know it almost died. Blame it on narcotics, Kermit Washington's right fist, Lionel Hollins's salary demands, discomfort with young black men running around with increasingly enormous amounts of cash on hand, the death of dynasties brought about by free agency.

While the rise of the street-smart ABA, custom threads in locker rooms, and personal politics expressed too loudly had caused a low rumble during the decade's first half, the second half of the seventies—visceral, strong, and profligate—almost seemed specially designed to alienate the population in Middle America, who compliantly averted their eyes. In this new climate, even small misdeeds were no longer tolerated; somehow an elbow from Maurice Lucas, Portland's audacious enforcer, became more dangerous to society than one by the generally reserved sixties big man Walt Bellamy. Lucas, a double-double power forward, was hardly unprecedented in physical play—Bellamy and others had played rough for years. But circumstances of the day made Bellamy seem just tough and Lucas a threat. True acts of creativity, such as Darryl Dawkins's unapologetic, even gleeful, backboard-smashing or the pet names he gave his own acts of destruction, were as much about racially charged public performance as they were about basketball.

Fans turned away from the game, complaining, sometimes in so many words, that it had gotten too black, violent, and money laden, presumably out of loyalty to the beatitude of basketball as a sport. And yet if they'd had the inclination to open their eyes, they'd have seen an explosion of innovation, energy, and talent.

In our collective memory, late-seventies ball exists in a state of fugue, as if, like the lockout season 1998–99, it didn't really count. Championships for Western outposts Seattle, Golden State, and Portland; a minor monarchy in typically destitute D.C.; star

Cause and Effect?

Black Players

NBA, percent by season

75%
70
65
60
'74 '75 '76 '77 '78 '79 '80 '81

TV Viewers

NBA Finals, households in milllions

10
8
6
4
'74 '75 '76 '77 '78 '79 '80 '81

Source: APBR.org, Nielsen

players shockingly stationed outside New York, Boston, and Los Angeles: These circumstances are anathema to the glitzy NBA we want to remember, the one that Bird and Magic and then Jordan ultimately gave us. If the seventies reemphasized the raw ingredients of pro football—Pittsburgh's lack of sheen, Oakland's uncomfortable ferocity, the newfound glow of big-money Dallas—the decade only killed all basketball's illusions. Sober meat-and-potatoes dominance by Hayes and Wes Unseld in the District? Aggressive confrontation from Dennis Johnson and Gus Williams amid the serene beauty of the Pacific Northwest? Utter smoothness in Buffalo, brought to you by Randy Smith and Bob McAdoo? None of it made a lick of sense.

POINT FORWARDS: The late 1970s NBA saw the rise of the point forward, with two of the most prominent exemplars strangely having the same last name: J. J. Johnson, of the Sonics, and Marques Johnson, of the Bucks. These players had forward size but often initiated the offense and even brought the ball up the court.

The NBA of the seventies was a dangerous place, frothing and combustible as a chemistry lab. Yet it was from these testing grounds that the next NBA emerged, and along the way there were pyrotechnics too unstable and impressive to remain burning for very long. Streaming video was invented, for the Buffalo Braves, two decades late. Smith, the team's 6′3″ lead guard, survived geographic anonymity to earn respect from his colleagues, if not the masses. Before ESPN, stars were made in the televised postseason, and the Braves weren't much of a playoff factor, losing twice to the Celtics (1974, 1976) and once to the Bullets (1975) before financial problems forced a move to San Diego. Few lasting memories of Smith remain; his 2009 death caused hardly a ripple even among devout basketball fans. Under today's scrutiny, a player with Smith's grace and athleticism would be a TV star by his sophomore year of college.

McAdoo is better remembered, thanks to his 1975 MVP award and his Hall of Fame career. But outside the first rank—McAdoo, Erving, Kareem, Unseld, Walton—the stars of the seventies were ultimately irrelevant to the game's history. No one's ever touted as the next Tiny Archibald or Bobby Dandridge. Each era has players like these, but in the seventies, they were as ubiquitous as camp family bands. Gar Heard's fame comes from a supporting role in the Greatest Game—a Sun, he hit the closing shot of the second overtime in Game 5 of the 1976 Finals. But before that he was a protozoal Josh Smith, a self-defined big man just as likely to stuff you at the rim as hit a long jumper. In '74, the 6′6″ Heard blocked more shots (230 total, 2.8 per game) than any player of that size before or since. Today, YouTube would have sainted him. But he, like so many seventies kinsmen, arrived too early.

Archibald perhaps stands as the most enduring of this group of ultimately fleeting stars. A prurient Kenny Anderson—nastier on the court, more excessive with the ball than his NYC kin—Tiny sped by defenders for no reason other than that's all he could really do. Archibald's numbers with the Kansas City Kings speak of midcareer Iverson, with copious shots and assists. But unlike Iverson in his prime, everyone understood Archibald's on-court limits and fatal flaws—you simply cannot watch Tiny play without foreseeing his doom. Iverson's imminent failure became evident only in his troubled gaze, not on his insane dribble-drives. AI's confidence won games, and Tiny's didn't. Archibald could never have won the 2001 MVP; the impact of his play was always limited. If you never make history, your name goes unrecorded.

In today's hypersaturated media environment, 20-point scorers rarely go unnoticed; there are blogs devoted to Richard Jefferson's bad tattoos. But a player like Bobby Dandridge, with four seasons over 20 points per game, exists only in footnotes to greatness. Dandridge began his career caddying for Alcindor and Robertson in Milwaukee, then wound up wedging himself under Hayes and Unseld in D.C. Few players win championships in two cities; today, these players become philosophies unto themselves ("Every winner must have a James Posey"). Whither the Dandridge Doctrine? If Dandridge had come twenty years earlier, he'd be in the Hall of Fame by default (see: Bill Sharman). Twenty years later, he'd have been paid by the victory parade, like Robert Horry. But Dandridge was lost to the Dark Ages.

But to forget Dandridge and Archibald is also to forget that the late seventies weren't all thrashing and grit. Aesthetes would have plenty to appreciate if they knew where to find it. Take World B. Free, an early poster boy for observation over instinct in basketball scouting. Free went to a tiny Carolina school, slipped into the second round in the '76 draft, and hovered in the background of Erving's 76ers before taking full flight with the newly minted San Diego Clippers in '79. There, World paired with Smith, the Southland version of Gus and DJ, beaming lasers over accomplices Swen Nater and post-Punch Kermit Washington. (Tell me that team wouldn't dominate NBA TV Fan Night voting in 2011.) And there, Free would average almost 29 points a game, performing incredible feats of decadence, an eternal heat check in sneakers. Pistol Pete Maravich was effectively Free's equal in audacity but several shades lighter and, as such, vastly more popular in Middle

PLANET LOVETRON: Sixers center Darryl Dawkins burst onto the scene in 1975 as one of the league's strongest personalities. In addition to breaking backboards and naming all his dunks, Dawkins claimed to be an alien from the planet Lovetron, a distant world far different from our own. Step inside and learn more about this strange land:

PRESIDENT: Chocolate Thunder, aka Darryl Dawkins (ex-Chairman of Interplanetary Funkmanship)

DISCOVERED: In the early 1970s, while Dawkins was in high school

ELEMENTAL COMPOSITION: "Love, love, love, and more love. That's it!"

DISTANCE FROM EARTH: One million billion light-years

FAMOUS VISITORS TO LOVETRON: World B. Free, Artis Gilmore, many beautiful women

SUPERPOWERS: Making sure things don't get bent

WEAKNESSES: Unlike the case of Kryptonians and kryptonite, Lovetronians are not weakened by love. In keeping with this trend, Chocolate Thunder loves chocolate—but he can be harmed by large quantities of white lightning.

LOVE TIPS FOR HUMANS: "Toes. Earthlings always forget about the toes."

America. But Maravich, too, was truly something to behold: a fundamentals-gone-wacky artist in short shorts and floppy hair. Memories of Maravich (universally positive), paired with those of fellow white seventies star Paul Westphal (dubbed the league's "blackest white player" by his contemporaries), make for an interesting test case in the decade's legacy. At each player's peak, Maravich was only slightly better and always played for far worse teams than Westphal's Suns. But Westphal's game was largely forgotten. Maravich made the Hall of Fame on his third ballot. Westphal is now known almost exclusively as an old H.O.R.S.E. champ and as Charles Barkley's favorite coach.

Even the Blazers, without question the most widely beloved of the late-seventies title teams, succumb to our collective bemoaning of the era. Memories of the Blazers can't be shared without the apologetic murmur about what might have been. Dr. Jack's castle in the sky—featuring the brilliant passing of Bill Walton, with extraordinary orbital support from Lucas and Lionel Hollins, floating so daintily above the mess the league had become—was eventually yanked down to the ground and infiltrated. In 1980, the Blazers fell victim to Billy Ray Bates, a chiseled, raw talent who grew up in the deep backwoods of Mississippi under antebellum conditions. Bates could dunk on anyone and knock down a shot from anywhere on the floor; no one ever bothered to teach him basketball because it seemed beside the point. His dominance at Kentucky State was viewed askance by the scouts, since there was no socially redeemable explanation for Bates's toiling away so far from the big time. After being drafted in the third round and paying dues in Maine for the CBA, Bates finally signed a ten-day contract with the Blazers in 1980. The antithesis of that championship team of a few years earlier, Bates earned the elemental nickname Dunk and reached the highest level of competition so quickly that he seemed immune to pressure—unless you counted his self-destructive behavior off the court. In the 1980 playoffs, he averaged 25 points per game; in the next postseason, Bates would be at 28.3. By 1982 he was in rehab and well on his way to a wild and woolly career as the "Black Superman" of Philippine basketball. The Blazers missed the playoffs that year.

IRRITATION AS FLATTERY: When Billy Ray Bates went to the Philippine Basketball Association in 1983, he entered a basketball subculture unlike anything in America. Rafe Bartholomew, author of *Pacific Rims: Beermen Ballin' in Flip-Flops and the Philippines' Unlikely Love Affair with Basketball,* explains: "The PBA was a league full of hoops autodidacts, guys who learned to play not in basketball camp but on neighborhood courts that often consisted of little more than salvaged two-by-fours nailed about ten feet high on coconut trees. These players had moves, like Francis Arnaiz's running scoop from fifteen feet, that didn't exist outside the Philippines. But Bates probably paid more attention to what passed for defense in the rough-and-tumble '80s PBA. Undercutting was frowned upon but not verboten; grappling was guaranteed. Local players knew Americans to be *pikon,* or easily pissed off, and they provoked imports by fondling them—literally groping their asses—or by cracking the sides of their mouths to surreptitiously shoot fine streams of spit at the foreign stars. Somehow, in the face of this trickery and despite the mischief Bates caused in the Manila streets, Billy Ray kept his cool on the court. Forty-six points per game was all the revenge he needed."

The '79 Sonics get even less credit. Lenny Wilkens's greatest team was the sane version of Gene Shue's Clippers, led by Dennis Johnson, Gus Williams, and Downtown Freddie Brown. DJ went on to fame elsewhere; he starred as the Ringo of Boston's Big

Three despite setting the early (pre-Magic, by a hair) standard for big point guards with brains. The Sonics were able to dominate defensively with a relatively odd roster: Jack Sikma was tall and Williams short, but the rest of the rotation was made up of tweeners, much like the mid-aughts Hawks (Billy Knight's famous collection of converted small forwards). Even without truly holy talents in hand, Wilkens saw the future and turned it into a surprising title run.

No moment did more to sully the reputation of the late seventies, of course, than when Kermit Washington of the Lakers put his fist through Rocket Rudy Tomjanovich's face during a game in December 1977. The basics are horrifying, with Tomjanovich nearly dying in the middle of a court in the middle of a game, motionless in a pool of blood. But the basics—black man assaults white man with fist—also gloss over the real lessons Washington and Tomjanovich have to offer fans. John Feinstein's detailed book on the incident lays bare Washington's struggle to make something of himself against all odds, his work to develop his mind so that his body could thrive. Though raw footage of the Punch makes him seem like a brute, Washington had actually been one of the most thoughtful, selfless players of his day, an incredible team player—one who stood up to fight only because teammate Kareem had been maimed in a previous game against the Rockets—and hard worker of the highest caliber.

Explosions tend to leave the air thick and impenetrable, and so it was with Washington, misunderstood for decades. Even those inside the game, those who knew the makeup of Kermit's soul, couldn't justify giving him a job. Look how long it took for even a subset of the world to realize Ron Artest was more menace to himself than others after the Brawl in 2004—things were worse in the less compassionate era Washington dealt with. It was easy to mark Kermit as an uninhibited thug, however inexact the accusation. But dozens of other big men would have swung in Washington's position. Once you've made it that far, it's easy enough to blame the whole decade. The world loves a villain, if only for the chance to play judge and jury. Shaking a reputation so entrenched is difficult, and so it is with late-seventies basketball. Viewed from afar, these years look like a black mark on the league. Or perhaps it was only a dense patch of color, too thick and heavy to see without a microscope. —*T.Z.*

IMMORTAL SOLES: Signature basketball shoes didn't reach widespread popularity until the '80s, but several stars of the '70s signed exclusive endorsement deals:

PUMA: Released in 1973, Walt Frazier's suede low-cut Clydes were the first shoe with crossover appeal and for a time were ubiquitous on the streets of New York. Rapper Doug E. Fresh has said, "Brooklyn loved the Puma. Harlem and the Bronx loved the Puma. The Puma was runnin' things."

CONVERSE: Building on their early success with the Chuck Taylors, Converse continued to dominate the basketball market throughout the '70s and released Julius Erving's popular Dr. J. model.

PONY: One of the more active companies of the era, Pony made signature shoes for both Earl Monroe and Darryl Dawkins.

NIKE: Nike was only a bit player during the '70s and early '80s, worn mostly by former ABA stars such as George Gervin and Moses Malone. In the 1980 Finals, Darryl Dawkins proceeded to wear a Pony shoe on one foot and a Nike shoe on the other, having signed deals with both companies.

LEGALIZE IT!

Court Cases, Contracts, and Caps

In 2008, the downtrodden Memphis Grizzlies sent their best player, Pau Gasol, to the championship-chasing Los Angeles Lakers at the trade deadline. Gasol was an impending free agent unlikely to re-sign with Memphis. In return for Gasol, the Lakers handed over three also-rans, a few draft picks, and whatever change they could find between the seat cushions.

The Lakers received an All-Star center capable of scoring, rebounding, passing, and blocking shots; their incentive for making the trade was obvious. The Grizzlies, meanwhile, left the untrained observer baffled. In return for Gasol, they received: Kwame Brown (a draft bust known mostly for being selected, and then ridiculed, by Michael Jordan) whose only real value was an expiring $9 million contract; Javaris Crittenton, a rookie point guard of limited ability; Aaron McKie, a broken-down guard whom the Lakers coaxed out of retirement and signed to a one-day, $750,000 contract just for the trade; first-round picks in 2008 and 2010, most likely too late in the draft to matter much; and the rights to Pau's younger brother Marc, a prospect considered serviceable but less gifted than his older sibling.

Outcry soon followed. Fans and journalists pilloried the Grizzlies for accepting such an obvious inequity among the basketball commodities exchanged. Grizzlies general manager Chris Wallace was deemed incompetent. The trade was regarded as a heist, even a conspiracy to help the megamarket Lakers. Dallas Maverick Dirk Nowitzki complained to a German magazine that winning a championship was difficult when other teams were benefiting from such "unfair trades." San Antonio Spurs coach Gregg Popovich told *Sports Illustrated*, "What they did in Memphis is beyond comprehension."

Despite all the consternation on everyone else's part, the Grizzlies were happy with the deal. Rather than ultimately losing Gasol without compensation through free agency, the team extracted value. It acquired an expiring contract that would create space under the salary cap, took back a low-cost rookie, and ingeniously navigated the NBA's byzantine salary rules. Ultimately, Memphis was really trading with itself, swapping competitive basketball for commercial viability.

In today's NBA, complicated legal constructs such as the collective bargaining agreement have become a part of everyday league dialogue. Teams routinely strike these questionable bargains between basketball's substance and its business, often leaving fans bewildered and angry. How did it get like this? How did a basketball league become as focused on the laws of the land as it is on the rules of the game? Blame the seventies, when it all went wrong.

The decade began under the specter of legal peril. When Connie Hawkins sued the NBA in 1968, he alleged that the league had violated federal antitrust laws, illegally colluding to prevent him from joining the Association. The NBA was caught off guard, incapable of producing a competent, orderly justification of its actions. This was a problem. A new front had opened up in the war between players and owners, and the league was newly vulnerable. Among those who saw the writing on the courtroom walls was a young David Stern, working for the NBA's firm, Proskauer Rose Goetz & Mendelsohn. If the Hawkins case launched the decade of legal mayhem, it also set Stern down the path to one day taking over the league.

The league settled with Hawkins, and that particular Pandora's box was never flung open. Had a court ruled in favor of Hawkins, it might have cast the NBA as a collection of conspirators who artificially suppressed the labor market. Contracts could have been voided, long-indentured players suddenly empowered, and anarchy elevated, with players and teams scrambling to establish a new order. No other blacklisted players sought to replicate Hawkins's legal triumph. But two years later, the fears that lingered in the background of the case were thrust into the foreground.

In 1970, Oscar Robertson, president of the National Basketball Players Association, led his union into a class-action lawsuit against the NBA, alleging additional antitrust violations and seeking to stop a merger with the ABA. The specific policies targeted were the reserve clause, which allowed any team to extend a player's contract year after year for as long as it chose; the draft structure, which awarded the rights of a drafted player to the selecting team in perpetuity; and the compensation rule,

(NOT) STRAIGHT CASH, HOMEY: Pro basketball saw the rise of many complicated legal and financial maneuvers during the 1970s, but one of the strangest was the ABA's Dolgoff Plan. A former pro player himself, Ralph Dolgoff became an accountant upon his retirement from the game and invented a deferred-compensation package to help the ABA's cash-strapped owners offer competitive contracts. Under the Dolgoff Plan, contracts included an annuity to be paid out over a twenty-year period beginning on the player's forty-first birthday, effectively turning portions of a salary into a pseudo-pension. For instance, a deal worth $1.4 million over four years would pay only $250,000 per season, plus $8,000 paid into the annuity every year for ten years. The annuity would then mature and be paid in annual installments of $20,000. Depending on who you ask, the Dolgoff Plan was either a legitimate pension or an underhanded plot designed to make the ABA look more legitimate than it actually was. Under the same name, the plan has become a common feature of contracts in the business world.

A MAN APART: The reserve clause was a standard part of sports contracts in 1967, but Connie Hawkins was able to have it removed from his ABA contract in case the NBA ever allowed him into the league.

which required a new team that signed a player at the end of his contract to remunerate the previous club that wasn't exercising its reserve option. A merger between the NBA and its chief competitor, eliminating even more options for players, surely would only make the problem worse.

Don't be fooled by the technical jargon. The Robertson suit was bold and aggressive, speaking truth to power. In fact, the glut of challenges to the system showed just how mercilessly the Players Association planned to go at its employers. At the time, it threatened to undermine the NBA's financial structure, its financial future, and even its outright existence. This was, in a sense, the point: The players would never have money on their side, but at the dawn of the decade, they were realizing they could appeal to the authority of the courts. Curt Flood had challenged baseball's reserve clause the previous year, but the Players Association took things even further.

Spencer Haywood sued everyone. Haywood had joined the ABA's Denver Rockets in 1969, after only two years of college. His first move was to target the ABA in 1969, seeking to break a contract that he claimed was consummated under the veil of fraud. Then he sued the NBA, which he sought to enter as a member of the Seattle SuperSonics before the NBA's age requirement would have otherwise allowed. Haywood was permitted to play after the Supreme Court found that the NBA's eligibility policy, which lacked any hardship-based exemptions, was too rigid. Once the league's rules were laid bare in front of an impartial judge, players had a fair shake at earning equal rights.

By 1975–76, it was all-out war. As long as the Robertson case remained unresolved, the merger was blocked. The NBA had lost the Haywood decision. Veteran Chet Walker also sought to tackle the reserve clause, demanding the right for players to break contracts easily, moving between teams when (as in his case) the current rights holders no longer had any use for him. He sat out the season in protest as his suit made its way through the court system. However, Walker abandoned his more radical challenge in 1976, when the Robertson suit was finally settled (as a player rep in the original suit, Chet couldn't be in two places at once). With the NBA-ABA wars having already inflated salaries, this agreement even further expanded player liberties. It eliminated the reserve clause, phased out compensation agreements, ended indefinite draft rights (at least as far as American players were

JUDGMENT DAY: The Oscar Roberston lawsuit was pushed toward its ultimate conclusion by federal judge Robert L. Carter, who upheld that the petitioning players had a valid class-action antitrust grievance. Carter was a fitting catalyst for a settlement that facilitated a burgeoning black upper class because he had spent his career along the legal front lines of the civil rights movement. Working for the NAACP as Thurgood Marshall's chief lieutenant, Carter directed strategy for landmark legal challenges, most notably *Brown v. Board of Education*.

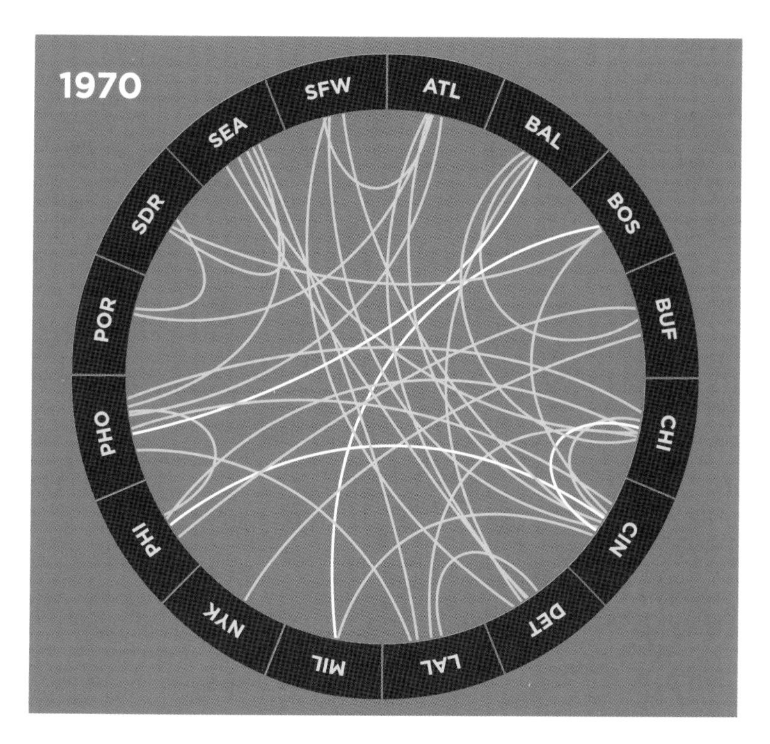

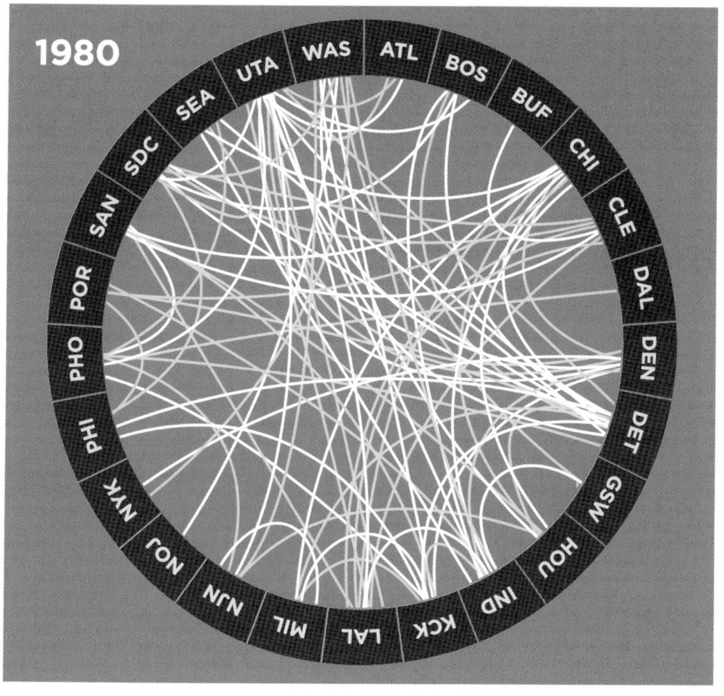

Player Movement Volatility Index

TYPE OF TRANSACTION

Trade between teams

Player signed as free agent or off waivers

In 1970, the NBA was a fairly sedentary place. There weren't many teams, trades were infrequent, and all players had a reserve clause in their contract that essentially bound the player to his team for life. When a contract expired, the team decided whether or not it wanted to re-sign the player. If it didn't, then he had the right to move on. But logically speaking, a player dropped by one team was unlikely to be picked up by another. In 1976, the Oscar Robertson suit settlement eliminated the reserve clause, giving players new freedom and creating true free agency. That same year, the NBA and ABA merged; more expansion would follow as the decade came to a close. With players free to come and go as they pleased, and more destinations than ever to call home, player movement increased exponentially. As the eighties began, the cluttered, often chaotic climate of today had just started to take hold, as is evident in a comparison of 1970 and 1980.

concerned), and awarded to Robertson's class $4.5 million in damages for lost wages. Bidding wars had been local; with the Robertson suit, the owners lost control on a global scale.

But beyond any specific legal victory, the lawsuits filed by players such as Hawkins, Robertson, Haywood, and Walker signaled a new climate in the league. Litigation had emerged fully as a weapon for the players, a means of waging asymmetrical warfare against the NBA. Amid this confusion and a rising tide of legal tension, Larry O'Brien had become commissioner in 1975. O'Brien stepped into this period of basketball upheaval and quickly recognized that the NBA required a strong legal framework if it was not only to defeat challenges in the present but also to guard against them in the future. The NBA might not have been prepared for the first wave of attack, but it wasn't going to surrender without a fight.

IN THE SHADOWS OF CAMELOT: Before becoming commissioner, O'Brien was one of the most effective campaign strategists of all time. As director of John F. Kennedy's presidential and two Senate campaigns, he spearheaded the use of campaign volunteers. He also instituted a system in which the Democratic National Committee communicated directly with each convention delegation and collected information on each delegate, a plan that has become the standard for both parties. O'Brien also headed up Lyndon Johnson's successful reelection campaign in 1964 and Hubert H. Humphrey's unsuccessful presidential bid in 1968. As DNC chairman in 1972, his office was the primary target of the break-ins that led to the Watergate scandal and Richard Nixon's resignation.

As one of his first orders of business, the commissioner sought out someone who could forcibly beat back a union. To stop the bleeding, David Stern was hired away from Proskauer as the NBA's general counsel in 1978. The Robertson settlement left the Players Association stronger and emboldened. The players had won changes that would allow them to wield greater market power and earn more money. Finally, the union could serve as a significant counterweight to the strength of the league's owners. Players were establishing themselves as partners to respect, not merely employees to control.

To restore law and order—and, of course, to get the owners back on stable ground—O'Brien, Stern, and league attorneys such as Russ Granik turned to an esoteric mechanism that could protect the NBA from unnecessary legal injury: the collective bargaining agreement (CBA). The CBA is a time-honored way of preventing intervention by courts, lawsuits, and other third-party intruders. If a CBA is consummated after good-faith negotiations, a court will reject nearly all legal challenges under the premise that both sides have already had the benefit of a fair hearing. Whether the NBA saw this strategy as the ideal form of compromise or a sneaky way to shut down the legal onslaught is subject to interpretation.

This new regime also discovered ways to use the CBA as a public relations tool. The seventies—and, for that matter, the eighties—was a period of rampant powder sniffing. What was essentially an image problem was hurting everyone—the league, the owners, the players—but instituting a comprehensive drug-testing program with the aid of a newly litigious union was no small feat. However, by inserting testing and suspension regulations into the 1983 CBA and thus guaranteeing the players' cooperation, O'Brien and Stern were able to achieve consensus and implement a program that helped clean up one of the league's biggest issues.

They didn't stop there. The CBA steadily evolved, growing to capture not only basic league rules, a drug policy, and a salary cap but also marketing considerations, employment guidelines, revenue distribution, eligibility for the draft, and nearly every other relevant factor. In short, it became an effective line of defense against both the labor concerns of the seventies and the image problems that threatened to drag the league down.

When O'Brien stepped down in 1983, it took the NBA's board of governors less than thirty minutes to unanimously endorse Stern as the league's next commissioner. In Stern, the owners saw not only a capable partner and advocate but also a lawyer who had offered structural fortitude. When questioned about whether someone who wasn't a basketball man could lead the league, Stern quickly (and profoundly) shot back that there would be no league without lawyers. As he later observed, "If you look[ed] across the landscape, everything seemed to be about confrontation, litigation and the like. The relationship between the teams and the leagues, between the players and the leagues, between the leagues and the cities . . . There was a lot of agitation."

Today's NBA is one without as much agitation, thanks primarily to the governing CBA. For all the advances made in basketball over the years, it's now the CBA—where all concerned parties sit down to hammer out law—that forms the backbone of the league. A lack of superstars, say, makes for good copy, but only impending CBA negotiations can send real shockwaves through the league. To say that the Grizzlies failed to think about their team (in the long run, acquiring Marc Gasol turned out pretty well) ignores that the CBA, and the lawsuits that gave rise to it, are the very DNA of today's NBA.

The Pau Gasol deal may not have been an equitable basketball trade, but it was an equitable NBA trade. If the CBA were less rigid, less exhaustive, and less a product of fear, things might be different. Trades almost certainly would be more fun and more satisfying. But after the seventies, that will never be the case. The law is here to stay. —*J.L.*

GIRL POWER IN A UNION:
Collective bargaining agreements don't exist solely in the world of sports. In 1996 dancers from the Lusty Lady peep show in San Francisco formed the first exotic dancers' union, the subject of the documentary *Live Nude Girls Unite!*. With the assistance of Service Employees International Union Local 790, they hammered out a CBA with the club that includes:

1. The right to "just cause" dismissals, which include "employer's opinion regarding employee sexiness while performing, customer interaction and/or customer satisfaction."
2. The right to family/personal leave, provided that "the dancer's appearance has not changed materially since she started her leave (i.e., employee has no additional tattoo or piercing . . . no significant weight gain or loss)."
3. Pay for dancers who undertake the "selecting, purchasing, and programming" of music.

	1980	1981	1982	1983	1984
NBA FINALS CHAMPION	LOS ANGELES LAKERS	BOSTON CELTICS	LOS ANGELES LAKERS	PHILADELPHIA 76ERS	BOSTON CELTICS
FINALS LOSER	76ERS	ROCKETS	76ERS	LAKERS	
MOST VALUABLE PLAYER	K. ABDUL-JABBAR	JULIUS ERVING	MOSES MALONE	MOSES MALONE	LARRY BIRD
POINTS per game leader	George Gervin **33.1**	Adrian Dantley **30.7**	George Gervin **32.3**	Alex English **28.4**	Adrian Dantley **30.6**
REBOUNDS per game leader	Swen Nater **15.0**	Moses Malone **14.8**	Moses Malone **14.7**	Moses Malone **15.3**	Moses Malone **13.4**
ASSISTS per game leader	M. Ray Richardson **10.1**	Kevin Porter **9.1**	Johnny Moore **9.6**	Magic Johnson **10.5**	Magic Johnson **13.1**

THE GOLD STANDARD

1980-1990

After finishing out the seventies with a swirl of discomfort, the NBA got the makeover to end all makeovers. Magic Johnson and Larry Bird entered the league in 1980, bringing their NCAA rivalry to the pros and setting off the Lakers-Celtics battles that would begin to bring back fans. These two franchises would pass the title back and forth for much of the decade, but it would be with the draft class of 1984 that the league really got back to full strengh, and then some. That June, Michael Jordan, Charles Barkley, Akeem Olajuwon, and John Stockton heard their names called by David Stern—who had become commissioner that February. This cohort, along with Magic, Bird, Isiah Thomas, Dominique Wilkins, and later additions Scottie Pippen, Karl Malone, and Patrick Ewing, gave the NBA a crop of stars unseen since the sixties—except this time they got the ratings, paychecks, and worldwide popularity they so deserved. And at the same time, international players slowly but surely left their mark, including one taken too soon.

1985	1986	1987	1988	1989	1990
LOS ANGELES LAKERS	BOSTON CELTICS	LOS ANGELES LAKERS		DETROIT PISTONS	
CELTICS	ROCKETS	CELTICS	PISTONS	LAKERS	BLAZERS
LARRY BIRD	LARRY BIRD	MAGIC JOHNSON	MICHAEL JORDAN	MAGIC JOHNSON	MAGIC JOHNSON
Bernard King **32.9**	D. Wilkins **30.3**	Michael Jordan **37.1**	Michael Jordan **35.0**	Michael Jordan **32.5**	Michael Jordan **33.6**
Moses Malone **13.1**	Bill Laimbeer **13.1**	Charles Barkley **14.6**	Michael Cage **13.0**	H. Olajuwon **13.5**	H. Olajuwon **14.0**
Isiah Thomas **13.9**	Magic Johnson **12.6**	Magic Johnson **12.2**	John Stockton **13.8**	John Stockton **13.6**	John Stockton **14.5**

CELTICS
33

CHOOSE YOUR WEAPON

Larry Bird, Magic Johnson, and the Real Merger

When Magic Johnson and Larry Bird went pro in 1979, the NBA was a dark, forbidding place. Clouded by the Punch and with Bill Walton sitting out the season, the NBA saw its audience withering away, both in the arenas and on television. Important playoff games, even the NBA Finals, were still broadcast on tape delay in most of the country, often not airing until late at night. The league was also still having difficulties assimilating (in every sense of the word) the players, teams, and styles from the ABA. The two leagues had merged only three seasons earlier and were still trying to figure out how to coexist. In a way, the two leagues fit together like puzzle pieces, with the ABA's rangy and athletic forwards filling in the middle spaces between the NBA's crafty guards, such as Paul Westphal and Dennis Johnson, and dominating big men, such as Kareem Abdul-Jabbar and Walton. But the frustrating thing about puzzles is figuring out exactly what pieces go where.

It would not be until the arrival of Magic and Bird that the NBA would finally accept the ABA. Stylistically, Magic and Bird were sons of the ABA, but they had been rendered palatable (or comprehensible) to mainstream fans. They would become the face of the NBA, laying the groundwork for its eighties success by bringing together a house divided. The bitter Lakers-Celtics feud may have split the nation along race lines, but it only mattered enough to do so because Magic and Bird had healed the league.

The only teams other than Magic's Lakers and Bird's Celtics that ever made it to the Finals from 1980 to 1988, when Magic and Bird were at their peak, were the Sixers and the Rockets, and only the Sixers won. During the eighties, Magic and Bird won a combined eight championships and faced off against each other three times between 1984 and 1987. They had a well-documented rivalry dating back to their college days, when they faced each other in the most-watched NCAA championship game in the history of the tournament, drawing forty million viewers

CONS MEN: Both Magic and Bird had endorsement deals with Converse, although they paled in comparison to the deals that NBA superstars have today. A Converse exec reportedly explained to Magic that "a player will never sell shoes," words that were soon made ridiculous after the immense popularity of Nike's Air Jordans. Before the 1986–87 season, Magic and Bird filmed a commercial for Converse that is a true '80s artifact. It features the two of them along with Isiah Thomas, Mark Aguirre, Kevin McHale, and Bernard King, awkwardly rapping about the greatness of the new Converse Weapon shoe.

ABA's Lasting Legacy

Composition of NBA All-Star Teams

(numbers that dwarfed that year's NBA Finals). When Magic and Bird first met in the Finals, in 1984, they again drew forty million viewers, the most ever to tune in for an NBA game. Clearly, there was something about these two players going at each other that captivated the public in a way that even the spectacular Dr. J could not.

Through his five championships with the Lakers, Magic revived the Auerbach/Cousy/Russell notion that the fast break could be a legitimate winning strategy, not just an entertaining style of play. Although the Lakers won a championship in Magic's rookie season, it took a few years for the curtain to really rise on Showtime. When Magic first joined the Lakers, it was still decidedly Kareem's team; Magic started alongside conventional point guard Norm Nixon and would even spend some time at forward when sixth man Michael Cooper came off the bench. Ultimately, the team realized that, despite his size, Magic was a bona fide point guard and traded Nixon for shooting guard Byron Scott in 1983. The following season, Magic led the league with an incredible 13.1 assists per game. (Nixon tied Isiah Thomas for second at 11.1.)

As Kareem entered the twilight of his career, Coach Pat Riley sped the game up, building the offense around Magic's playmaking, Scott's sharpshooting, and James Worthy's swooping dunks. The height of the Showtime Era was the back-to-back championships in 1987 and 1988, which were also the finest individual seasons of Magic's career. In 1986–87, Magic led the league in assists, at 12.7 per game, while scoring 23.9 points per game and almost out-rebounding Kareem, averaging 6.3 boards to Kareem's 6.7.

But what elevated Magic beyond even superstardom was the way his personality showed itself in his play. Magic's near-permanent smile underscored the genuine delight he felt when a teammate scored off one of his passes, and his joie de vivre provided a counterweight to both the moodiness of his teammate Kareem and, more generally, the more confrontational blackness that had been associated with the turbulent late seventies. Bird, meanwhile, displayed little of Magic's infectious charisma and was actually much closer to Kareem in temperament. Although he was devoid of Kareem's self-seriousness, he was equally disdainful of most reporters and members of the public. But Bird won over fans with his grittiness, competitive drive, and, above all, his swagger—a trait that marked him as a scion of the ABA.

BEYOND THE NORM: Although he was a two-time All-Star, Norm Nixon may be unfamiliar to younger fans. Here's a quick guide to get them up to speed.

1. While with the Lakers, Nixon once faked a free throw, leading to a double lane violation and a jump ball. The Lakers won the jump and eventually won the game in overtime. But since Nixon never actually shot the ball, the refs should never have called a lane violation. To correct the error, the Lakers and Spurs replayed the final three seconds of the game several months later, with the Spurs winning this time.

2. When Magic first joined the Lakers, Nixon was the team's leading playboy. Magic was once approached in a hotel lobby by three women who each gave him her number and then asked him to pass it on to Nixon.

3. Nixon missed the entire 1986–87 season after stepping in a hole during a softball game and damaging a tendon in his leg.

4. In 1984, Nixon married actress/dancer Debbie Allen of *Fame* fame. Allen is Phylicia Rashad's sister, which made Nixon the brother-in-law of NBA fanboy Ahmad Rashad.

5. Following his career, Nixon became an agent, counting among his clients Jalen Rose and LL Cool J.

Like Celtics teammate Dave Cowens, Bird was tough and hard-working almost to the point of psychosis. But he combined that blue-collar ethic with attitude and flash that would have been right at home in the ABA.

While he had all the basketball fundamentals expected of a Hoosier, Bird talked trash like the king of the playground. He rebounded like a power forward, but also had remarkable court vision, used a variety of crafty ball fakes, and could fill up the basket like few in the league. Pistol Pete Maravich, with his arsenal of gimmicks and prima donna posture, had been something like the basketball version of Norman Mailer's "White Negro" at its most hollow, a practitioner of a soulless, decontextualized version of playground ball. By contrast, Bird's no-look passes weren't mere showmanship or an expression of personal identity through competitive creativity. They were just smart basketball with the added bonus of being mean, a quality that came right out of Cowens. It was Bird's hard-knocks individualism that made his creativity into something authentic. (Interestingly, a washed-up Maravich turned up on the 1980 Celtics team in a reserve role.)

Bird was the first NBA superstar to really take advantage of the three-point shot, which had been popularized by the ABA and adopted by the NBA during Bird's rookie season. The three-pointer was considered something of a novelty even in the ABA, and its most prolific shooters were specialists like Les Selvage in the ABA or Craig Hodges and Dale Ellis in the NBA. By the 1986 season, however, Bird was leading the league in threes, and he dominated the inaugural 3-Point Shootout held during All-Star weekend. He won the contest in its first three years, from 1986 through 1988, completing the three-peat by hitting the moneyball on the final rack and raising his index finger in the air before the ball even hit the net. Even in a meaningless exhibition setting, Bird's swag was phenomenal.

From his first days in Boston, Bird put his stamp on the team. As recently as 1976, the Celtics had been one of the best teams in the league, winning two championships with a team built around Cowens, John Havlicek, and Jo Jo White. It was these teams that fixed the image of the Celtics as old-school and methodical. But by the 1978–79 season, they had aged considerably, winning only 29 games. As a rookie, Bird energized the squad and opened up the Celtics offense with his daring, passing, and long-range shooting, leading the team to 32 more victories than the previous season. By

THE MAGIC KINGDOM: Once upon a time, Michael Jackson actually hung out with other adults, among them Magic Johnson. Whether it was their shared Midwestern heritage or their race-transcending universal popularity, there was a special affinity between the two kings of the '80s. Magic traveled on multiple tours with the Jackson 5 and appeared in the video for the 1992 single "Remember the Time." Magic spoke movingly at Jackson's memorial service, saying, "He was my idol. He was everything to me."

BIRD'S ONLY FRIEND: Larry Bird is a notorious loner, but in the first half of his career, he would often carouse after games with Rick Robey, a backup center with the Celtics. In the late '70s and early '80s, the home team was required to provide the road team with a case of cold beer in the locker room after each game. Players drank what they wanted and left the rest, but Bird and Robey would stuff pillowcases with cans of beer to take on the road with them. Bird quit drinking beer after Robey was traded to the Suns in 1983 and, not coincidentally, won his first MVP award the following season.

THE REAL SHOWTIME: Although the name Showtime is forever associated with the fast-break offense, the Denver Nuggets went to extremes not imagined by Paul Westhead or Pat Riley. With stars Alex English, Kiki Vandeweghe, and Fat Lever, they went 136 consecutive games with more than 100 points and set an NBA record by averaging 126.5 points per game during the 1981–82 season. The Nuggets also played in the highest-scoring game of all time, a 186–184 triple-overtime tilt against the Detroit Pistons. The most notable thing about the strategy is that it worked, with the Nuggets winning 54.8 percent of their games during Doug Moe's tenure as coach.

TEARING DOWN THE MYTH: In his 2003 memoir *Chocolate Thunder*, Darryl Dawkins calls bullshit on the legend of Magic playing center in the 1980 Finals, claiming that he didn't guard him the whole night. While Magic did jump at center, starting power forward Jim Chones was mostly matched up against Dawkins, and reserve Mark Landsberger also saw time at the 5 spot.

the 1981–82 season, the Celtics were fourth in the league in points scored, at 112 per game. When the Showtime Lakers defeated the Celtics in the 1987 Finals, Bird lamented that the Celtics had not run enough, saying, "We had no fast break. When we got a rebound, we'd hold it and show everybody we got a rebound."

When they faced off in those three NBA Finals, Magic and Bird redefined the concept of NBA rivalry. Russell and Chamberlain and West and Robertson had engaged in memorable duels on the floor; Magic and Bird were so cosmically antagonistic that they didn't even have to guard each other to dominate the league. Although they were similar in size, each team would often use its best defender, such as Michael Cooper for the Lakers or Dennis Johnson for the Celtics, to keep the other team's star in check. Magic and Bird's rivalry was based less on an actual head-to-head match-up than on a contest of wills and to show who could lead his team to victory. Both players also admitted that the first thing they did in the morning was check the box scores to see how the other had performed. Those box scores contained the kind of remarkable all-around stat lines that harked back to Robertson. Incidentally, Magic finished second to the Big O in career triple-doubles, with a total of 138, while Bird stands at fifth with 59.

The similarity to Robertson was more than stat deep. Magic and Bird's influence on the league's future was, in some ways, a throwback to the glory days of the 1960s NBA. In turn, they set into motion a new NBA epoch that, when it came to style and production, was even more ambitious and complex than anything that had come before. During the seventies, the trend toward specialization had reached its absolute zenith (or nadir). Even stars such as George Gervin were specialists of a sort, expected to do little more than make sure they scored. Magic and Bird, on the other hand, were capable of doing it all. As a rookie, Magic started at center, replacing an injured Kareem in Game 6 of the 1980 Finals. By the time the game was over, he had also played minutes at guard and forward. Bird's versatility was less formal; although he never lined up at center, he was able to do whatever his team needed, seemingly at will. On the Celtics' run to the 1986 championship, Bird nearly averaged a triple-double for the playoffs, including 29 points, 11 rebounds, and 12 assists in the series-clinching Game 6 against the Rockets. He was everywhere on the court, draining outrageous three-pointers, making clutch steals, and even winning a jump ball from Hakeem Olajuwon.

Magic and Bird raised the bar on versatility. Both standing 6′9″ and possessing neither the power of a big man nor overwhelming athleticism, they set a new standard for NBA superstardom and deconstructed the very nature of positionality in the process. The two had an immediate effect on the league, even on players who were just a few years younger, such as Isiah Thomas, who has stated that he studied the Lakers and Celtics and learned from them the value of sharing the ball. Wing players such as Clyde Drexler and Michael Jordan evolved into more dynamic and well-rounded players than their predecessors George Gervin and Dr. J had been, and Charles Barkley learned to handle the ball, pass, and shoot very well for a power forward. Magic and Bird made it clear that if you wanted to lead a team to a championship, you had to be multidimensional. Certainly, the eighties had stars who came from the old paradigm, such as Dominique Wilkins (an ABA-style scoring forward) or Patrick Ewing (an NBA-style center), but then again, neither of those players ever won a championship.

The legacy of Magic and Bird is most clearly seen in the generation of players that came after them, the eighties babies who grew up emulating their all-around mastery. Big men like Derrick Coleman and Kevin Garnett refused to be chained to the post, and 6′8″ athletes like Jalen Rose and Penny Hardaway wanted to play point guard—all as a direct result of Magic Johnson and Larry Bird. Many young black kids idolized the Showtime Lakers and therefore hated the Celtics, but Larry Bird is their ancestor, too. Take, for instance, Chris Webber, who as a member of the Fab 5 was one of his generation's most important signifiers of a "black" game. As much as his baldie and baggy shorts said Michael Jordan and his Michigan upbringing and zeal for passing said Magic Johnson, his craftiness, love of the jump shot, and peak stat lines of 25, 10, and 5 unmistakably said Larry Bird. *—B.R.*

HOW TO SUCCEED IN BUSINESS: Since his retirement, Magic Johnson has had remarkable success in the business world, building an estimated $700 million portfolio. Impressed with Magic's business acumen, Kareem approached him looking for tips. Magic explained, "To be like me, you've got to shake hands, hug people, attend luncheons. You've got to be nice to people all the time." Kareem's response was, "Well, maybe I can do it another way."

THE INVENTION OF AIR

The Brash, Brilliant Doodles of Young Jordan

AND HE SHALL DELIVER THEM: Prior to Jordan's rookie season in 1984, players on the Bulls were asked in the team media guide, "What was the worst time or biggest disappointment in your life?"

DAVID GREENWOOD, Forward: "The basketball season of 82–83."

JAWANN OLDHAM, Center: "1983."

SIDNEY GREEN, Forward: "Last year . . . the whole year."

THE PERFECT PLAY: When Jordan got to Chicago, he so badly wanted to supplant Dave Corzine as the team's best Pac-Man player that he bought a machine for his house.

In 1987, four young, hopeful ladies from the Washington, D.C., area entered the studio to record a sassy, if wan, R&B single they hoped would bring them fortune and fame. Through the almighty mandate of the remix, LaDawn Brown, Lachelle Baker, Crystal Torez, and Anissa Moody stretched their "Everybody Use Your Imagination" to occupy two sides of an otherwise forgettable twelve-inch. Under the name Hot Butterfly, they released it on the local City Groove Records, no one noticed, and, presumably, they all went on with their lives. Hot Butterfly was forgotten until intrepid record collectors dug the single up more than two decades later, when it gained some small notice as a curiosity.

What made for the newfound interest in Hot Butterfly, as well as the group's presumably high expectations, was the involvement of Michael Jeffrey Jordan in the record. "Imagination" begins with Jordan's name, intoned by heavily processed, high-speed vocals; next, MJ himself drops in for a sliver of a spoken intro: "The pressure's on. Most people panic for a way out. But myself, I imagine a thousand different ways to get myself out." He returns at song's end, as if to reassert his dominion or remind us that he approves. The sleeve depicts Brown, Baker, Torez, and Moody with matching Salt-N-Pepa hairdos, door-knocker earrings, and oversize Air Jordan sweatshirts. A large image of His Airness hovers overhead. Moses Malone Jr. and Ray Leonard Jr. helped out on the background chant, but this was unquestionably a Michael Jordan joint. And yet it vanished without a trace.

It's inconceivable now that a Jordan-branded commodity would disappear like this. In 1987, though, Michael Jordan was a very different kind of superstar. Edgy, dangerous, even controversial, he was far from safe, even as the public hung on his every highlight. He put up huge numbers and regularly ransacked the realm of possibility; quite often it looked like Jordan was inventing a sport on the spot to suit his gifts and everyone around him was trying to play catch-up. "Everybody Use Your Imagination" was the first

"Be Like Mike," except that it taunted rather than encouraged its audience. Jordan's mind came up with a thousand different ways out; the imagination of the title was his, as was the gift that had allowed him to get on this record in the first place. To many, though, Jordan was a showboat, a ball hog, and a team killer whose one-man freak show paled in comparison to the small-scale societies one found with the Lakers, Celtics, or Pistons of the eighties. Jordan the corporate entity was just as unrefined. When else in his career would the consensus Greatest of All Time (GOAT, for those adept at holding back laughter) ever get behind a scruffy local musical act from a city he had no ties to?

As a public figure, Jordan's great achievement has been his ability to stay on message—to craft a narrative for himself and then cram it down our throats at every opportunity. Doubted, he repeatedly triumphs through hard work and the restorative, vindictive power of destiny. Jordan as we know him, and as he wanted himself to be represented right up through his Hall of Fame speech in 2009, is a series of cycles, which only adds to the bullying power of his story. But due diligence reveals that many of them depend on exaggeration, fabrication, or repression. That has also required forgetting early missteps like Hot Butterfly—for all we know, he's bought up and destroyed copies himself—and it's meant forgetting who the young Jordan really was and how the league perceived him.

In Jordan's script, a skinny sophomore is left off of the varsity basketball team at Laney High, with the last spot going to his friend Leroy Smith. Yet as David Halberstam explained in his Jordan biography *Playing for Keeps*, the decision was based almost entirely on size. The team's coaches agreed that Jordan would get his chance and was clearly the superior player—they just neglected to tell him. While Jordan was selected behind big men Akeem Olajuwon and Sam Bowie in the 1984 draft, there was no shortage of teams hankering to move up and take him second. Even the Rockets had considered it. The preference for big men was just too ingrained. As with the high school story, the basic facts check out. Yet in both cases, there was also a lingering sense that Michael Jordan would still likely end up Michael Jordan.

We're now supposed to see his first years in the league as an NBA bildungsroman, with Jordan paying his dues and working his way to the ultimate prize. In fact, Jordan was in the eyes of some a radiant dead-ender who might never win a championship.

THE JAZZ-O-METER

1980s RATING: Kinda jazzy (55/100)

MY MELLOW MY MAN: Conservative columnist George F. Will once wrote an essay titled "The Athletic Jazz of Michael Jordan." MJ himself is a big jazz fan, saying, "I'm a mellow type of dude. Jazz slows down the pace of my life." While at UNC, Jordan was once introduced to Wynton Marsalis, a meeting both men still like to mention in interviews.

THE CHIEF OF SMOOTH: Robert Parish was a big jazz fan, although his tastes veered toward the soothing sounds of jazz guitarists Earl Klugh and George Benson, whose sound incorporated elements of pop and R&B.

DEEETROIT: Jazz drummer Roy Brooks was offered a basketball scholarship to play at Detroit Institute of Technology, but turned it down to join Yusef Lateef's band. Throughout his career playing with such luminaries as Charles Mingus and Max Roach, he kept up his love of basketball. One of his later compositions, "Basketball," features the sound of him rhythmically dribbling a basketball alongside an African drum. His Aboriginal Percussion Choir once performed a concert in the '80s with a small basketball court set up in front of the stage so kids could shoot hoops while the band played.

THE FIRST VICTIMS: At North Carolina, Jordan used to follow every practice by marking on a blackboard how many times he'd dunked on each of his teammates during one-on-one drills.

THE ILLEST THINGS: When Jordan and agent David Falk negotiated shoe contracts in 1984, Nike made the best pitch by far. However, Jordan still had to be convinced to sign because he much preferred to wear Adidas.

Michael Jordan wasn't the first player to jump to the rim or abuse defenders. But there was something different about MJ. Not only could he get higher and do more whilst hanging in the air than anyone who had come before, Jordan was outright vicious in the way he used this exquisite ability, careening around the court and knifing his way to the basket with recklessness—as expansive as Magic, but replacing Johnson's glee with a kind of freewheeling, vigilante menace. To say that Jordan had a playground-style game was to suppose it could be contained or assigned its own argot. Jordan jetted up the court, around, over, and through defenders, with an organic, ecstatic ease that made a mockery of "moves." The ball leapt out of Jordan's hands as if imbued with his spirit, understanding for the first time what the rest of its life would be like. The burnished fadeaway that would later become MJ's calling card, that ultimate beam of reckoning, was yet years away.

Make no mistake, Jordan was a shock to the system. But if this onslaught had been predicted by some scouts and executives, it was practically assumed by David Falk, Jordan's agent. Falk was in his own way as seminal as MJ, leveraging for his rookie client a deal on par with the league's biggest stars and a sneaker contract that nearly matched Jordan's salary. Falk, of course, took a sizable cut, when in the past agents had been lawyers hanging around the margins of the sport for kicks. Nike, in turn, invested in Jordan not merely as a star basketball player but as a movement. Young Jordan was, by virtue of the way he played the game, a rebel, a change agent. The Jordan 1 shoe was banned by the league for violating rules regarding footwear and uniform color schemes; Nike promptly released an ad that used the ban as metaphor, implying—perhaps rightly so—that the ban had as much to do with Jordan's impact on the sport as any simple violation of rules. Shrewdly, the Bulls phenom paid the fines and continued to wear his signature shoes, an investment that paid itself back thousands of times over. At this point, Jordan wasn't selling excellence, he was all about defiance.

During Jordan's first three seasons, the Bulls were a sub-.500 team that nevertheless stumbled into the playoffs. Jordan missed most of the 1985–86 season with a broken leg, so it's not fair to hang that one on him. But the idea of a team for whom the postseason was a given despite obvious deficiencies was a fitting, even snide, commentary on Jordan's position in the league then. He was viewed as sublime but entitled, lacking the gravitas that eventually made his prowess seem earned. He returned in time for the 1986 postseason, putting up a playoff-record 63 points in a double-overtime Game 2. Jordan's outlandish effort, which came against the gritty, proud Boston frontcourt of Bird, Kevin McHale, Robert Parish, and a rejuvenated Walton, was in vain, as the Celtics swept the Bulls. In 1986–87, Jordan averaged 37.1 points per game for the year but again lost to the Celtics, in three games, in the first round. The losses to the Celtics today are seen as the growing pains of a brilliant young star trying to carry an entire team by himself because he had to. Jordan was, according to the legend, as fated to fall to the Celtics as he was to one day overcome them. But at the time, these battles were about more than waiting for the torch to be passed.

Many older players thought of Jordan as a showy punk meaninglessly piling up point after point against the consummate respectable vets. That it was so easy for Jordan, but so hard for his team, was the ultimate sign of tastelessness. You just didn't leave the boys behind like that, having so much and spreading so little of it around. You wouldn't exactly call MJ irreverent. He showed respect to no one not because he felt destiny would prove him right, but because his play let him get away with whatever he wanted. That's the paradox of Jordan's career, and while the early years have been carefully reinterpreted, it nevertheless felt this way at the time. While he had yet to prove himself to the older generation or win any titles, he was already, in a sense, godlike. The mantra of hard work and determination was at odds with the effortless exuberance that marked the days before Scottie Pippen (who was drafted in 1987) and Phil Jackson (who joined Doug Collins's staff as an assistant that same year). He would also never get a chance to say "I told you so," because to win championships, he had to accept the triangle and Phil's guidance.

While the Celtics were NBA royalty looking down their noses at a petulant Jordan, the Pistons presented a more evenly matched battle. When the Bulls and Pistons met, it was also a final battle of sorts, a clash of basketball civilizations in which Detroit represented the true believers. The Bad Boys were mean, even sadistic, earning their two titles with hard-nosed, physical play. Coach Chuck Daly's expensive suits gave him the air of a mob boss directing hired toughs. Center Bill Laimbeer wasn't just physical, he was a thug in the Blackshirt sense who took the court with the express goal of agitation. Even the Pistons' most lyrical player,

BROKEN SHAPES: Although the Bulls later rode the triangle offense to championships under Phil Jackson, they actually attempted it several years earlier with diminishing returns. When Doug Collins took the Bulls coaching job in 1986, Jerry Krause informed him that they would run Tex Winter's triangle as the team's offense. However, Jordan despised it and Collins never seemed fully committed to the system, leading to its disposal after only a few months. Toward the end of Collins's tenure with the team, Winter had so little sway with the head coach that he would often spend practices taking notes apart from everyone else.

WHAT FRIENDS ARE FOR: In 1988, Jerry Krause traded Jordan's on-court protector and good friend Charles Oakley to the Knicks for true center Bill Cartwright. Jordan was furious and immediately started belittling Cartwright, referring to him as "Medical Bill" because of his injury history and making especially hard passes in practice so Cartwright would be recognized as having terrible hands.

point guard Isiah Thomas, was a bastard who had orchestrated a boycott of Jordan at the 1985 All-Star Game. Jordan started the game but finished with only 7 points; it's long been rumored that Isiah asked his Eastern Conference teammates to keep the ball out of the rookie's hands. This virtual embargo not only spoke volumes about how MJ was seen by his elders, but also set up an opposition between him and the Pistons.

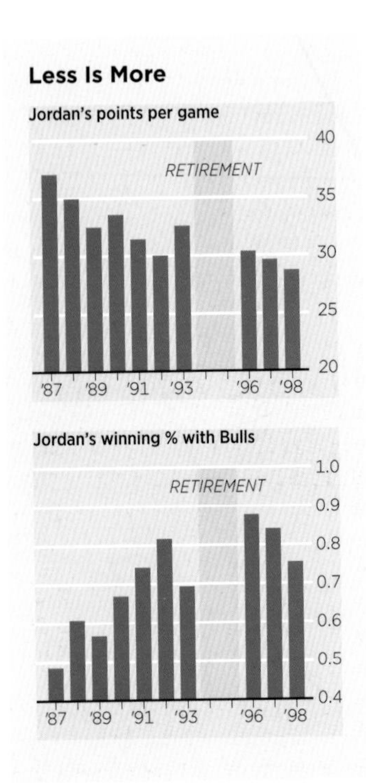

In 1988, the Bulls got out of the first round for the first time; in 1989, Jordan hit the Shot, his high-flying game winner over the Cavs' Craig Ehlo, officially beginning his pro tenure as a winner. But in 1988, 1989, and 1990, the Pistons stood in their way, beating the Bulls in the second round once, and then twice in the Conference Finals. When the Bulls finally got past them in 1991, en route to their first championship, the Pistons left the court without shaking hands. That's now regarded as the ultimate display of both poor sportsmanship and the subhuman place the Bad Boys occupy in NBA history. However, that's in a post-Jordan world. At the time, it represented the frustration, even disgust, that older players felt at the thought that Jordan had superseded them. They were hung up on what he represented and ignored what Michael Jordan had lost along the way. It's almost like the Pistons won after all.

That young Jordan, for whom all things seemed possible, had to give himself up for the story as we know it to continue. He's a hiccup, a roadblock, that like the embarrassment of Hot Butterfly had to go away for the legend to ring out. Jordan even seemed to recognize this at the time. The greatest dunker the world had ever seen, the man whose logo was himself midflight, competed in (and won) his last dunk contest in 1988. Then Jordan claimed he didn't want to be known as a dunker anymore and went so far as to compete in the three-point contest in 1990 to officially signal a shift in his game. No longer the madman who could level any arena with his dynamism, he was now a shooter.

The dunk takes an instant and an eternity; it's both completely frivolous and totally domineering, a flash of light so blinding and brief that it might as well have never happened. A shot was the stuff of narrative; it was itself a story with a built-in arc, climax, and resolution. It also served as the perfect punctuation to any possession, game, season, or career. That kind of player, the one who seized the past and carefully etched the present, was the athlete MJ had learned to become. *—B.S.*

Golden Oldies

NBA Musical Moments for the Ages

Basketball may or may not be jazz, once moved to the rhythms of funk and soul, and now partners with hip-hop. Over the long, synergistic history between music and hoops, though, few performances can match the might of "Everybody Use Your Imagination." Here are five.

WILT CHAMBERLAIN

In 1961, the year he was busy laying waste to the NBA record book (which he'd already laid waste to several times over), Wilt took some time out to step into the studio and lay down his one and only single, "By the River." Painfully un-hip, jaunty, and drastically simple pop-soul, it's Wilt having a good time without having to try too hard. Coincidentally, the song was played over the PA system during warm-ups the night he scored 100 in Hershey.

TABRON

Manute Bol stood 7′7″, was built like a Giacometti, and had few equals when it came to swatting shots back at opponents. He was the kind of striking, one-dimensional figure bound to be immortalized in song, especially when he first entered the league. Enter D.C.'s Tabron, whose electro-boogie "Block the Ball" tells Manute's story—including a very special encounter with some Lakers cheerleaders at the mall.

MEADOWLARK LEMON

Lemon was one of the Globetrotters who wasn't actually much of a basketball player, but this 1979 oddity more than makes up for that. Taken from his *My Kids* LP on Casablanca, it uses the ol' "What if aliens came to destroy the human race?" conceit to argue for mankind's essential unity. Imagine a cross between the Chairmen of the Board, Brook Benton, Scott Walker, and Tracy Morgan, with some really crappy laser-battle sound effects turned way up in the mix.

PAULETTE REAVES

Taken from Reaves's 1977 *All About Love,* her second album for Miami's TK Records, "Flesh" is hard-hitting, yet sophisticated, soul. It's got one foot in disco, one in gutsier rhythms, and is a prime example of what this unjustly forgotten soul diva was capable of. The NBA connection? Today Reaves is best known as the mother of Atlanta's Josh Smith. She appeared in the memorable television series *The Rookies* and sometimes sings the national anthem at Hawks games.

ULTRAMAGNETIC MC'S

In 1989, the NBA decided it needed rappers to do an intro for that year's All-Star rosters, with a couple of lines for each player and coach. For reasons known only to a select few, the league recruited the Bronx's totally out-there Ultramagnetic MC's. With a start-and-stop flow that makes every line opaque, Kool Keith, Ced Gee, and Tim Dog somehow make Michael Jordan sound unexceptional and Mark Price a high priest of the game. Nine minutes of quizzical brilliance.

SIXERS
34

LOUD, FAT, AND GIFTED

The Irrepressible Charles Barkley

There are people distinctly suited for the life and profession they are drawn to. They are gifted with a mental or physical makeup that makes their fantastic successes not exactly easy but at least explicable by a combination of hard work and the natural way of things. Then there are those for whom the fit is wrong (or at least slightly off), and yet it doesn't matter. Although their glories and ultimate achievements may not be as all-encompassing as those of men fated for their purpose, they can provide an even deeper meaning. They are the misfits and outcasts who storm the gates and plant their flags.

In Michael Jordan's mythology, a teen cut from his high school team builds himself into a basketball god. While Jordan was a man of pure will, he also had greatness carved into his very body. While it makes for a great story, it's akin to a geological event—awesome but scientifically predictable. Jordan's contemporary, Charles Barkley was the real deal. Barkley was a 6′4″ power forward—half rage and half ass that could move mountains—and he would tell you about it.

He grew up in the projects of Leeds, Alabama, raised by a mother who worked as a domestic. Barkley made the varsity team only as a high school senior. He went to college at Auburn, one of his few options and a basketball backwater at the time. He dominated the paint and the conference—he led the SEC in rebounding and became an attraction—but Barkley was as much a curiosity as he was a star. This was not without good reason. Barkley was fat and wore incredibly short shorts; his outsized brilliance seemed like the plot of a silly eighties teen comedy. Even his nickname, the Round Mound of Rebound, was a jab at the impossible as well as a snicker at the absurd.

ROUND MOUND: While at Auburn, Barkley's weight sometimes climbed close to 300 pounds, earning him his famous nickname as well as others, such as Lard of the Rings and Boy Gorge, which never stuck. When he traveled to Philadelphia in advance of the NBA draft, he weighed in at 292 pounds, which greatly concerned Sixers owner Harold Katz, who happened to have made his fortune with the Nutrisystem weight-loss program.

Barkley won the SEC Player of the Year award and was drafted by the Philadelphia 76ers in 1984. He joined a squad of aging veterans, and one wonders what Julius Erving, Moses Malone, and Maurice Cheeks thought of the young Barkley. He had the uncontrollable tongue of a schizophrenic, bulging self-belief, and a pneumatic waistline. He wanted more than was proper and he wanted it quickly.

Barkley's transition to the NBA wasn't particularly painful, but the joys of binge eating had to come to an end. The natural talent and ferocity had been enough at the college level, but against the elite of the NBA, Charles had to get fit, and fortunately, he had a knowledgeable tutor in the ways of the big man. Charles said, "Thank God for Moses Malone. He taught me the ropes about getting in shape. I've always said Moses was probably the most influential person in my career." Malone and his teammates also showed Barkley the importance of toughness. Only a few games into his career, Malone, Dr. J, and Barkley triple-teamed Larry Bird in a wild brawl, one of the most star-studded fights in league history. Barkley had landed in the right place.

Newly fit and supported by seasoned pros, Charles was an early NBA success. To watch him play in those first years was a strange combination of rooting for both the underdog and the bully. Nothing ever seemed to fit properly. The explosion and quickness of the legs coupled with an enormous upper body was a combination almost impossible to believe. He moved so fast once he started that you wondered if he would ever be able to stop, or, more accurately, if he would topple over as he careened down the court. If big men before or since have been able to rebound and lead a break with as much skill and dexterity, none did it with as much ferocity and abandon. Charles frequently said no one would ever dare to take a charge on him because they knew the pain he would bring.

Above all else, though, there was the rebounding. Particularly on the offensive glass, Barkley had an uncommon gift. Often competing against players taller by a half foot or more, Charles would manage to create space and find the ball. His low, sturdy center of gravity allowed him to root out larger players and gain position; his explosive leaping meant he was rarely troubled from above. He was a master of the put-back, where his seemingly unnatural powers harmonized. He had historically great hands for a big man and it was nearly impossible to strip him once he had possession. When he landed, defenders seemed to shed off of him, leaving him clear for the easy bucket. Barkley swung his elbows and snarled. His huge mass and the force of his personality sent out a sonic blast that left him free. It didn't matter if he was surrounded; if Charles had the ball close to the hoop, he was going to score.

Inch for Inch

Top 250 career rebounders by height
drafted 1975–2000, averages through '09

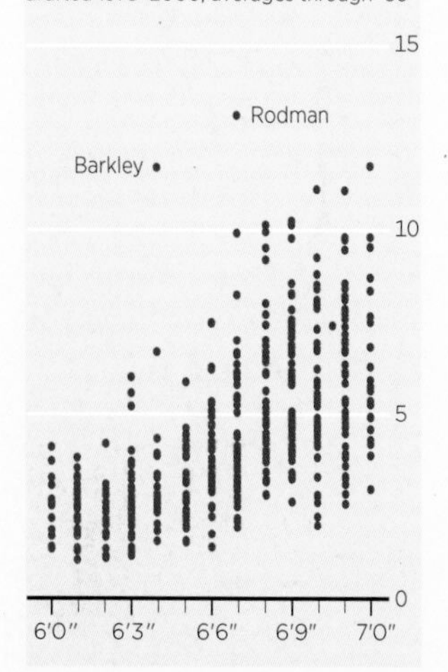

Career rebounding leaders by height
drafted 1975–2000, averages through '09

	Height	Rb Avg
Mookie Blaylock	6'0"	4.1
Mark Jackson	6'1"	3.9
Andre Miller	6'2"	4.2
Fat Lever	6'3"	5.8
Charles Barkley	6'4"	11.7
Adrian Dantley	6'5"	5.7
Larry Johnson	6'6"	7.5
Dennis Rodman	6'7"	13.1
Elton Brand	6'8"	10.0
Karl Malone	6'9"	10.1
Hakeem Olajuwon	6'10"	11.1
Kevin Garnett	6'11"	11.2
Tim Duncan	7'0"	11.8

It was so improbable that Barkley could do such things that his brute strength and power became moving. When Sixers legends Chamberlain or Erving changed the rules of the game, it seemed a matter of course. For Charles it came from a deeper and less settled place, closer to the next Sixers hero, Allen Iverson, than to those who preceded him. It was the mixture of Wilt's unlikable, unstoppable Goliath within the confines of a recognizably human frame that made him sympathetic. He also had much in common with a contemporary in another sport, Mike Tyson. While Charles was battling giants on the glass, Tyson was battering larger opponents in the ring with a comparable passion and otherworldly ferocity.

Tyson, too, was supposed to be too small but had a power and menace that grew from an internal fire. Tyson was an untamed rage that seemed the result of an intelligence that hadn't found an outlet and went looking for a fight. Barkley was smart and curious and willing to grow in ways that few athletes can. The intelligence was always groping for an outlet, however, and that left him open to moments of both cathartic realizations and dangerous, barely controlled explosions.

Charles was less unhinged and dangerous than Tyson, but he was no less eager to fight. His only rule seemed to be that he solely picked on those bigger than himself, and in the NBA of his day there was no shortage. He tangled with noted bruisers like Bill Laimbeer, Charles Oakley, and, in his dotage, Shaquille O'Neal. It was the incidents with non-players that were more troubling, though. He famously tossed a man through a plate-glass window, not the first of his late-night confrontations. The most embarrassing and longest-lasting incident involved Charles's attempting to spit on hecklers during a game in New Jersey and instead hitting a young girl. He later said, as only he could, that the problem was his inability to "get enough foam." Charles, of course, apologized profusely and for one of the few times in his career seemed genuinely contrite. He would later acknowledge that it was a life-altering experience, finally pushing him a step back from the fine edge at which he played.

During his years in Philadelphia he spoke openly and angrily of the city's racial politics. He lacked some of the charm and incisiveness that he would later gain as a cultural critic and TV personality, but his rawness and willingness to speak honestly and at length about any subject was just as profound then. Charles was

SIR CHARLES: While Barkley was listening to a Philly sports talk-radio show, he heard an elderly woman call in to complain about what she considered to be his selfish and overly aggressive play. He called the station repeatedly over the next few days, trying to make contact with the woman. When he finally got hold of her, he arranged for a limousine to drive her and her family to a game and treated her to courtside seats.

ANYTHING LESS WOULD BE UNCIVILIZED: During Chris Webber's 1993–94 rookie season, Nike ran a memorable ad showing Webber and Warriors teammate Latrell Sprewell hanging out in a barbershop recounting Webber's devastating behind-the-back showboat move and dunk on Charles Barkley. When the Suns and Warriors matched up in the first round of that season's playoffs, Barkley got his revenge, averaging 37.3 points per game on 60.5 percent shooting in a three-game sweep. In the final game, Barkley scored 56 points and regularly taunted the bench with cries of "Put that in a commercial!"

VIRTUAL CHUCK: Barkley was one of only two players not included in the original *NBA Jam* video game due to his involvement in *Barkley Shut Up and Jam!*, another two-on-two game built around playground basketball. But the truly notable Barkley video game is 2008's *Barkley, Shut Up and Jam: Gaiden, Chapter 1 of the Hoopz Barkley SaGa*, an unofficial sequel made by a small company called Tales of Game's Studios. Charles is on the run in post-apocalyptic Neo New York, where he encounters adversaries such as Bill Cosby's character from *Ghost Dad*. He dispatches Cosby with the help of Juwanna Mann, the main character of the WNBA cross-dressing comedy of the same name.

always firm in his convictions; he also proved himself willing to listen and learn. He railed against an unfair media and the injustices of racism while openly discussing interest in a Republican Party seemingly unfriendly to many of his views. However flawed and problematic, Charles was never one to hide. He was willing to make mistakes and take abuse, when warranted. His ability to laugh at himself and to be open about his failures has given him special license in our culture of hasty and severe judgments.

He was often loved or loathed. Barkley served as an inspiration and as a lesson in pushing beyond the possible. Perhaps he was a figure of bacchanalian fear and subdued regret for those who hadn't and didn't want to go there themselves. He was wild and hungry and fully alive. That he never made any attempts to suppress his personality, or appetites, lent him a certain authenticity. Ironically, this authenticity has proven a more valuable commodity than corporation-friendly good conduct; Barkley has remained the most marketable and relevant of his peers because of rather than in spite of it. This twist may be the most ticklish part of his complicated history.

Still, it was those early years on the court in Philadelphia that were the most athletically affecting. As the veterans faded away and Barkley took over, he became a fully realized force. Some of those seasons are statistically shocking to remember. In 1986–87 he won the rebounding title by averaging 14.6 per game and an incredible 5.7 on the offensive glass. He did this while shooting 59 percent from the floor and scoring 23 points a game. It's worth noting here, again, that while he's listed at 6′6″, Barkley has himself acknowledged he is closer to 6′4″.

Those types of numbers would become the norm for Charles. In Philadelphia he would frequently average 25 points and more than 12 rebounds, with field goal percentages approaching 60. While his game would later become more dynamic and complete, it was in these early years that he was the most purposefully efficient and exacting. Defense was never his strong suit, but he could often make the spectacular play. He made six consecutive All-Star Games and, more impressively, was selected to either the first or second All-NBA team seven consecutive times. Unfortunately, management did little to reload, and Barkley labored on teams unfit for his mighty efforts.

Charles performed heroically in the postseason but was ultimately outgunned against teams with more consistent talent throughout the lineup. His statistics for his deepest postseason runs in Philadelphia contradict the popular conception of Charles as a playoff failure. For the 1986 postseason, Charles averaged 25 points and 15.8 rebounds; in 1989, 27 and 11.7; and in 1991, 24.9 and 10.5 as the Sixers lost to Jordan's first championship Bulls.

Barkley grew increasingly frustrated during his later years in Philadelphia as he saw his star contemporaries across the league having playoff success while he was largely a one-man team. You couldn't exactly feel sorry for him—he was too proud and brutal for that—but you did sense he was becoming depleted out there as he fought valiant losing battles as the sole hero on the court. He brought to mind William Faulkner, who wrote, "Nothing can look quite as lonely as a big man going along an empty street."

Charles would finally force himself out of Philadelphia and into the desert of Phoenix in the 1992–93 season and got a team to accentuate his talents. He was still great, perhaps better than ever, but he would ultimately come up short, losing again to Jordan's Bulls in the Finals.

The latter third of Barkley's sixteen years was plagued by injuries. He fought through them, but his explosiveness wasn't there. One wonders if his desperate hunger and the necessary heroics of the Philadelphia days didn't drain him in his later years. He would go on to say that his only regret was not demanding a move sooner. Perhaps he might have had more success before the other superstars of his generation were settled. Charles was not only the victim of a body not exactly suited to his purpose but also of being born during the wrong time, only days apart from Michael Jordan, and in the same draft class as Hakeem Olajuwon.

Ultimately, though, his eventual failures are part of his enduring legacy and charm. Barkley never gave a damn and he never stopped trying. He wasn't polished enough for perfectionists, but to those who were fond of lost causes and doomed romance, he held a deeper value than solemn victory. If basketball is a sport dominated by genetic freaks and those with regal grace, then Barkley was the chain-smoking, beer-drinking loudmouth who somehow ascended to the throne. Sure, he had a talent that can't be taught, but he was human and had an appetite that we could all relate to.

Or, as Barkley's been known to say, "We ain't here for a long time, we here to have a good time." —*A.K.*

HOPPEN MAD: At the start of the 1991–92 season, Barkley was asked if he thought backup center Dave Hoppen would make the team's final roster. Barkley predicted that he would, with the rationale being that the Sixers would want to keep at least one white guy on the roster to placate the city's white fans. Predictably, the media and fans went crazy with allegations of reverse racism, but Barkley defended his statement, saying, "It was no dig at the 76ers organization and it was no dig at Dave Hoppen. It was a dig at society," and "I wouldn't try to open a soul food restaurant in Salt Lake City or field an all-black team there or in Phoenix. That would be idealism but bad business." Hoppen did start the season with the team, but later was injured and placed on the reserve list.

IT CAME FROM CROATIA

Drazen Petrovic and the NBA's Intercontinental Exchange

As the first international player to really have an impact on the NBA, Drazen Petrovic helped set the stage for the international influx of the late 1990s and aughts. However, he remains best known for his tragically premature death. In 1993, at age twenty-nine and just four years into his American pro tour, Petrovic died in Bavaria. He was asleep as a passenger in a VW Golf driven by his German model girlfriend, Hilal Edebal, when the car collided with a truck on the misty, slippery autobahn. The headline of a newspaper in his native Croatia read, IMPOSSIBLE! Chuck Daly solemnly stated, "You know, there is a saying that we have about John F. Kennedy: 'You know, Johnny, we never got to know you.' And I kind of feel that way about Drazen. I felt that the whole year that I was with him went by too fast and I really never got to know him the way I would have liked to." Given what Petrovic was on the verge of achieving, there could not have been a more powerful eulogy.

Petrovic's numbers suggested that he was poised to break through a glass ceiling for European players. His points-per-game average increased each year to the point that in his last season, 1992–93, he averaged 22.6 points on 52 percent shooting. In that final season, Petrovic had also become more aggressive at getting to the free-throw line and had developed feistier defensive skills, two attributes that clearly indicate his growing NBA maturity. Petrovic could have been the first Euro to emerge as a star. No gimmicks, all game. He cited xenophobia as the reason he did not make an All-Star team—hard to imagine now, in this age of Dirk Nowitzki and Yao Ming. But given the reputation of Europeans from Petrovic's era (a reputation he did his best to shake), no one expected the foreigners to rise to the level of American stars. Maybe fans and coaches just couldn't believe what they were seeing—a familiar trope in the story of pro basketball.

While by and large NBA stars still hail from America, and the fervor over European, then Latin American, players turned

SLAVIC SOUL PARTY: The Slavic basketball tradition extends much further back than Drazen Petrovic and Vlade Divac. George Mikan was of Croatian descent, as was former player and coach Rudy Tomjanovich. Celtic great John Havlicek was half Czech and half Croatian. Although you would never guess based on his name, Kevin McHale, another famous Celtic, is also half Croatian (on his mother's side). Representing Serbian roots are "Pistol" Pete Maravich and Spurs coach Gregg Popovich. When he was head coach at Pomona College, Pop would sometimes invite the team over to his house to eat "Serbian tacos."

WILT PLUS TWELVE: As a twenty-one-year-old, Petrovic scored 112 points in a Yugoslavian League game for Cibona Zagreb against Smelt Olimpija. Perhaps the most impressive thing about his tally was that he needed only 60 field goal attempts to get it, making exactly two thirds of his shots.

out to be in large part wishful thinking, the United States is no longer master of the universe. The Dirks, Pau Gasols, and Tony Parkers of the world have proved that Euros can compete, make All-Star teams, and win championships. Commissioner David Stern's persistent interest in European expansion (and beyond) acknowledges the immense international influence on the NBA. What's more, with perfectly worthy players like Josh Childress choosing to spend time overseas rather than re-sign with their NBA teams, parity across continents may not be so far off. In 2002, Petrovic was inducted into the NBA Hall of Fame, the ultimate testament to his contributions and his unfulfilled promise.

Still, the stereotype of Euros largely remains that they are soft, unwilling to bang knees and elbows down in the post, weak on defense, and generally spacey rather than maintaining a tough mental resolve. These descriptors could not be further from Petrovic's demeanor. Kenny Grant, an agent who helped bring Petrovic to the United States, said of him, "He was a basketball hermit. He didn't have a lot of social life other than basketball." Grant also noted that while playing in Europe before joining the NBA, Petrovic lived across the street from the gym where his team practiced and took five hundred shots every morning before the rest of the team even arrived.

Petrovic also had a boldness to his character, unlike the many other imports who seem resigned to riding the pine and playing in garbage time. He began as a bench player in Portland but was so confident in his abilities that he requested a trade—Portland soon dealt him to New Jersey, where his career skyrocketed. Petrovic's bravado was eulogized by *Sports Illustrated*'s Jerry Kirschenbaum, who called Petrovic a "provocateur who spat at referees, taunted opposing fans and once emptied a bottle of mineral water over the head of a courtside official," and recalled that after receiving an elbow from Blue Edwards, Petrovic told him, "You play correct, or we will fight!"

Petrovic played during a time of extreme unrest in his homeland, which no doubt contributed to his stone-serious demeanor. During the off-season when Petrovic was traded from Portland to New Jersey, he snuck away to Croatia to visit family and friends for three days, telling the team that he was visiting his brother in Florida. "I'm playing basketball," he once said, "and my friends are getting killed." Petrovic joined the NBA just as the Berlin Wall fell, when both he as an individual and his homeland were

VLAD TO THE EXTREME: No recent player has embodied the stereotype of the ineffectual Euro better than forward Vladimir Radmanovic, and no event typifies his nature quite like "Snowboardgate." Radmanovic spent the 2007 All-Star break at the Park City, Utah, home of fellow Serb Vlade Divac and returned with a separated shoulder. Vlad Rad initially said he sustained the suspicious injury after falling on ice with his hands in his pockets, but it was later revealed that he hurt himself snowboarding.

THE UNIVERSAL LANGUAGE: In a 1992 game, Petrovic made a lasting impression on Knicks guard Rolando Blackman: "I have a lot of respect for him," said Blackman. "But he has to stop the flagrant stuff. He was pushing and shoving too. He's a trash talker with an accent."

CONQUISTADOR: Fernando Martín Espina is little remembered in this country, but he was one of the first Europeans to play in the NBA. The Spanish center was selected in the second round of the 1985 NBA draft. Due to injuries, Martín played only a total of 24 games for the Portland Trail Blazers in 1987 and returned to Spain at the end of the season to rejoin his pro team Real Madrid. In a tragic harbinger of Petrovic, Martín died in a car accident in 1989, crashing his custom Lancia Thema. Current Trail Blazer and fellow Spaniard Rudy Fernández paid tribute to Martín in the 2009 slam dunk contest, wearing Martín's #10 Blazers jersey for his first dunk.

HOLY HAND: Arguably the greatest player never to play in the NBA, Brazilian legend Oscar Schmidt gained fame in the basketball world anyway by decimating opponents in international competition. Schmidt was the leading scorer in three of his five Olympics (including a 42.3-point average in 1988 in Seoul), famously led Brazil to a gold medal with 46 points in a stunning comeback over a star-studded American team in the 1987 Pan American Games, and is the leading scorer in basketball history, with 49,703 total points. Drafted by the Nets in 1984, Schmidt turned down several opportunities to play in the NBA during the '80s in order to maintain his amateur status so he could play in the Olympics. He has also been an outspoken critic of what he perceives as the "cowardly" European style of play, instead preferring to play an open, attacking style reminiscent of his country's legendary soccer teams.

beginning to escape the strangling grip of Communism and sort out the challenges that lay ahead.

Petrovic and his contemporaries embodied the familiar narrative of a rise out of poverty and violence to a better life. This trajectory mirrored the American Dream and provided an easy comparison to the backgrounds of the domestic pros who knew so well blacktops and hoops with missing nets. The Eastern Bloc players came from war. Maurice Cheeks came from the Robert Taylor Homes. The parallels are easy to draw, but also far oversimplified; they don't do justice to either side's struggles. The NBA is a far more interesting place when we also take the time to both note these similarities and be accurate about their differences.

Eastern Europeans had been a part of the NBA at least since 1985, when the Suns picked Bulgarian Georgi Glouchkov in the seventh round. Glouchkov's most notable achievement was his mysterious rookie-year weight gain, attributed to everything from fast food to candy to steroids. But the region was already home to the best basketball players outside of America. The unified Yugoslavian national team was legendary; Petrovic first played on it in 1984. Vlade Divac, Toni Kukoc, and Dino Radja would also all end up playing in the NBA. The Soviet team, with Lithuanian stars Arvydas Sabonis and Sarunas Marciulionis, was perhaps even more influential. Sabonis, in particular, was something of a holy grail for the NBA, a gigantic, supremely athletic center who could both throw the breeziest no-look passes you'll ever see and dunk over a young David Robinson in the 1988 Olympics. The USSR took the gold that year, despite the presence of Robinson, Danny Manning, and Mitch Richmond on Team USA. It's a straight line from this Soviet team and its Lithuanian standouts to the changes in rules about amateurism and the inception of the Dream Team.

The 1992 Olympics belonged to the Dream Team, but they played Petrovic and the Croatian team (Kukoc, Radja, Zan Tabak, and the inimitable Stojko Vrankovic) for the championship. Lithuania, another breakaway basketball powerhouse, had the misfortune to play the USA early on, thus landing them in the bronze-medal game—where they had the satisfaction of besting what remained of the Soviet Union. When asked right before the championship game how Croatia might take the gold medal from the United States, Kukoc paused, then said, "Heh, heh . . . joke." Language barrier aside, it was an odd way of answering, but Kukoc's sarcasm was fitting: With no difficulty, USA dispensed with Croatia in the Olympic final game, 117–85. Still, the silver medal was more than a consolation prize for the proud Croatians. Before Croatia's clash with Russia to determine who would play the United States, the head of the Croatian delegation, Toni Vrdolljak, climbed aboard the Croatian team bus and told the players, "You better win this game." Squeaking by Russia, 75–74, was the Croatians' gold medal. They were set to finish second in international basketball's most important tournament yet, the one that brought the NBA face-to-face with the rest of the world for the first time.

But there's another side to this story. NBA players had long been heading overseas at oblong points in their careers. One of the most notable examples was Bob McAdoo—the "Doo" of the two NBA championships and an MVP award—who after a groundbreaking NBA career shuffled off to Italy, playing for Olimpia Milano, Filanto Forli, and the very literal-named Teamsystem Fabriano. With Fabriano, McAdoo won the Euroleague final-four MVP at age thirty-seven and ended up playing until he was forty-two. Perhaps taking a cue from McAdoo, thunderous dunker and outsized personality Darryl Dawkins also made his way around Italy after his injury-shortened NBA career. Even Dominique Wilkins played in Europe. In 1994–95, Nique moved to the Celtics and saw his scoring average drop from 26 points per game to 17.8. Upset with his role, he moved to Europe the next season and led Panathinaikos to a Euroleague championship and Greek Cup. When he returned to the NBA the following year, he averaged 18.2 points per game for a terrible Spurs team, shuttled back to Europe the next season to play for Teamsystem Bologna, and then decided to play one last lackluster season with the Orlando Magic.

Lesser NBA talents also became legends overseas: Mike D'Antoni, for one, had a brief NBA career, making the NBA All-Rookie second team in 1974 despite averaging only 4.8 points a game for the Kansas City–Omaha Kings and then floundering back and forth between the ABA's St. Louis Spirits and the NBA's San Antonio Spurs. D'Antoni found greatness, though, in Europe, where he won five Italian League titles, two Euroleague titles, and was named the league's top point guard of all time. Another international transplant star came in the form of Billy Ray Bates, who had a name and a story fit for a Johnny Cash song. The newly, and only briefly, sober Bates became a legend, bringing his sublime, overpowering high-wire act to a Philippine Basketball

LOVABLE LITHUANIANS: Although the Dream Team was the dominant story of the 1992 Olympic basketball tournament, the Lithuanian team was not far behind. Starring Sarunas Marciulionis and Arvydas Sabonis, the Lithuanians took to the court wearing tie-dyed warm-ups paid for and designed by the Grateful Dead, featuring a slam-dunking skeleton. When they defeated their former oppressors, the Unified Team (the rest of the former Soviet Union), for the bronze medal, President Vytautus Landsbergis joined the team in the locker room and emerged covered in champagne and wearing one of the famous tie-dyed T-shirts.

Association that had never seen a player like him before. The lesser competition didn't hurt, either. Bates had a condo, a bodyguard, and an Uzi. Bates became known as Black Superman and had his own Black Superman sneaker line made by a local company. Bates would also play in Uruguay, Switzerland, and even Mexico. What these stories amount to is an asymmetry between the United States and the rest of the world in the basketball exchange program. Basketball players began coming to the NBA from impoverished Eastern Bloc war zones to live out fantasies while battling prejudices about their abilities. NBA players' overseas trips, on the other hand, largely constituted bloated, hobbled victory laps around exotic locales, most often to Mediterranean countries or other resort destinations. This difference in motive partially explains why it took so long for overseas players to have an impact in the United States: Americans on their overseas tours weren't exactly writing home about any of the competition they faced there.

DIRTY DANCING: In the run up to the 2001 draft, it was often mentioned that lanky Georgian prospect Nikoloz Tskitishvili had training in ballet. The truth was a little more complicated: As Skita explained in his draft-night interview—in perfect hip-hop-inflected English, no less—he had actually participated in a traditional Georgian folk dance performed "with knives and bullets in our inside pockets."

Perhaps there is more to the story of the Euro delay. International players just didn't seem in a rush to invade the NBA en masse. Plenty of the most famous Euros—Russia's Sergei Belov, Serbia's Radivoj Korac, Italy's Aldo Ossola, or Spain's Emiliano Rodríguez; Kresimir Cosic from Yugoslavia, Nikos Galis from Greece, Israel's prized boychick Moshe "Miki" Berkovich, or Mexico's favorite hijo Manuel Raga—never bothered to come over. They just didn't seem all that interested in making their mark in the NBA. Sabonis is the most curious case. Had he shown up once the Wall fell, there's little doubt he would have been among the NBA's best centers. Instead he waited until he was bloated, slowed, and badly needed the money. Even then, you could see what might have been.

Petrovic may be better known for his death than for his life, but it is because of him that every country has its own Shaq, because of him that general managers visit unpronounceable places. It will likely take another few decades until the stereotype of the European softy disappears, and the true tragedy of Petrovic's death is that he could have erased this stigma like no other player from that sector of the world. *—Dr. L.I.C*

FANTASIA NO. 84

How the 1984 NBA Draft Changed Everything

On May 12, 1985, the NBA draft changed forever. That was the night the draft first asserted its independence from reality. That's not to say that the draft had previously been a farm for objective thinking and sound decisions. But coming on the heels of the majestic Class of 1984 (Jordan, Olajuwon, Barkley, Stockton), 1985 marked the year that the draft's connection to the rest of basketball began to fray—when it became a phenomenon unto itself. Once a casual business transaction that reinforced the boys'-club atmosphere of the league, the draft was now a magical place, an enchanted valley where dreams came true. This process culminated in the high-schooler and Euro-laden draft boards of the millennium, pure gibberish to all but the most wistful executives.

This transformation began during the waning weeks of the 1983–84 season, when several teams appeared to be intentionally losing games to ensure they landed the top pick in the upcoming draft. At the time, it was to be used to select Akeem (later Hakeem) Olajuwon, or perhaps Georgetown's Patrick Ewing, if he could be enticed into leaving school a year early. (It would not be until later that summer, at the Olympic Trials, that Michael Jordan would really blow scouts out of the water and enter into consideration for one of the top spots.) Throwing games for the draft was a time-honored practice in sports, more tradition than transgression; wallowing in muck, bad teams were allowed to drop one or two contests late to ensure they picked first (and, paradoxically, regain some measure of dignity). It was a matter of courtesy.

Yet something about 1984 was different. That year's tanking was so aggressive and obvious that it offended the sensibilities of many around the league. It's one thing to have a mistress, another yet to take her to lunch at the country club. Tanking, it turned out, could be more than insurance for the league's worst team—it could turn "worst" into a competition. This realization was the

CAN'T STOP, WON'T STOP: Back in the day, there was no set number of rounds for the NBA draft. Team executives could basically keep drafting players as long as they wanted. The 1958 draft, for example, went seventeen rounds, but the last four rounds consisted of only one pick per round, all by the Cincinnati Royals. Of the last seven players taken by the Royals, only one ever made the team: Adrian Smith, who went on to win the 1966 NBA All-Star Game MVP.

KICKS AND GIGGLES: Before the draft went to two rounds in 1998, GMs often used the later rounds to amuse themselves:

DAVE WINFIELD: *5th round, 79th overall, by the Hawks in 1973.* The eventual Hall of Fame outfielder was such a superb athlete that after college he was drafted by the Hawks (NBA), the San Diego Padres (MLB), the Utah Stars (ABA), and the Minnesota Vikings (NFL).

LUSIA HARRIS: *7th round, 137th overall, by the Jazz in 1977.* A three-time All-American at Delta State University and a member of the 1976 Olympic team, she was the first and only woman selected in the NBA draft. She was pregnant at the time.

VIC SISON: *10th round, 206th overall, by the Nets in 1981.* Standing 5′7″, Sison never played college or even high school ball. A former student manager at UCLA, his selection was "a graduation present from Larry Brown," who had just left UCLA to become the head coach of the Nets.

CARL LEWIS: *10th round, 208th overall, by the Bulls in 1984.* The legendary sprinter and long jumper joined his fellow 1984 Olympic gold medalist Michael Jordan as a selection of the Bulls. Chicago GM Rod Thorn thought it would be "cute."

first spark in that it turned hope for the future into a commodity as valuable as playing with honor.

Imagine if anyone had really known what fruits the 1984 draft would bear! With teams fighting tooth and nail to out-wither each other, how ugly could it have gotten if it had been a race to the bottom for *four* prizes? The Class of 1984 had success above and beyond reasonable expectations, with four players being named either first- or second-team All-NBA within four years of draft night. Between them, Jordan and Olajuwon were responsible for every championship won between 1991 and 1998, and Barkley and Stockton both made the Finals. When everything was said and done, the class boasted the greatest player ever, the premier center of the next fifteen years, the all-time leader in assists, and a power forward of unmatched intensity and capability. Most important, this onrush of talent catapulted the league into a period of popularity and prosperity that has yet to be matched, finishing the work Magic and Bird had started some four years earlier.

Good thing that the league, by then under the control of master showman-cum-authoritarian David Stern, had devised a solution to tanking. The lottery, a random selection of oversize envelopes that would determine which of the worst teams in the league got to pick in the top seven, would be a more than adequate deterrent. It was meant to be all-business, a slap across the face in the name of rational behavior. The worst record guaranteed nothing more than a chance at one of these picks; the only superstition meant to enter the picture was a healthy fear of bad karma—what might happen if a team dared tempt fate by gunning for the bottom of the standings anyway.

Unfortunately, this was a classic case of treating the symptom, not the disease. Tanking may have disappeared, but its root cause—a belief in magic and nymphs and the possibility that the future is always on your side—was only exacerbated. The lottery turned what had been a matter of fact, with the occasional polite nudge, into some wish-upon-a-star, rub-my-rabbit's-foot shit. There is absolutely no way that you can set something up as a prize decided by chance—a form of gambling—and not set off certain receptors in the human brain that scream "fun," "thrills," and "Why not me?" The league's cure for tanking only made its underlying impulse worse, more grandiose. The draft of Patrick Ewing ended up being a world-historical event because it was the fulfillment, and the release, of all the energy that had been mounting. For the time being, what actually happened with Ewing was an afterthought. In that moment, anything was possible. On the eve of the draft lottery, one NBA executive was quoted as saying, "We've had the Mikan Era, the Russell Era, the Kareem Era, and now we'll have the Ewing Era." And while the Knicks had won, the dream belonged equally to all teams in the league.

From the beginning, the lottery has been a televised event, laying it bare as the ritual it is. Superstition is now a heavy presence, working against, not in concert with, the lottery's original, sober intent. Team representatives bring all manner of talismans to Secaucus with them, from lucky horseshoes to bottles of holy water. In 1990, the league introduced a new weighted lottery system featuring fourteen numbered Ping-Pong balls used to determine the draft order. Although the Ping-Pong balls were drawn behind closed doors, the viewers were shown ample shots of them, casting team owners in the role of a bunch of helpless old ladies playing bingo at church. For perennial lottery teams, returning again and again with a thoroughly selfish prayer, the analogy was a little too apt.

PROPHECY OF THE OVERMAN: In the early-to-mid '90s, the NBA played Richard Strauss's *Thus Spoke Zarathustra* after many first-round draft picks. Playing off the music's use in Stanley Kubrick's *2001: A Space Odyssey*, it's a fitting pairing of image and moment, but a little ridiculous when used as the score to the Lakers taking career-long role player George Lynch with the twelfth pick in 1993.

The resultant hype machine is not some conspiracy on the part of dark forces up at the commissioner's office, as some have suggested. If it were, it's been a pretty bad idea—if fans and executives alike approached the draft with more reasonable expectations, teams could make more intelligent decisions, players could be viewed for what they really are, or realistically might become, and many jobs might be spared. A healthy skepticism might replace goofy fetishization. The world would be a better place, and the NBA a more sanguine business. Had this foundation been installed, then the years of high school and European picks might have been less farcical; after all, the damage these picks have done to rosters has always been greatly exaggerated, and the real toll taken by the image of front offices the league over. Instead, chasing ghosts and speaking tongues replaced calculated risks as the lingo of the inevitable risk built into draft picks.

How can 1984 continue to haunt us, even when it's acknowledged as an exceptional draft? That's the secret of 1984's legacy: Watching the rookie Michael Jordan or Hakeem Olajuwon must have made opposing teams sick with envy, but also giddily anxious for their chance at the next superstar. In the wake of 1984, daring to dream was as human as a gag reflex; that summer, the lottery seemed to reify the dream of the next big thing. Today, that period exists

FUCK YOU, I'M GOING TO ITALY: Brandon Jennings made headlines in 2008 by going pro in Italy to circumvent the age limit, but he wasn't the first to do so for leverage.

DANNY FERRY: Drafted by the dreaded Clippers in 1989, he decided he would rather play for Il Messaggero Roma of the Italian league. After Ferry spent one season in Italy, the Clippers traded his rights to Cleveland, who signed him to a ten-year guaranteed contract.

BRIAN SHAW: When negotiations with the Celtics broke down after his rookie year, Shaw opted to take a more generous offer to join Ferry with Il Messaggero Roma. The following year, he signed a new five-year contract with the Celtics.

beneath the surface of draft-day consciousness. It's the trauma that started it all, the kernel from which the draft's hermetic, frequently daft outlook developed.

It was only a few seasons before the draft attempted to quixotically tear down more walls, expanding its reach and, as was to be expected, its capacity for foolishness. Contrary to popular belief, international and pre-college prospects were first taken seriously by the draft in the mid-eighties. In 1986, the Portland Trail Blazers selected Soviet center Arvydas Sabonis with the last pick of the first round, the first time an international player had gone that high. The symbolism of cracking the first round was unmistakable: Portland was, in effect, saying that the rights to Sabonis were more valuable to them than an NBA-caliber player who could join their team right away.

Whatever struck those Blazers must have crept through the Pacific Northwest, because three years later, Seattle used the seventeenth pick of the 1989 NBA draft to select Shawn Kemp, an ultra-athletic forward who had never played a single game in college or even junior college. Kemp had been kicked off the team at Kentucky and spent time at juco before entering the draft, making him a mysterious entity that most fans had never witnessed. Kemp's immediate impact set the stage for Kevin Garnett, who in 1995 became the first high school player to go straight to the pros since Moses Malone in 1974 and Darryl Dawkins and Bill Willoughby in 1975; Kemp's crazed, raw play and eventual lack of discipline also made him the prototypical preps-to-pro flameout. Garnett had failed to receive a qualifying test score and, rather than sit out a year as a Prop 48 casualty, decided to enter the draft straight out of high school—really, not so far from Kemp's situation.

But if Sabonis and Kemp had proven to be isolated instances, and Garnett could claim special circumstances, it was the 1996 draft that grabbed the wheel and sent teams down the road to oblivion. Before, there had been socially imposed limits, none of which had any real legal standing. Now teams had only as many possibilities as they dared imagine in front of them. It was there, hidden in plain sight, back-to-back picks at the end of the lottery. At number thirteen, the Charlotte Hornets selected Kobe Bryant, an honor-roll student from suburban Lower Merion High School with SAT scores that well exceeded NCAA requirements. Bryant's situation was markedly different from Garnett's, since

Bryant could have attended any university in the nation but chose to turn them all down and go straight to the NBA. Were it not for Bryant, the impact of Garnett's decision may have been substantially limited, possibly creating a new sort of hardship category for exceedingly talented high school players who didn't meet NCAA requirements, such as Jermaine O'Neal, who joined Bryant in the 1996 draft, going seventeenth overall. But Bryant's bold decision ensured that for the top high school players, no matter what their collegiate prospects, going straight to the NBA became the rule rather than the exception. From 1997 until the NBA enacted an age limit in 2006, at least one high school senior was selected in the first round of every NBA draft.

Pedrag Stojakovic, taken immediately after Kobe, became the first European player ever selected in the lottery. Unlike Sabonis and Petrovic, veterans who had already proven themselves in international competition, Stojakovic was still a child, only recently turned nineteen and with little experience playing against top international competition. Although Stojakovic remained in Europe for two more seasons, he was still only twenty-one when he made his NBA debut in 1998, along with a lanky twenty-year-old forward out of Würzburg, Germany, named Dirk Nowitzki. Stojakovic and Nowitzki soon emerged as two of the best young players in the league, and from there, everything began to spin out of control.

It took time for high schoolers and Euros to become automatic presences in the lottery; even then, it was those agreed upon as "the next KG" or "the next Dirk." However, once these players became mainstays of those rarefied regions, gradually the "maybe the next KG" and "possibly maybe the next Dirk" crept into the first round. This is how you got Josh Howard and David West going at the end of the first round in 2003.

Still, was it really that much worse than a draft-day bust from a Big Ten program? All draft picks are gambles. The draft-day suits of players, the more flamboyant the better, have become an integral part of the event. They lend the same air of unreality to the process as seeing GMs explain their lucky charms on national television. However, at this point you wonder why only the players show up in lavish, improbable costumes. Why not encourage all involved to dress in bright colors, and turn the whole thing into the masquerade of fun and fantasy that, for one special night, they can feel their jobs to be? —*B.R.*

FOOLS RUSH IN: Not all the high schoolers who followed Garnett and Kobe into the draft were prepared for NBA life:

KORLEONE YOUNG: Fortieth overall in 1998. The improbably named Suntino Korleone Young surprised even his high school coaches when he declared for the draft. He played in only three games for the Pistons and was waived the next summer due to injury.

LEON SMITH: Twenty-ninth overall in 1999. The ultimate high schooler horror story, Smith was released by the Mavericks before ever playing a game. Just a few months after being drafted, he had already been arrested twice for misdemeanor assault charges against girlfriend (and current WNBA star) Cappie Pondexter, swallowed 250 aspirin tablets, and was committed to a psychiatric ward for several weeks. He eventually played in 15 games for the Hawks and Sonics.

KWAME BROWN: First overall in 2001. Brown has had a nine-year career in the league, but as a rookie with the Wizards, he was so unprepared for NBA life that he would buy new clothes every day, not knowing how to do laundry or have suits dry-cleaned.

OTHER CASES: Ndudi Ebi (2003, 19 games), Ousmane Cisse (2001, no games), James Lang (2003, 11 games).

Decoding the Draft

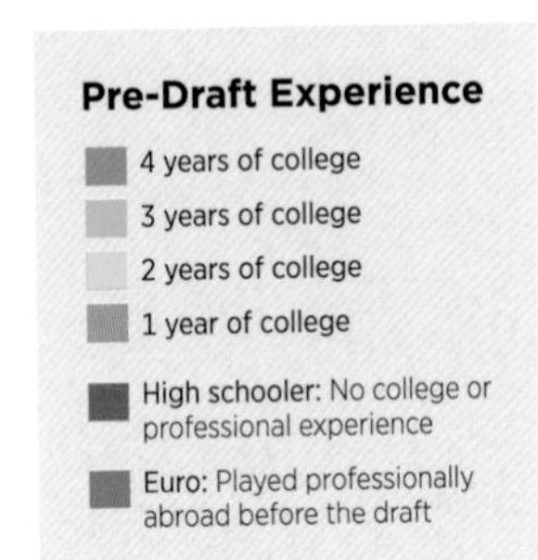

There have been many changes in the culture of the NBA draft since 1980. There was the introduction of the lottery in 1984 and Kevin Garnett's jump from high school in 1995, followed by the imposition of the age limit before the 2005–06 season, to name a few. Even before KG, underclassmen weighed the decision of how soon to go pro. International players went from barely understood fliers to number-one overall picks in Yao Ming (2002) and Andrea Bargnani (2006). Scouting has expanded to every corner of the country at the college and high school level; internationally, the focus on Europe has been equalled by an interest in players who hail from Latin America, Africa, and Asia. But this chart of first-rounder performance shows that one thing has remained the same: No matter what kind of pick is in vogue, being a general manager is never easy.

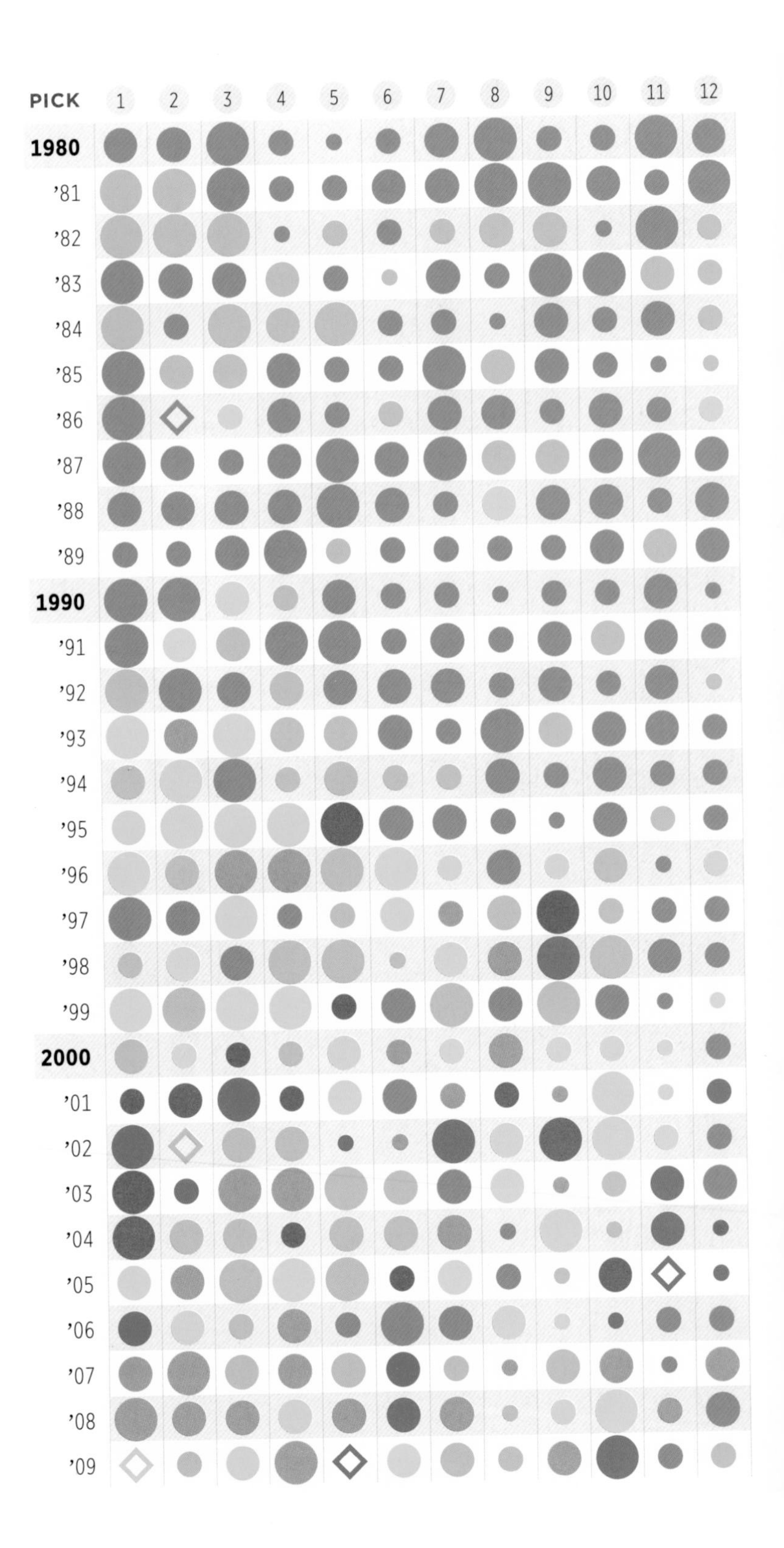

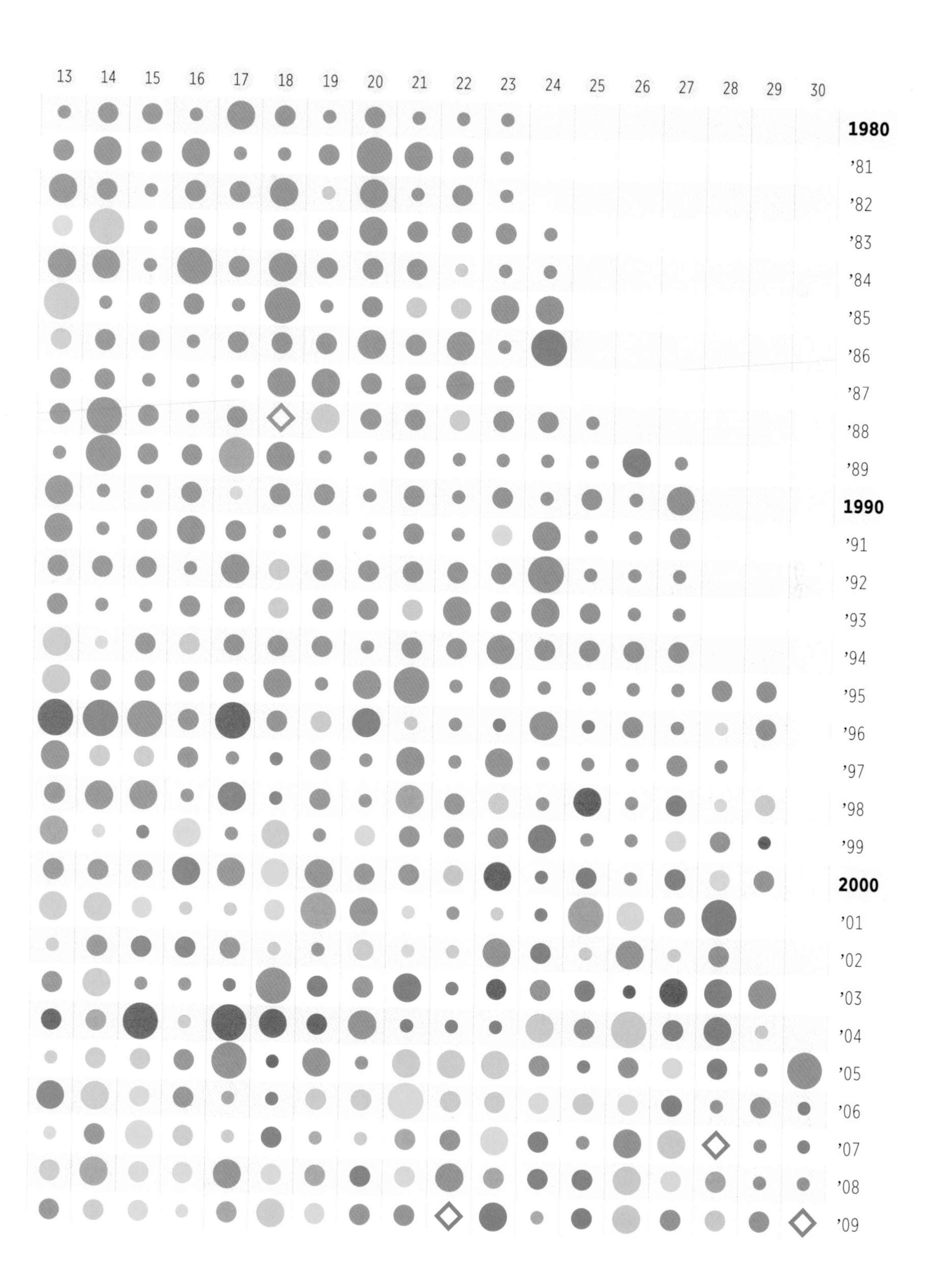

13
14
15
16
17
18
19
20
21
22
23
24
25
26
27
28
29
30
1980
'81
'82
'83
'84
'85
'86
'87
'88
'89
1990
'91
'92
'93
'94
'95
'96
'97
'98
'99
2000
'01
'02
'03
'04
'05
'06
'07
'08
'09

	1991	1992	1993	1994
NBA FINALS CHAMPION	CHICAGO BULLS			HOUSTON ROCKETS
FINALS LOSER	LAKERS	BLAZERS	SUNS	KNICKS
MOST VALUABLE PLAYER	MICHAEL JORDAN	MICHAEL JORDAN	CHARLES BARKLEY	HAKEEM OLAJUWON
POINTS per game leader	Michael Jordan **31.5**	Michael Jordan **30.1**	Michael Jordan **32.6**	David Robinson **29.8**
REBOUNDS per game leader	David Robinson **13.0**	Dennis Rodman **18.7**	Dennis Rodman **18.3**	Dennis Rodman **17.3**
ASSISTS per game leader	John Stockton **14.2**	John Stockton **13.7**	John Stockton **12.0**	John Stockton **12.6**

A TALE OF TWO THREE-PEATS

1991–1999

This was Michael Jordan's time. Jordan became the most popular athlete in America, and then the world; his Bulls won six titles and might have won more, had MJ not taken time off to pursue baseball and then walked away when he could have kept on winning. But, as with the Red/Russell Celtics, this dominance meant that the other major figures of the day had to content themselves with second-best. They did, however, join Jordan on the first team of NBA players to win Olympic gold in 1992. Yet if the first three-peat captured the league still at its late-eighties zenith, the second one masked the ugliness and controversy that would overrun the NBA as soon as Jordan exited. The Knicks and Heat turned basketball into a thankless slog; a generation of wild egoists emerged, many of whom found their way onto the reviled Dream Team II. The decade ended with a lockout, a harsh reprieve that may have only exacerbated tensions and that suggested that had it not been for Jordan, the league might have collapsed several years earlier.

<table>
<tr><th>1995</th><th>1996</th><th>1997</th><th>1998</th><th>1999</th></tr>
<tr><td>HOUSTON ROCKETS</td><td colspan="3">CHICAGO BULLS</td><td>SAN ANTONIO SPURS</td></tr>
<tr><td>MAGIC</td><td>SONICS</td><td colspan="2">JAZZ</td><td>KNICKS</td></tr>
<tr><td>DAVID ROBINSON</td><td>MICHAEL JORDAN</td><td>KARL MALONE</td><td>MICHAEL JORDAN</td><td>KARL MALONE</td></tr>
<tr><td>Shaquille O'Neal 29.3
Dennis Rodman 16.8
John Stockton 12.3</td><td>Michael Jordan 30.3
Dennis Rodman 14.9
John Stockton 11.2</td><td>Michael Jordan 29.6
Dennis Rodman 16.1
Mark Jackson 11.4</td><td>Michael Jordan 28.7
Dennis Rodman 15.0
Rod Strickland 10.5</td><td>Allen Iverson 26.8
Chris Webber 13.0
Jason Kidd 10.8</td></tr>
</table>

JORDAN AND HIS DISCONTENTS

When Second-Best Was Good Enough

REFUSE TO LOSE: Michael Jordan was never involved in a three-game losing streak from November 1990 until his second retirement in 1998, a stretch that covers 626 games across the regular season and playoffs. The Harvard Sports Analysis Collective found that a team with the Bulls record (and Jordan) would have a 1-in-150 chance of never losing three games in a row during such a stretch.

Lord forgive the Clutch City Rockets. Led by megacenter Hakeem Olajuwon, entouraged by Otis Thorpe, Mario Elie, and personal bodyguard Vernon Maxwell; blessed with the naïve gutsiness of rookie Sam Cassell, the ever-welcome whiteness of Matt Bullard and Scott Brooks, the calm and savvy of early Robert Horry; and led to battle by basset-hound-eyed Coach Rudy Tomjanovich, the 1993–94 and 1994–95 Rockets had the misfortune of winning two titles during the years when Michael Jordan had temporarily retired from the NBA.

Olajuwon would never meet Jordan on the NBA's biggest stage, and for this, we should all feel emptiness. For although Jordan was the best guard of the day (and, yes, likely of all time), Olajuwon was the era's greatest big man—something he proved in the most clear-cut manner possible: In the Rockets' two title years, Olajuwon stepped on, and then over, the other three Hall of Fame big men of the 1990s: Patrick Ewing, David Robinson, and Shaquille O'Neal. In the 1994 NBA Finals, against Ewing's Knicks, Olajuwon rebounded, scored, stole, blocked, and free-throwed his way to a first championship. In 1995, his Rockets bested Robinson's Spurs in the Western Conference Finals and then beat Shaq's Magic for the title.

THE VOID: Coach Don Nelson didn't even watch the Jordan-less 1994 NBA Finals between the Rockets and Knicks, saying, "I decided to play golf. It was just so boring . . . They're taking skilled players and keeping them from doing exciting things. Guys pound it inside and take time off the twenty-four-second clock. It's become so predictable, it's almost sickening occasionally."

The 1994 Finals achieved infamy for two reasons: (1) the famous O. J. Simpson white Bronco chase that interrupted the Game 5 telecast, and (2) Olajuwon's last-second block of John Starks's attempted three-pointer that prevented a Knicks championship. This was one of many do-it-all plays that Olajuwon authored during the series to lead Houston to its first franchise title. Just moments before the game-ending block, with the Rockets protecting a two-point lead, Olajuwon stole the ball from Starks, lured a foul from Ewing, and calmly hit two free throws. We envision most NBA titles surrounded by a top-to-bottom team of notables or an outstanding star tandem. But with all due respect to that supporting cast, when we think about the Rockets' titles of 1994 and 1995, we fixate on Hakeem.

Beyond his immense skill, Olajuwon was known for his piety. Hakeem had been thoroughly Americanized at the University of Houston, but as his NBA career progressed, he embraced his faith and became a devout Muslim. He changed—in his words, "corrected"—the spelling of his name from Akeem in March of 1991. Starting that year, Hakeem began donating 2.5 percent of his yearly income to the poor and always traveled with a compass so that he could pray toward Mecca in any NBA city. His religiosity and his proclivity for speaking in proverbs ("God comes first," "Paradise is not cheap") lent a spiritual authority to the Rockets' championships.

HARDER BETTER STRONGER FASTER: Olajuwon fasted from dawn until sunset every Ramadan throughout his career. Many observers believed that Hakeem actually played better during the month, and in February 1995 he received the Player of the Month award even though Ramadan had started on the first of the month that year.

Yet with Olajuwon's former teammate Kenny Smith sitting next to him in the TNT studios, Charles Barkley routinely jokes that Jordan "loaned" the Rockets the title during his two-year hiatus between three-peats with the Bulls. And although those Rockets were really, really good, what rings true in Barkley's joshing is that Michael Jordan's absence is the closest thing the NBA has to an asterisk. Michael Jordan adds another level of meaning to anyone else's achievements during his time in the league. Jordan might as well be present on every plaque and trophy, on the pages of the record books, or in the rafters of any arena in pro basketball from roughly 1984 to 1998.

Jordan's dominance was so overwhelming that his presence (or absence) determined the worth of all wins, losses, awards, and other achievements during his reign. If we follow the logic that Jordan's 1993–95 absence mars the Rockets' mid-nineties titles, so too should Jordan's presence in each of his championship years soften the defeats of his greatest competitors. The Drexler Blazers, the Ewing Knicks, the Stockton/Malone Jazz, the Payton/Kemp Sonics—all were good enough to have won titles were it not for Jordan. But none were more worthy than the 1992–93 Phoenix Suns.

The Suns were an oddball cast of characters, but not one to gawk at like some real-life *Fish That Saved Pittsburgh* roster. These Suns were an NBA Haley's comet that emerged for but a season, never to reappear. These eclectic talents were not brought together by astrological fate but by design. Oliver Miller, the roundest man ever to play the game, excelled for this one year only. Dan Majerle and Tom Chambers collectively defied the

CAVS
HEAT
SONICS
SUNS
PACERS
JORDAN
23
SIXERS
MAGIC
BLAZERS
RAPTORS
NETS
HAWKS
BUCKS

00.1
PISTONS
JAZZ
HEAT
HEAT
NEW YORK
33
SUNS
32
BLAZER

SOLAR ECLIPSE: The success of the 1992–93 season was also fleeting for Suns coach Paul Westphal. As a player for the Suns, he had been one of the organization's earliest stars, leading them to the 1976 NBA Finals and making three All-Star teams. He returned to Phoenix in 1992 as a rookie head coach and guided them to the Finals for the first time since the '76 run. Although they made the playoffs the next two seasons, Westphal was fired in the middle of the 1995–96 season for not getting the team back to the Finals.

stereotype of Caucasians lacking athleticism. Richard Dumas had returned to Phoenix after a drug suspension forced him to play in Israel for what would have been his rookie year; while his career would ultimately be relegated to the could've-been heap, for 48 games this season he fulfilled his promise. Negele Knight was named Negele Knight. Danny Ainge was championship-proven with the Celtics. Cedric Ceballos famously won the slam dunk contest by dunking while wearing a blindfold through which he could clearly see. And then, of course, there was the man whose outsized personality cast a shadow across the entire desert.

"Charles, I hear you're one of the baddest dudes in the NBA. You're so tough on the court. Show me how tough you are."

Those were the words allegedly spoken to Charles Barkley by Joseph McCarthy in a Milwaukee parking lot shortly before McCarthy got his face beat in by Barkley, then a member of the Philadelphia 76ers. That incident occurred in December 1991. Approximately six months later, Barkley was acquitted of charges stemming from the fistfight. On the same day, Barkley received news that he was traded to the Phoenix Suns. Sam Smith wrote in the *Chicago Tribune* that Barkley was now the "Suns' problem." Sixers owner Harold Katz noted of the trade, "We won thirty-five games with this superstar. Nobody can tell me we're not going to win more next year." The 76ers won 26 games that next year, while Barkley led Phoenix to a historic season.

Barkley won the MVP award in 1993. He had the best year of his career, averaging a career high in points per game in what was his ninth season, at an age (twenty-nine) when most NBA players begin to decline. He brought leadership and an edge to a team that had previously seemed content with scoring a million points a game and never contending. Barkley's campaign made for one of the greatest man-on-a-mission endeavors of all time, even though he never realized his objective.

The Suns' banner season brought them as far as a Game 6 versus Jordan and company. After staving off elimination in Game 5, beating the Bulls 108–98 and sending the series back to Phoenix, Barkley, channeling his version of Olajuwon, boasted, "I talked to God the other day. He said: 'Charles, hang in there. It's your destiny to win.' " MJ—ever a divine vessel himself—retorted, "He's been saying that business since he got here. We're here to say his destiny is to have a long summer thinking about what he should have or could have done."

We all know how it ended, with the dagger driven in by John Paxson, of all people, and Jordan merely acting the decoy. Phoenix led 98–96 with 14.1 seconds remaining. The Bulls had floundered in the fourth quarter, failing to score for the first six minutes: Up until Paxson's shot, MJ had scored all of Chicago's points in the quarter. Phoenix took advantage but missed six of their last seven shots, any two of which could have easily iced the game. On one side, Phoenix slowly burned, desperately trying to "not lose" instead of stepping on the throat of their opponent. On the other side, the Bulls flailed but were always anchored by their captain.

On the game-winning play, MJ barely touched the ball. Of course he brought it up court, but he quickly dished to Scottie Pippen, who dribble-penetrated the lane perfectly, completely breaking down the Phoenix defense. Pippen then passed to Horace Grant, who swung the ball to Paxson, who nailed the defining three-pointer of his career. The play spoke to the greatness of Jordan's supporting cast and to the genius of coach Phil Jackson's craftsmanship, but MJ put his metaphysical imprint all over those waning seconds. Jordan's presence loomed so large in the collective consciousness of the Suns that they could barely attend to the eventual assassin, Paxson. For Phoenix, it must have felt like they had successfully dismantled a bomb only to choke to death on a celebratory cupcake.

The year before, Team Jordan had devoured two other championship aspirants, the New York Knicks and the Portland Trail Blazers. The Bulls defeated Patrick Ewing's Knicks in the Eastern Conference Semifinals. Ewing dominated his mismatch with Bulls center and Jordan whipping boy Bill Cartwright, and the Knicks gave Chicago a level of physicality rarely seen from other, more intimidated competitors: In Game 3, Charles Oakley—the NBA's very own Suge Knight—mugged the goggles damn near off the saintly Horace Grant's face. Rotten apples John Starks, Xavier McDaniel, and Anthony Mason fought the Bulls with plenty of bark and muscle but were left on planet Earth when Jordan went for 42 points in Game 7 of the series.

In the Finals, the Bulls trounced a Portland Trail Blazers team that, in any other era, might have had a shot at multiple championships. The 1991–92 Blazers boasted one of the best starting fives to never win a title: Clyde Drexler, Terry Porter, Kevin Duckworth, Buck Williams, and Jerome Kersey. Athletically,

SAY IT WITH THUNDER: Jordan sought to embarrass many opponents throughout his career, but his pettiest feud was with Dan Majerle. Jordan didn't hate Majerle for any personal reason. Instead, Jordan tried to kick his ass at every opportunity because Jerry Krause loved him so much, and MJ considered the praise excessive. According to David Halberstam, Jordan took things so far that he exclaimed, "Thunder Dan Majerle—my fucking ass!" after Paxson's game-winning shot.

PHIL'S BOOK CLUB: Coach Phil Jackson gave the following players the following books while in Chicago:

MICHAEL JORDAN: *Fever: Twelve Stories*, by John Edgar Wideman

SCOTTIE PIPPEN: *The Ways of White Folks*, by Langston Hughes

WILL PERDUE: *On the Road*, by Jack Kerouac

STEVE KERR: *All the Pretty Horses*, by Cormac McCarthy

STACEY KING: *Beavis & Butthead: This Book Sucks*, by Sam Johnson

B. J. ARMSTRONG: *Zen Mind, Beginner's Mind*, by Shunryu Suzuki

CRAIG HODGES: *Way of the Peaceful Warrior*, by Dan Millman

Drexler was Jordan's closest match in the league—he was a high-flying dunker with flair, but in the presence of the man himself Drexler was just a *Homo sapiens* to MJ's demigod. In 1984, the Trail Blazers drafted Sam Bowie over Jordan *because* they already had Drexler. MJ had never forgotten this slight and used this series as an opportunity to once and for all prove Drexler inferior. (An older Drexler would eventually chase down a ring with the 1995 Rockets.)

The 1998 Bulls completed their second three-peat by defeating the Utah Jazz of Stockton and Malone. These two ringless soldiers were the embodiment of the big-man/little-man strike force, that most sacred of NBA templates. Malone was an exemplar of physicality in basketball. And yet Jordan, with one quick shove of Jazz defender Byron Russell and a series-winning shot, both subsumed and dismissed the Jazz's counterphilosophy.

Jordan could serve to elevate even teams that might not have ever had a legitimate shot at a title. In 1996, the Gary Payton/Shawn Kemp Seattle SuperSonics stepped into that hallowed circle of the NBA Finals only to fall to the Bulls 4–2. The Sonics were associated as much with Kemp's riveting dunks and Payton's notorious in-game jawing as the gravitas of championship play. As an alley-oop combo, the two stars' synchronicity was so extrasensory that Payton could toss the ball from the half-court line to Kemp in mid-leap. The Reign Man's dunking style defied conventions of the day—rather than using the majestic elevation of Jordan or Clyde Drexler, Kemp put his knees, feet, and crotchal region in his opponent's grill. Before facing Jordan, these Sonics had a reputation as chokers. They rode a tremendous 1994 regular-season performance to the first seed in the playoffs, only to lose to the eighth-seeded Denver Nuggets in the first round. In 1995 they were defeated by the seventh-seeded Lakers. Soon, the team fell apart. But they were among Jordan's victims; this alone grants them nobility. They were touched by a fucking angel.

By comparison, the failure of Barkley's Suns to derail the Michael Jordan Experience at the height of its powers does not seem to be that much of a disappointment. Their attempt was a noble one, and it came down to a single fireball of a season. In fact, if you squint, you may even be able to see the Suns winning it, a shimmering illusion always just at the edge of the Phoenix desert. Losing to the nineties Bulls was all but preordained, a matter we can't erase but only debate the cosmology of, like loss or death.

RON HARPER'S INDEX:

Number of points Ron Harper scored in his college career: **2,377**
Number of points Michael Jordan scored in his college career: **1,788**

Number of turnovers Harper had in his rookie season: **345 (led the league)**
Number of steals Harper had in his rookie season: **209 (3rd in the league)**
Number of players ranking in the top 3 in both turnovers and steals that year: **1**

Number of players who have had ten or more steals in a single game: **19**
Number of players other than Harper who did it in their rookie season: **0**

Percentage of Los Angeles Clippers playoff appearances that happened when Harper was on the team: **50%**
Number of starters on the 1990–91 Clippers roster who tore their ACL: **2**

Drop in Harper's scoring from last season with Clippers to first season with Bulls: **13.2 points per game**
Rise in wins by Harper's team from final season with Clippers to first season with Bulls: **20**

Number of consecutive seasons the Chicago Bulls had a Dayton, Ohio, native on the roster: **14**

Thankfully, the advent of the Olympic Dream Team in 1992 allowed the great players of Jordan's era—Patrick Ewing, John Stockton, Karl Malone, Chris Mullin, Charles Barkley, Reggie Miller—to win a championship without winning one of *his* championships. The USA's Olympic gold medals of 1992 and 1996 cemented each of these players' status as winners, and the ease with which they dominated the rest of the world allowed MJ's mortal foes to bask in his glory. At the same time, this team belonged to Jordan simply because they dominated. There is a well-known hypothesis that Isiah Thomas's omission from the team (even though Pistons coach Chuck Daly led the squad) was at the behest of Michael Jordan. If it's true, that decision is perhaps the most poignant reminder of Jordan's clout at the time. MJ decided not only who won or lost, he decided who played.

Few things define the confident perception of comfort in the 1990s as well as the Dream Team. This group of players represented the basic outlook that things would go well. Even when adversity lurked, it quickly dissipated. America's success in the Gulf War was never in question, and following the war the country rebounded from a recession that made way for the prosperity of the Clinton years. We had a blithe confidence that there was nothing much in the world to fear. Anthrax in the mail, a bomb hidden in a shoe—these were as inconceivable as Argentina's fielding a basketball team that would beat America's finest roundballers. The NFL gave us leaders in Aikman, Favre, and Elway, while Major League Baseball gave us the Jeterian Yankee dynasty. The NBA gave us the Dream Team and Michael Jordan, indicators not only of American prominence but of all being right with the world.

This ultimate obfuscation of reality, not his tangible achievements, honors, titles, or even the highlight clips, is what makes Michael Jordan Michael Jordan. His greatness took a torch to NBA history; the rest are left to pick through the ashes. We now must decide the value of the achievements by Malone, Barkley, and Ewing in the same way that we try to determine the life spans of characters in the Old Testament. Michael Jordan provides a lens through which we view the game during his time, and it is through that lens that his contemporaries must be perceived and analyzed as well. —*Dr. L.I.C.*

THE MICHAEL JORDAN OF:

Jordan has become such a cultural icon that his name is invoked in the most bizarre of comparisons. Here are some of the stranger examples (all from actual sources):

PUGET SOUND: The Michael Jordan of ecosystems

MARY BARTH: The Michael Jordan of accounting

WINSTON TABB: The Michael Jordan of librarians

RICHARD C. HOLBROOKE: The Michael Jordan of global diplomacy

STEPHANIE PEARL-McPHEE: The Michael Jordan of knitting

STEVEN RAICHLEN: The Michael Jordan of barbecue

JENNA JAMESON: The Michael Jordan of porn

THE "TIAN CHI" CHINESE WASHING MACHINE: The Michael Jordan of washing machines

ALASDAIR FRASER: The Michael Jordan of Scottish fiddling

MILTON FRIEDMAN: The Michael Jordan of economics

BILL CLINTON: The Michael Jordan of late-twentieth-century politicians

EDWARD R. LACHAPELLE: The Michael Jordan of avalanche forecasters

Basketball on Film

The Evolution of an Idea

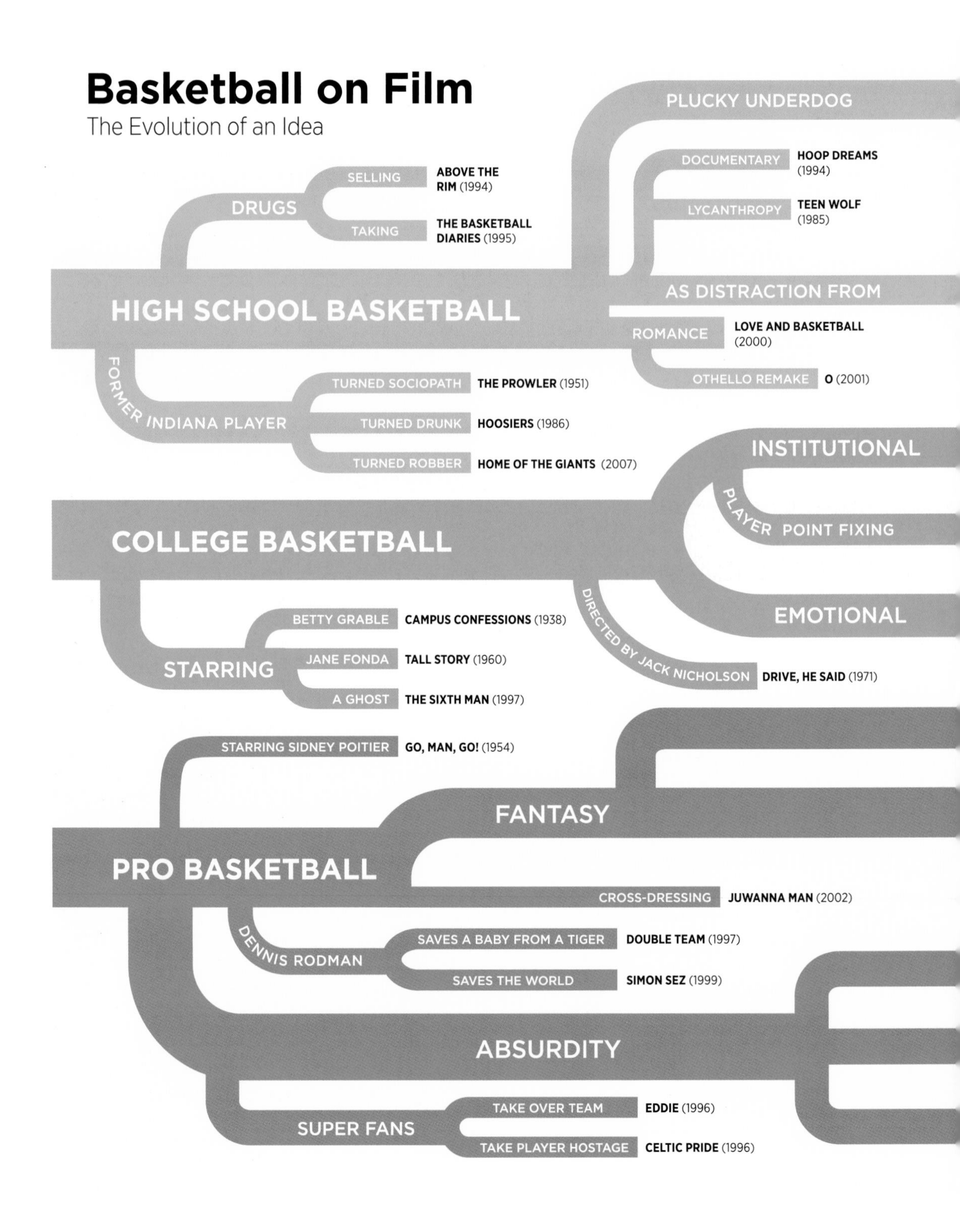

FACTS AND FICTIONS

Life imitates art, art justifies life, and Denzel schools Ray Allen.

CAMPUS CONFESSIONS, 1938: One of the first basketball movies, and maybe the only one to originate a move, *Campus Confessions* costarred Stanford's Hank Luisetti, an early proponent of the jump shot. During one scene, Luisetti dribbles the ball behind his back as a gag. After watching the film, eighteen-year-old high school senior Bob Davies was so inspired by Luisetti's behind-the-back dribble he began practicing it obsessively, and would eventually be credited with introducing it to the NBA. If you squint, that makes Luisetti the inventor of both the jumper and any and all behind-the-back moves.

SPACE JAM, 1996: By the time Jordan was ready to return to basketball after a brief stint in baseball's minors, he was not simply an athlete. He was also a corporate entity who had some explaining to do. *Space Jam* provided MJ with a ready-fit narrative, justifying why he should return to the sport (to save the world from aliens), reaffirming his commercial clout (it grossed $2.3 billion), and making his baseball hiatus seem as forgettable as the movie itself (Bill Murray has called *Space Jam* his least favorite of his own films).

HE GOT GAME, 1998: The climactic scene pits ex-con father (Denzel Washington) against high school star son (Ray Allen) in a game of one-on-one that will decide Dad's fate in the justice system. The script called for a 15–0 drubbing, but then Denzel went and got a few buckets, and Ray Ray ended up having to dig in more than he had counted on. Of course, in the end Allen triumphed, but it's a story he has never been able to shake.

MILLER
10
KEMP
7

DREAM TEAM II

Our Brief National Nightmare

When the Dream Team returned home from the 1992 Olympics in Barcelona, they arrived stateside as conquering heroes and were welcomed back as triumphant warriors. They'd been dispatched to Iberia to restore honor to their bruised native land, whose 1988 team of amateurs managed only a bronze medal. So the pros were sent to set the record straight, as it were. This they accomplished. It was Dream Team II that screwed everything up.

In some ways, Dream Team II was John Thompson's fault. The syrup-voiced Georgetown coach headed up the 1988 U.S. men's Olympic basketball team, and he selected some curious players while leaving off, among others, Danny Ferry, who was at the time the reigning College Player of the Year. Thompson's handpicked team lost to the Soviet Union in the semifinals. Though they did win the bronze medal, it was the first time the United States, the land that invented basketball, had *ever* failed to reach the gold-medal game.

After the loss in '88, an embarrassed USA Basketball decided to take action. For decades, the Olympic basketball teams had been selected by the head coach. USA Basketball defused any selection controversies by taking the roster out of the coach's hands and making it the responsibility of that most democratic of traditions, a committee. Simultaneously, FIBA, the governing body for international basketball, changed its rules to allow NBA players to participate, so the United States could now send its top professional talent instead of hastily assembled teams of college kids. For the 1992 Olympics in Barcelona, USA Basketball and the NBA got together and coproduced a monster. Instead of a name, they gave it a blockbuster movie title: the Dream Team.

Soon after Dream Team I conquered the world, USA Basketball and the NBA began preparing for the 1994 World Championships, to be held in Toronto. Upholding Hollywood tradition, they billed it as a sequel: Dream Team II. They began by approaching Michael

EGOS COLLIDE: As soon as the rosters were named, the debate began about who would win if Dream Team I and Dream Team II played each other. The MGM Grand in Las Vegas even tried to make it happen but was unsuccessful in its bid.

MAGIC JOHNSON: "They would never beat us ... It's not even worth talking about ... We'll put Larry in a wheelchair ... then have him stand out behind the three-point line and bust them out. Me and Mike would penetrate and just kick it back out to him."

MICHAEL JORDAN: "Not only was Dream Team I better, but we could beat them right now. Those guys are on the right team, because they're definitely dreaming."

SHAQUILLE O'NEAL: "That was an old team. We're a young team with young legs. Best-of-one, best-of-three, best-of-seven, it really doesn't matter. We'd beat them."

REGGIE MILLER: "Let's get it on. I'll put up the money, we'll sell out the Hoosier Dome. [Michael Jordan] wants to challenge us, we'll accept that."

JOE DUMARS: "I respect them, but I won't ever say they would beat us. I'd play them in a heartbeat."

THE ADMIRAL'S CLUB: As an officer in the U.S. Navy, David Robinson has always been willing to serve his country. Robinson is the only American basketball player to play in three Olympics: Seoul '88, Barcelona '92, and Atlanta '96.

THE FILM'S LAST REEL: Dominique Wilkins was the odd man out on the '94 World Championship team, a player clearly more at home with the generation of stars that populated the first Dream Team. It was also his final moment as one of the league's top stars, coming after a midseason trade to the Clippers that ended his time as the face of the Hawks.

Jordan, asking him to reprise his starring role, but he promptly turned them down. Without MJ, they decided to reboot, finding a dozen new players to represent the red, white, and blue. Going into the 1993–94 NBA season, Jordan had won seven consecutive scoring titles and was established as not only the best player in the NBA but the most dominant athlete on the planet as well as a corporate behemoth. Jordan, however, unexpectedly retired on the eve of the 1993 season, and the chokehold he held on all things NBA was suddenly loosed. Larry Bird retired around the same time, betrayed by his back, and Magic Johnson edged away as well, to wage a public battle for HIV awareness.

With Bird, Magic, and Jordan all gone, the guys from Dream Team II saw themselves springing into that void as the basketball world's new alpha dogs or, at the very least, stepping into the NBA's newly vacated upper echelon. The World Championships, with a worldwide basketball community looking on, had the promise to punch Dream Team II's tickets to immortality.

As the first team of NBA players in the Olympics, Dream Team I somehow managed to meet everyone's expectations. They had ostensibly been selected to restore the United States' designation as the world's foremost basketball power. Yet they were also sent to Barcelona to help present David Stern's grand scheme of globalization, to not only create NBA fans around the world but to subsequently slip a hand into their wallets; Stern's NBA was the first American sports league to understand that expanding its appeal worldwide created previously unrealized revenue streams.

Dream Team II was tasked with just as many goals. They were supposed to maintain the USA's basketball supremacy and extend the NBA's brand farther beyond America's borders, while simultaneously establishing themselves as the next generation of NBA stars. It wasn't as simple as just winning every game they played, though it remains unclear whether the players actually understood this. Dream Team I will be remembered as the greatest collection of basketball talent ever assembled on one team. Unfairly or not, Dream Team II will mostly be remembered by the antics of their genial knuckleheads.

As Dream Team II head coach Don Nelson told *SLAM* years after the Worlds, "I remember Kemp would do a thunder dunk or something, and he'd grab his testicles or some stupid thing, make a bit of a fool of himself. I had a couple guys do that."

No kidding. Dream Team II's style of play was loud and indulgent, which was mostly entertaining to watch, if a little unseemly. Dream Team II spent much of the 1994 World Championships in Toronto slam dunking, grabbing their aforementioned testicles, arguing with the refs, thumping their chests, talking trash. In some ways, Dream Team II was the most American team USA Basketball could have assembled, much more so than Dream Team I's politically correct business professionals. They were candid and unapologetic, speaking honestly even when it was probably unnecessary. (From a story in *Sports Illustrated* at the time: "The U.S. players had even more fun away from the court, sampling the Toronto nightlife extensively. 'Look at how bloodshot my eyes are,' said Larry Johnson. 'The guys on this team will keep you up until four or five in the morning.'")

Dream Team II did have several squeaky-clean players. A few years after playing with Dream Team II, Steve Smith would donate $2.5 million to Michigan State University, his alma mater, the largest single donation from any athlete to his former school in history. Mark Price grew up a choirboy, literally, in Enid, Oklahoma. Joe Dumars was such a strident moralist that the NBA would eventually name its annual sportsmanship award for him. Kevin Johnson retired from basketball and went on to become the mayor of Sacramento, California.

PRICE IS RIGHT: Along with brothers Matt and Brent, Mark Price is a member of the Price Family Singers, who specialized in barbershop, patriotic tunes, and Christian gospel.

On the flip side were guys like Shawn Kemp, Derrick Coleman, Shaquille O'Neal, and Larry Johnson. They were all still in the early stages of their careers, known mostly for playing with more style than substance. They attacked the rim, fired up ill-advised jumpers, and often felt it was so important to celebrate these achievements that they'd be late getting back on defense. While this made them endlessly entertaining (and unpredictable) for fans with an appreciation for the new school, it was not a style of play that would endear them to fundamentalists, those who valued things like sportsmanship over things like windmill dunks. For the players of Dream Team II, validation was an immediate goal—from the NBA, from the world, from wherever they could get it. Most of them had yet to be embraced in America, much less anywhere else. None of the players had won any championships in college, and only Dumars had won an NBA title.

PROBLEM CHILD: Nets forward Derrick Coleman might be the epitomical Dream Team II player. When new Nets head coach Butch Beard entered the 1994–95 season looking to bring discipline to New Jersey and promised to fine players for dress-code violations, Coleman handed Beard a blank check. That same season, Coleman escalated his long-running feud with Karl Malone: "He's an Uncle Tom, an Uncle Tom since the beginning of time. He's not real. He talks a good game."

The problems started before the games even began. Shaquille O'Neal, perhaps the biggest star on the team, almost didn't play in Toronto because he had established marketing ties with Pepsi,

RED, WHITE, AND SHOE: Dream Team II was not the only Olympic squad to prize commerce over country. In Barcelona, Jordan, who was endorsed by Nike, famously draped himself in the American flag to cover the Adidas logo on his Olympic uniform while accepting the gold medal. Nike later supplanted Adidas as the team's sponsor, but the team photo for the 2008 gold-medal-winning team shows Coach Krzyzewski blocking the Adidas shoe of Dwight Howard—the only player on the team not to endorse Nike—with his leg.

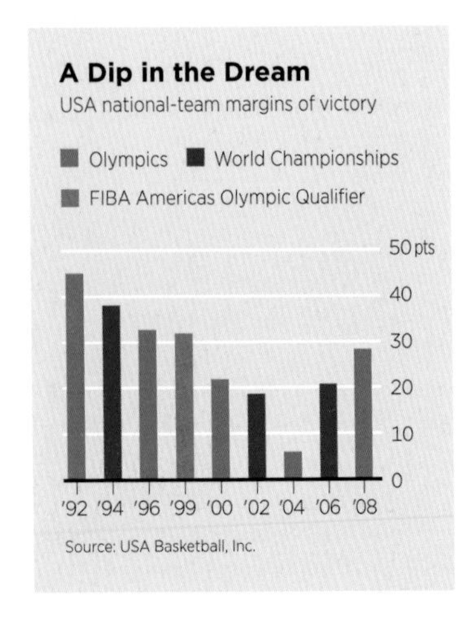

which didn't want USA Basketball to be able to promote him. (USA Basketball had a deal with McDonald's, which sells Coca-Cola.) A détente was eventually reached, the solution being that Shaq was provided with clear plastic cups on the bench so that he wouldn't be seen drinking from the same red Coca-Cola cups the rest of the team used.

Striving to prove their worth, Dream Team II was relentless. In the first half against Puerto Rico, Reggie Miller outscored their entire team by himself, 26–25, draining 8 threes from the relatively short international three-point line. After they won the game, by 51 points, Larry Johnson summarized: "We're basically taking a lot of countries to school." After they beat China by 55 points, Dominique Wilkins told the *Boston Globe*, "We were trying for 60 or 70 tonight, and we came close. We were definitely predicting 60." In the tournament final, they crushed Russia, 137–91. During a time-out late in the game, Dream Team II eschewed a huddle in favor of watching NBA mascots do acrobatics on the court. When Shaq was subsequently named to the All-Tournament team, which was sponsored by a drink company other than Pepsi, Shawn Kemp had to accept the award on his behalf. Dream Team II played 8 games and won them all, by an average of 37.8 points. (Dream Team I had won their games by an average of 43.8 points.) Dream Team II had accomplished their most fundamental job, winning the World Championships. But they never received the rousing hero's welcome that awaited Dream Team I upon their return. Because the World Championships were talking place in Toronto, the American media was able to cover the tournament in real time, unlike the Barcelona games. Because the Dream Team predated the Internet, we didn't see cell-phone videos of Charles Barkley carousing on Las Ramblas or read tweeted reports of Michael Jordan popping in to Spanish casinos; we mostly just assumed they were on their best behavior away from the games in Spain, faithfully representing the best America could offer to the world; we liked the Dream Team as much for what we didn't know as what we did.

Never known for fully understanding the larger basketball culture that produced most of these players, the mainstream media roasted Dream Team II rather than attempt to explain them. Writing in the *Chicago Tribune*, Bernie Lincicome asked, "And the point of Dream Team II is? Choose one: to sell hamburgers; to gloat; to sell T-shirts; to strut; to sell soft drinks;

to scowl." Most of the media selected all of the above. If the first Dream Team represented the NBA and David Stern's marketing triumph, Dream Team II quickly became their nightmare. This was everything the NBA did not want their league to be associated with: greed, anger, self-absorption. "It seems like we can't win," Dream Team II center Alonzo Mourning told *Sports Illustrated*. "If we don't win by a ton of points, everybody says we're not as good as the Dream Team. And if we do win by a lot, people say, 'Yeah, but it was more fun when the Dream Team did it.' "

That's because it *was* more fun when the original Dream Team did it, at least to a casual sports fan. Jordan, Magic, and Bird were all charismatic and well known, and America was rooting for them to prevail on its behalf. Nobody had ever seen NBA players go up against the best of the rest of the world, so a natural curiosity factor provided a delicious hook.

Dream Team II was focused, maybe too focused. They not only wanted to win in convincing fashion, like Dream Team I, but there was an unshakable sense that the members of Dream Team II were there to validate their own long-term greatness, perhaps too soon. Dream Team I had older players, established legends, their places in history secure; they were content to play roles within the larger team concept. As Dream Team II seemed intent on using the World Championships for their individual coming-out parties, they began grumbling about playing time after the first game of the tournament. (Accordingly, it was Dumars, the lone guy who'd won an NBA championship, who eventually volunteered to sit out a game to create more minutes for everyone else.)

Dream Team II was probably an embarrassment to some, entertaining to fewer, forgettable to most. For better or worse, Dream Team II served to inspire the NBA's coming generation, a generation that would be defined as being concerned primarily with self: J. R. Rider, Glenn Robinson, Stephon Marbury, Antoine Walker—these guys would all follow in many of the Dream Team II players' expensively endorsed footsteps, finding fame and fortune but winning little of importance in the NBA. Dream Team II wasn't a team of agitators so much as it was a team of the aggrieved. Their country asked them to pick up where a group of legends had left off. What they lacked in charisma and corporate skills they attempted to make up with sheer audacity.

And as it turned out, winning doesn't cure everything. *—L.W.*

DREAM ON: When it came time to select the players for the 1996 Olympic team (aka Dream Team III), USA Basketball president C. M. Newton vowed that the team would be full of "character, not characters." The committee bypassed most of the 1994 team, keeping only Shaquille O'Neal and Reggie Miller, while bringing back five members of the original Dream Team (Barkley, Malone, Pippen, Robinson, and Stockton), plus Hakeem Olajuwon, who would've been on the first team had he been a U.S. citizen at the time. Notably, the new additions were either model citizens (Grant Hill, Mitch Richmond) or too low-key to cause trouble (Penny Hardaway). Only trash-talking point guard Gary Payton had a hint of Dream Team II's menace.

CULT OF PERSONALITY

Lil' Penny, Grandmama, and the House of Mutombo

THE RIGHT TO REMAIN STYLISH: In the mid-'90s, Nike promoted its new stars by casting them as the Fun Police, a group of yellow-raincoat-clad players who went around town telling less hip people what's fun and what's not. Featuring up-and-coming stars such as Kevin Garnett, Jason Kidd, Damon Stoudamire, and Gary Payton, the ads had them weigh in on everything from no-look passes (fun), leading off *SportsCenter* (fun), and country line dancing (surprisingly fun). With the exception of line dancing, the "fun" things in these ads were related to what the athletes did on the court—a rarity in this era of advertising.

FOR THE LOVE OF HEATHER LOCKLEAR: The basketball ads of the '90s inspired similar campaigns in other sports. Nike's "Chicks Dig the Long Ball" series featured pitchers like Greg Maddux and Tom Glavine acting self-deprecating about their hitting skills and trying to get Heather Locklear to notice them.

In 1993, Michigan's Chris Webber and Memphis State's Anfernee "Penny" Hardaway entered the NBA draft, were picked consecutively at one and two, and then were immediately swapped for each other. Hardaway and three draft picks went to the Orlando Magic, while Webber went to the Golden State Warriors. At Memphis State, Hardaway's lithe, multipurpose game had drawn rave reviews. But Webber entered the NBA as a full-fledged celebrity, the ringleader of the University of Michigan's Fab Five. Picking up where the UNLV teams of a few years earlier had left off, the Fab Five hit college ball with an NBA-ready arsenal of both skill and style, sporting a trademarked look of baggy shorts and high black socks with black shoes. Hardaway was a truly unique player who single-handedly put his school on the map; in the pros, he instantly became one of the NBA's brightest young stars. But not even a player of Hardaway's caliber could glitter as brightly as Webber. Penny was a professional athlete who did amazing things; Webber was a cultural figure.

Then, in 1996, Nike gave Hardaway a television commercial with a talking puppet, and abruptly his fame became the equal of Webber's. Webber's Nike ads let him do the talking—the most notable featured him in a barbershop bragging to teammate Latrell Sprewell about dunking on Charles Barkley. The barbershop setting portrayed Webber as boisterous and, more importantly, himself. For Hardaway, on the other hand, it was not as clear who "himself" was. At the height of their fame, the puppet wrote a book, with a foreword by his older brother, the NBA star.

Penny's ad campaign endowed him with an auxiliary persona so large that it rivaled that of rapper/movie star/macro-celebrity Shaq (who, interestingly, had indicated that he did not want to play with Webber when Webber emerged from college). Yet Hardaway achieved his status with a whisper and a smile, letting the puppet—and his fans—do the talking. The Lil' Penny campaign also turned Hardaway's hints of personal swagger into greater aesthetic trademarks. He had a cool-sounding first name and a cooler-sounding nickname. He popularized wearing a Band-Aid above the eyebrow.

The term "character"—both in the sense of personal traits and of the figure in his Nike commercial—is the key word in Hardaway's story. Penny was a tabula rasa until Nike *gave* him a character, masking his actual *lack* of personality. The Nike spots consisted of a Chris Rock–voiced wooden puppet as Hardaway's shit-talking doppelgänger/sidekick/spokesman. Lil' Penny/Rock would shoot his mouth off at whoever was in the vicinity ("You can't guard me! The Secret Service couldn't guard me!") while the real Hardaway would remain largely silent throughout the spots. These ads provided Real Penny with charisma and a sense of humor while simultaneously granting him a certain level of mystery (provoking the question, Why is a puppet doing all the talking for him?). The campaign was extremely popular, no doubt contributing to the admiration he earned from many future NBA stars such as Joe Johnson, Tracy McGrady, LeBron James, and Gilbert Arenas.

ONE BIG FAMILY: Before the 2006–07 season, Nike introduced "The LeBrons," an ad campaign depicting LeBron James as several embodied aspects of his own personality: Wise LeBron, Business LeBron, Athlete LeBron, and Kid LeBron. The commercials reinforce the common theme of James's career: He can be everything to everyone and constitutes the field. By playing all demographics, LeBron shows that he can appeal to all demographics, too.

Penny was a great basketball player on his own, and he was a celebrity because all NBA players are. But he owed his *phenomenon* to Nike. The branding of Penny Hardaway was a bit like Don DeLillo's "Most Photographed Barn in America." Penny was a cultural figure, elevated above other All-Stars, because . . . he was a cultural figure. And it was Nike that made it so. The puppet said it all.

Nike knew it could make Penny bigger. After all, it had already figured out a way to make *more* out of Michael Jordan. From the very beginning of Jordan's career, his deal with Nike, and that company's use of him as a nouveau-basketball icon, had been key to establishing his brand. Then, in 1986, the Air Jordan campaign reached new heights with ads featuring Mars Blackmon. Spike Lee—pre-icon, pre–MSG courtside, pre–*Do the Right Thing*—reprised his fast-talking, thick-rim-bespectacled character from his film *She's Gotta Have It* as the perfect foil to Jordan's debonair dunk maestro. Employing Mars Blackmon was gutsy—selling Michael Jordan by way of a character from a critically championed independent film about gender dynamics among the black middle class. But it worked. Penny, the personality, came out of an (non-)interaction with a squawking marionette; Michael Jordan, the smooth-talking advertising juggernaut, was birthed alongside the transplanted Mars Blackmon.

MORE BARKLEY: Perhaps the strangest of Barkley's many commercials was the "Barkley of Seville" Nike spot, a parody of Gioachino Rossini's opera *The Barber of Seville*. Called for a foul by a dandified ref, Sir Charles shouts, "Enough!" and slaps the offending official in the face. The ref dies from the blow, causing Charles to lament his action and to claim it was a mere accident.

Just as Nike refined Michael Jordan, it somehow managed to push the outrageous Charles Barkley even further. In the early 1990s, Barkley, chock-full of quotable hilarity and on-court vitriol, was already a character in his own right. His infamous "I am not a role model" ads used a single quote to cast him as the ultimate iconoclast, but the ads pitting Barkley against Godzilla made him larger than life. Barkley balled against the radioactive dragon, swinging his posterior and elbows around with fury and ultimately winning the game. These spots proved prescient, as articulating Barkley's edge suited him much better in the long term than any Jordan-like politesse would have.

Converse's best effort called on truculent, gold-toothed Hornets forward Larry Johnson to portray an alter-ego, Grandmama. In this campaign for Converse's React series, Johnson, in drag, played a little old lady who happened to live in a shoe and, with the power of Converse on her feet, was able to juke past anyone on the court. Johnson even reprised the character for an episode of *Family Matters* in which he teamed up with Urkel in a two-on-two tournament, with predictable results. The ads brought Converse into the two-horse race between Reebok and Nike, at least as far as starmaking was concerned.

LJ predated the craze of vaudevillianly subverting black masculinity through big-boned drag roles: Tyler Perry's Madea, Martin Lawrence's Big Mama, and Eddie Murphy's Rasputia among them (with Flip Wilson's Geraldine, of course, pioneering this genre). The Grandmama spots effectively neutralized the threat of the intimidating player on the court. Ironically, late in Johnson's career, his real-life persona became the complete opposite of the one projected by Grandmama, particularly when he shifted teams from the Hornets to the Knicks. He became a more outspoken and controversial player, exhibiting the type of acerbic racial pride that was generally absent from professional sports. Johnson grew a beard of Abrahamic proportions to signify his conversion to the Nation of Islam, called his Knicks teams a group of "rebellious slaves," and remarked that he and Avery Johnson were from the "same plantation." However, having endeared himself to (white) America in years previous, Johnson would forever be seen as Grandmama.

Penny and LJ also shared a remarkably similar career path. Each showed Hall of Fame promise early in his career before becoming hobbled by injuries, wandering the NBA like some thirsty nomad.

The glorification of fallen athletes was nothing new, and certainly the younger Penny and LJ were more memorable—and more fun to recall—than their later, debilitated forms, but for this generation, that mythology was inseparable from their advertising campaigns. For some of the NBA's greatest couldabeens of the 1990s, those Teddy Riley–soundtracked Thurman Munsons, taken from us too soon, fame results at least as much from these commercials as from their status as athletes.

Dikembe Mutombo, on the other hand, has over his long career shown that sheer force of personality can in effect exorcise sneaker mythos if one so desires. In 1992, Adidas used the Congolese rookie to market a pair of multicolor shoes that looked like an exoticized answer to the Cross Colours aesthetic. African-patterned textiles were criss-crossed every which way, and a shield and spears, along with Mutombo's number, 55, graced the tongue. As hideous as the shoes were, the ads outdid the product. One featured Dikembe, wearing ugly-ass zebralike-print shorts (which matched the shoes), running in place to tribal drums accompanied by either a snake hiss or unidentified percussion instrument. In the spot, Mutombo suddenly jumps up to block a shot (in an empty gym) and returns to the ground to state, in broken English, "Man does not fly in the house of Mutombo." Since then, Mutombo has gone on to serve as the game's most multilingual and internationally savvy ambassador, an erudite statesman and a far cry from the Adidas-crafted demon. This image has disappeared altogether; Mutombo's career has become his own, albeit in large part due to his gimmicky finger-waving after blocking a shot.

Whereas Mutombo gained independence from his shoe, others have become completely subsumed by their footwear. Take the Celtics' Dee Brown, who is remembered for one thing: winning the 1991 dunk contest by covering his eyes with his forearm, ostensibly completing the first "no-look" dunk the contest had ever seen. The dunk was only half of the performance, though. In a move that would change the dunk contest and NBA branding forever, Brown preceded the dunk by taking a moment to inflate his black Reebok Pumps. Reebok would soon after commemorate this feat in a commercial with Brown, replaying the famous pumping of shoes. Of course, Brown was never as skilled as Hardaway, Johnson, or Mutombo, all All-Stars in their own right. But Brown also differed in how he was branded. Whereas Hardaway was puppetized, Johnson transgendered, and Mutombo primitivized,

THE JAZZ-O-METER

1990s RATING: Oddly jazzy (65/100)

IN THE ZONE: Wayman Tisdale gets bonus points for being a recording artist himself, playing bass guitar and keyboards. In total, the Oklahoma-bred big man released eight smooth-jazz albums, many of which have unfortunate basketball-related puns as titles (*Power Forward*, *Hang Time*, *Rebound*, etc.). Tisdale was invited to perform at numerous jazz festivals as well as on Warren Hill's Smooth Jazz Cruise.

TENOR MADNESS: David Robinson is also a talented musician, playing both the piano and the saxophone. While in Barcelona with Dream Team I, Robinson engaged in an old-fashioned tenor battle with Branford Marsalis at a downtown hotel.

TAKE THE A-TRANE: Branford Marsalis is himself a Knicks fan, once bizarrely comparing the 1992–93 team to the classic Coltrane Quartet: "When Patrick slams, when Anthony Mason grabs a rebound and knocks somebody on their ass—it's Coltrane, man, 'A Love Supreme.' The Knicks have that vibe, that aggression. This team is tailor-made for New York."

MISTER MAGIC: Magic Johnson wrote the liner notes for saxophonist Gerald Albright's 1994 album *Smooth*.

CREPUSCULE WITH SCOTTIE: A cryptic 1997 Nike ad featured highlights of Scottie Pippen on the court interspersed with clips of a cheetah running and Thelonious Monk playing the piano.

Brown merely *was* his shoe. And this blurring of man and clothing article enabled sneaker companies to continually convince people that they could purchase flight and superhuman strength in these products.

"Nike don't own n*ggas, n*ggas own Nike": KRS-ONE made this remark after being confronted in *Rap Pages* magazine about ostensibly "selling out" to Nike. An elder statesman of hip-hop, he had reinterpreted Gil Scott-Heron's black-power anthem "The Revolution Will Not Be Televised" as "The Revolution Is Basketball/Basketball Is the Truth" for a 1995 Nike commercial. Whether or not this statement holds true, it speaks to something symbiotic about the relationship between sneaker brands and their pitchmen. The immense skill of a player like Penny provided Nike with the power to push sneakers, while shoe companies provided myths to players that in many cases gave them popularity, even longevity, beyond what their playing careers could alone.

In the twenty-first century, sneaker ads no longer push creative boundaries toward crafting cultural icons. The talking puppets that represent LeBron and Kobe in *their* Nike ads are just stand-ins, likely because the real LeBron and Kobe are busy shooting other commercials. And yet, when we see Chris Webber offering analysis of a game at halftime, we see a tragic figure. Although Webber was perennially in the conversation alongside Tim Duncan and Kevin Garnett as the power forwards of the era, he came within inches of the NBA Finals multiple times and had to contend with accusations of being "soft" or a "choker" throughout his career. Webber is seen as a great but tainted player.

PUPPET REGIME: In 2009, Nike itself reintroduced the Lil' Penny concept in the form of Kobe Bryant and LeBron James puppets voiced by David Alan Grier and Kenan Thompson. Neither comedian is Chris Rock's equal, and the commercials are generally considered more annoying than endearing.

We sympathize, though, because he has always seemed a whole person. Hardaway underwent the same surgery during his career and never regained form; he never sniffed a championship. But if Penny ever were to pop up on television, even as a series of breathtaking highlights from his All-Star years, the first question any of us would ask is, "Where's that puppet?" *—Dr. L.I.C.*

ROTTEN ISLAND

Knicks-Heat, the Rivalry That Made Hate a Virtue

As Michael Jordan put the finishing touches on a hardware-laden legacy that had included its fair share of acrobatic flourishes, there flourished a rivalry that reminded us of everything ugly and profane about basketball. The late-nineties battles between the New York Knicks and the Miami Heat represented a retrograde, junkyard form of the game that remains reviled for its ugliness. Both teams were committed to aggressive, physical defense. Not content with merely frustrating an offense, they wanted to eradicate it. And both teams were thoroughly unapologetic. Knicks-Heat games were tense, violent, stilted, low-scoring, and unattractive. Yet their anti-style was brutishly effective, and it was driven by authentic hatred. It captivated the NBA community like a bar fight, slasher flick, or car accident—there was just no turning away from this least elegant form of basketball.

It was surprising that we watched Knicks-Heat when there were so many more appealing alternatives out there. The 1990s had begun with the Detroit Bad Boys' muscularity vanquishing Showtime, only to see Michael Jordan (however toned-down) and the Chicago Bulls signal the league-wide rise of a more beautiful game. Colorful basketball that either improved upon or circumvented the sport's more physical past flourished. Signature teams and players of the decade were distinguished by their fluid and innovative games: Olajuwon and the Dream Shake; the crushing alley-oops of Payton and Kemp; Barkley's evolution from Round Mound to All-Around; the Admiral's lithe jumpers and leaners; the vision of a new jack Magic Johnson, as central as the original model but far more explosive, embodied by Anfernee Hardaway. By and large, the NBA was viscerally exciting in a way that depended little on body blows or macho posturing.

And yet few NBA games, players, rivalries, or spectacles could arouse the same level of passion as Knicks-Heat, the sport's ugliest iteration. This rivalry was a scrum, fans hooting with titillation as

GRITTY CHIC: It initially seems odd that the same man could be responsible for the Showtime Lakers and the hard-nosed Knicks and Heat of the '90s, but Pat Riley has always been a man at the intersection of glamour and grit. Riley went from a working-class background in Schenectady, New York, to becoming a close friend of Giorgio Armani and an occasional model in the designer's shows. Riley's allegiance to the workingman has been a little mixed up, as he both supported George W. Bush ("I'm pro-American, pro-democracy, I'm pro-government. I follow my boss. He's my boss.") and loves gutter poet Bruce Springsteen, even closing his 2008 Hall of Fame speech with a quote from the Boss.

BIRTH OF BOWEN: It's only fitting that the dirtiest player of his generation came of age in the midst of the Knicks-Heat rivalry. After years as a journeyman playing in France and the CBA, among other places, Bruce Bowen found a home with the 1999–2000 Heat. Under the tutelage of Pat Riley, he picked up an array of dirty tricks and forged his reputation as a defensive stopper. The following season, he emerged as a full-time NBA starter and was voted onto the All-Defensive Second Team, where he would later become a fixture as a member of the San Antonio Spurs.

muscle-bound men gashed each other over and over, occasionally taking breaks for time-outs and fistfights. The basketball, slow, sloppy, and incensed, was nearly incidental, the stuff that happened in between the next flare-up. Anchored by Patrick Ewing and Alonzo Mourning, respectively, the Knicks and Heat attacked each other methodically, working from the inside to create post isolations, open perimeter looks yielded by collapsing defenses, and trips to the free-throw line. All the while, defenders would counter by lowering their shoulders through picks, grabbing at arms and torsos and jerseys, crashing into dribble penetrators, and driving post players from the blocks by burying knuckles and elbows in whichever unfortunate lower backs were in the way. How else could all those foul shots came about? Characterizing Knicks-Heat basketball as bruising has become hackneyed and, anyway, inaccurate: There were also breaks, sprains, and bloodletting.

This ugly, malevolent basketball nonetheless aroused so much passion because the theater was authentic and the enmity real. Miami's Tim Hardaway once said of the Knicks, "I hate them with all the hate you can hate with." Michael Jordan and the other pretty things of the 1990s may have been beautiful and esteemed, but they also held themselves beyond reach, sacrosanct, like works of art. The Knicks and the Heat played different basketball, the sort that, for all of its flaws, was terrestrial, tangible, attainable. It invited fans to experience the rivalry in a more personal manner. Knicks-Heat had an empathic quality: The players didn't do anything special—they were just like us, only more so. A common fan probably couldn't bang with Charles Oakley, but he certainly understood the floor-bound brutishness in a way that he couldn't understand David Robinson's assault on physical laws. Fans were free to see the Knicks and Heat as human—humans engaging in a conflict filled with raw, recognizable emotion, especially anger.

Indeed, the fuel for the rivalry was a seething, inbred hostility. This closeness had been missing from the Knicks' rivalry with the Indiana Pacers a few years earlier. Though the teams played similarly brutish basketball, they were far from the same. The Knicks, with the oft-maligned Ewing in the middle, gave their all for playoff wins that they—or at least their fans—felt entitled to. The Pacers, on the other hand, rallied behind the snide, impudent Reggie Miller to demonstrate that they (and their basketball-crazy state) belonged. The rivalry peaked in 1994 and 1995, when

Michael Jordan was playing baseball and the NBA food chain was in flux. The Knicks and Pacers clawed at each other as though only one could survive to fill the niche. But having a similar style is not the same as kinship, or, as with Heat/Knicks, being actual kin—and hating each other like only relatives can.

The central figures in this war were Pat Riley, whose departure from New York to Miami incited the conflict, and the two centers, Ewing and Mourning, who shared an alma mater, a mentor, and a lineage as seminal Hoya big men. In 1994, the Knicks lost the NBA Finals to the Houston Rockets in seven games after taking a 3–2 series lead. Pat Riley was New York's coach. For a team that had toiled in shadows cast by the greatness of others—at once the championship Knicks of the 1970s and their present-day Eastern Conference rivals—it was devastating to come so close and fail. The following year, New York fell in the Conference Semifinals. Riley resigned that summer, only to resurface as coach and president of the Heat in September. Riley's actions were taken as defection. He had not given up on winning a championship, only on doing so with the Knicks. Worse, he had opted to command a strangely similar set of new troops.

CROSS TO BEAR: In April of 2000, the *New York Times Magazine* published a story in which Knicks players Charlie Ward and Allan Houston made comments about Jews killing Jesus Christ and persecuting Christians. Their comments were immediately condemned by the Anti-Defamation League and David Stern, and they were booed in Madison Square Garden. Ward initially defended his comments, saying, "My best friend is Jewish, and his name is Jesus Christ, so therefore I have no reason to offend any religion," but he later sought counsel from Rabbi Yechiel Eckstein, who accepted Ward's apology and declared that he was not anti-Semitic. Houston was also repentant and visited Israel in 2009 with a delegation of community and political leaders from New York.

By 1997, during Riley's second season in Miami, the Heat supplanted the Knicks atop the Atlantic Division, and that year the war began. The opening shot was appropriately violent and ridiculous: In Game 5 of the Eastern Conference Semifinals, Charlie Ward aggressively boxed out P. J. Brown. Retaliating, Brown flipped Ward into the stands, literally head over heels. Benches cleared, suspensions crippled both teams, and the Heat survived an attrition contest for the rest of the series. The violence, absurdity, and animus continued in ensuing years. In 1998, Mourning and Knicks forward Larry Johnson staged a fistfight in the middle of Madison Square Garden as Knicks coach Jeff Van Gundy, Riley's disciple and successor, hung from Mourning's leg. In 1999, eighth-seed New York improbably defeated top-seeded Miami on a miracle shot in a deciding Game 5 of the opening round. In 2000, the teams traded low-scoring (72–70!) tension fests, with the Knicks outlasting Miami in seven. Regular-season games were the same: low scoring, rough, almost out of control, and fascinating.

SHOWBIZ AND LJ: Upon hearing of Larry Johnson's 1999 "rebellious slaves" comments, Bill Walton called Johnson a "disgrace to the human race," to which Johnson retorted, "That's not the same Bill Walton who was at UCLA smoking pot and [being a] hippie, was it? Not that one."

Riley's presence on both sides of the rivalry—the scars he left in New York and the controlling figure he cut on the Miami sideline—provoked the genuine disdain each team felt for the

6 DEGREES OF CHRIS GATLING:

In the mid-'90s, everyone was talking about the new party game Six Degrees of Kevin Bacon, where you attempt to link actors through their film roles to the prolific actor Kevin Bacon in six steps or fewer. Around the same time, Chris Gatling was in the midst of an NBA career that saw him play for nine different teams—including two stints with the Miami Heat—making him something like the Kevin Bacon of the NBA.

We were able to link George Mikan to Chris Gatling in six steps:

1: George Mikan played with Clyde Lovellette on the Minneapolis Lakers from 1953 to 1956.

2: Clyde Lovellette played with Lenny Wilkens on the St. Louis Hawks from 1960 to 1962.

3: Lenny Wilkens played with Spencer Haywood on the Seattle SuperSonics from 1970 to 1972.

4: Spencer Haywood played with Frank Johnson on the Washington Bullets from 1981 to 1983.

5: Frank Johnson played with Joe Kleine on the Phoenix Suns from 1993 to 1994.

6: Joe Kleine played with Chris Gatling on the New Jersey Nets in 1997.

other. The Knicks could fold Riley's defection into their long-running story of desperation and disrespect: To beat Miami was to vindicate New York's honor. The Heat, generally moribund prior to Riley's arrival, could not only validate their coach but also accomplish the twin goals of establishing the franchise and curing the NBA of the Knicks' seemingly endless psychodrama. Looking on at two teams locked in deep kin strife—employing an unapproachably grimy style of basketball and playing out their weary narratives—made it hard for basketball fans to escape the rivalry. Riley sat atop the junction of divergent branches from the same family tree.

But this was about more than just the Riley schism. It was also about fratricide. New York's franchise player was Patrick Ewing, a sad hero throughout a decorated career. The pattern for his basketball life was established in college, at Georgetown. Despite leading the Hoyas to three NCAA championship games and the NCAA title in 1984, the center's accomplishments were overshadowed by his failures: chiefly, losing to North Carolina in the 1982 championship game after a teammate made a historically bad pass, and then losing to unranked Villanova in the 1985 championship.

Ewing went on to a similar professional career: A perennial All-Star and a Hall of Famer, Ewing never won a title, and, as he toiled under the pressure of championship expectations and bad knees, he regularly encountered fan ambivalence fueled by his faulty guarantees and near misses.

Sibling rivalry also tormented Ewing. As a younger brother can, Alonzo Mourning offered the promise of succeeding where his big brother had failed. Mourning took up Ewing's legacy at Georgetown, emerging as the Hoyas' next great hope at center. With Ewing he shared a mentor, Georgetown coach John Thompson, who taught him to play the same dominating defense and effective, if not explosive, offense. Mourning arrived in the NBA touted as the kind of Georgetown center with whom a team could win a title. Ewing and Mourning had always been united by their shared heritage and a friendship that waxed and waned during their playing careers. Upon Mourning's ascendancy and Riley's defection, their relationship became even more thorny and intertwined. The father had opted for new hope over eldest dignity. The Knicks-Heat rivalry was a Civil War, and Ewing and Mourning were like brothers on opposing sides.

Though Riley, Ewing, and Mourning were the rivalry's signature figures, Tim Hardaway—an innocent bystander polluted by the bad blood—was perhaps its saddest participant. After seven joyful, rambunctious years with the fast-paced Warriors, Hardaway took on a different role. On the Heat team, Hardaway became gritty and devious, the sort of point guard who would rather judiciously pick his spots than initiate offense freely. His notorious crossover slowed, devolving from reliable weapon to sometime threat. The one constant was his knuckleball jump shot, an ugly and improbable "asset" that opponents invited him to use, then cursed when it would drop. Miami's Hardaway was tenacious but muted, the ultimate proof that not even someone from outside the family could escape the rivalry's inbred corrosiveness.

While playing for the Warriors, Hardaway was a symbol of progress, the sort of gem who might have earned a place alongside Jordan and the era's other signature players. On the Heat, Hardaway was a useful mercenary, a leader of trudging men whom opponents respected but did not quite fear. He was suddenly a player who aroused particularized anger in opposing fan bases when he led the Heat to victory, a steep step down from his previous, stylized stardom. Hardaway's descent from the glistening courts of Golden State to this Eastern Conference battlefield gave him greater depth and dimension, though. Just as Riley's narrative allowed fans to witness betrayal and scorn, and as the sibling rivalry invited projections of the most intimate hostility, Hardaway's story took on elements of maturation, redemption, and remorse.

In the end, it never was about the basketball. What the Knicks and Heat played could hardly even be called that at times. Their rivalry, staged over ninety-four feet of hardwood, was nonetheless about strength and frailty, about the many costumes in which passion arrives. Humanity, sometimes beautiful, sometimes hideous, and oftentimes just passable, was truly on display. Not basketball. And such an honest depiction was a riveting counterweight in an era filled with the soaring victories and freakish successes of so many superheroes. —*J.L.*

6 DEGREES OF CHRIS GATLING, CONTINUED: To prove this game is not limited to NBA players, we connected President Obama to Chris Gatling in only four moves:

1: Barack Obama plays regular pickup basketball games with Arne Duncan, the secretary of education.

2: Arne Duncan played with Muggsy Bogues on the Rhode Island Gulls of the U.S. Basketball League in 1987.

3: Muggsy Bogues played with Dell Curry on the Charlotte Hornets from 1988 to 1997.

4: Dell Curry played with Chris Gatling on the Milwaukee Bucks in 1999.

Just for the hell of it, we folded the universe over itself by going from Kevin Bacon himself to Chris Gatling, again in four moves:

1: Kevin Bacon was in *Murder in the First* (1995) with Christian Slater.

2: Christian Slater was in *True Romance* (1993) with Michael Rapaport.

3: Michael Rapaport played with Chris Mullin on the West team in the 2010 All-Star Celebrity Game.

4: Chris Mullin played with Chris Gatling on the Golden State Warriors from 1991 to 1995.

A History of Violence

Fights Between Players

Players with five or more fights or altercations and their opponents. Fights between opponents are also shown.

We began with 23,000 game recaps provided by the Associated Press, covering nearly 75 percent of all regular-season and playoff games between 1980 and 2009. We then identified and coded all incidents of on-court violence reported in the recaps—from mere shoving matches to bench-clearing brawls. We then supplemented this data set with information on fines and penalties provided by Patria Bender and www.ProSportsTransactions.com. The final database includes over 500 incidents involving 430 different players and represents what we believe to be a near-complete tally of every on-court incident from the past thirty years of NBA play.

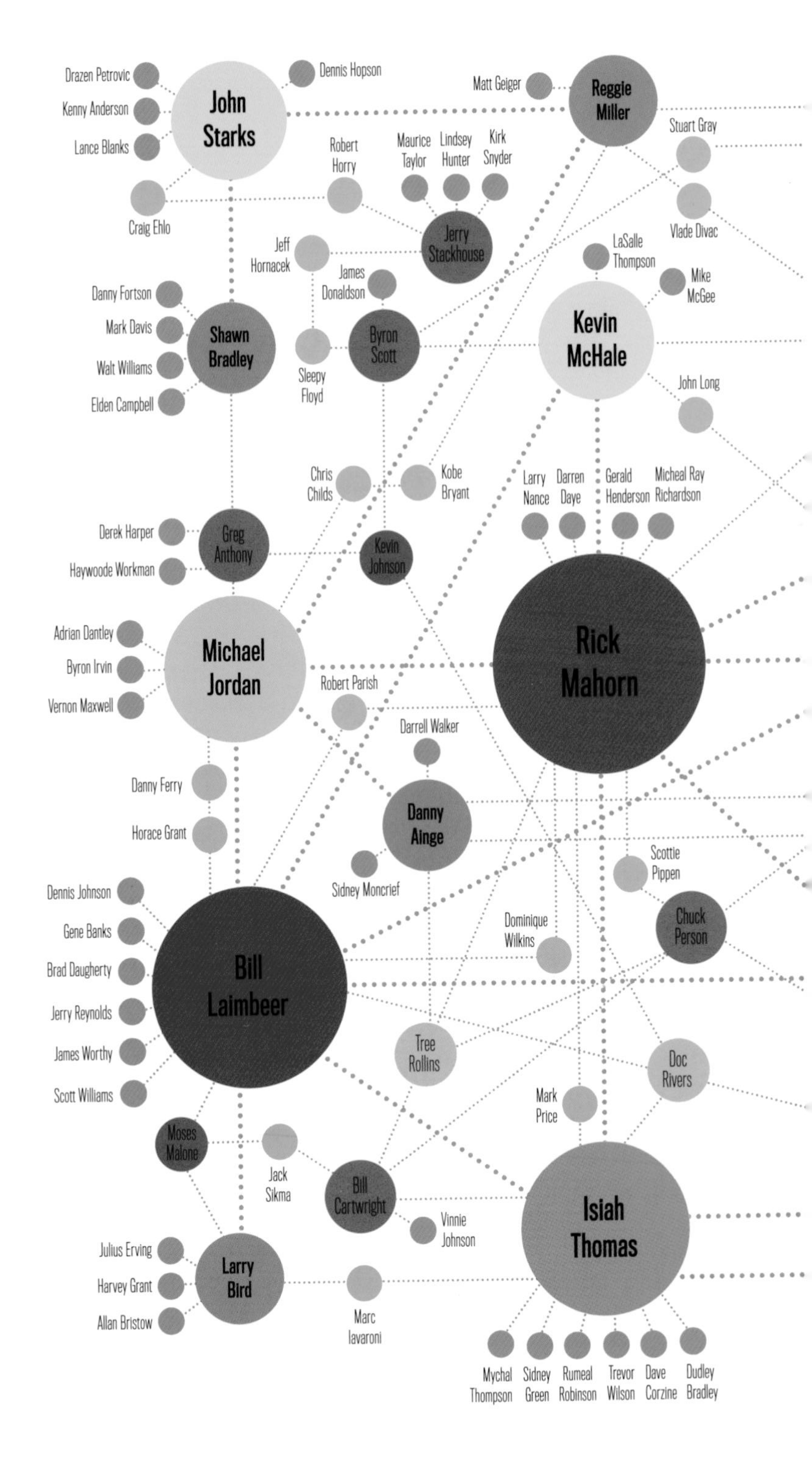

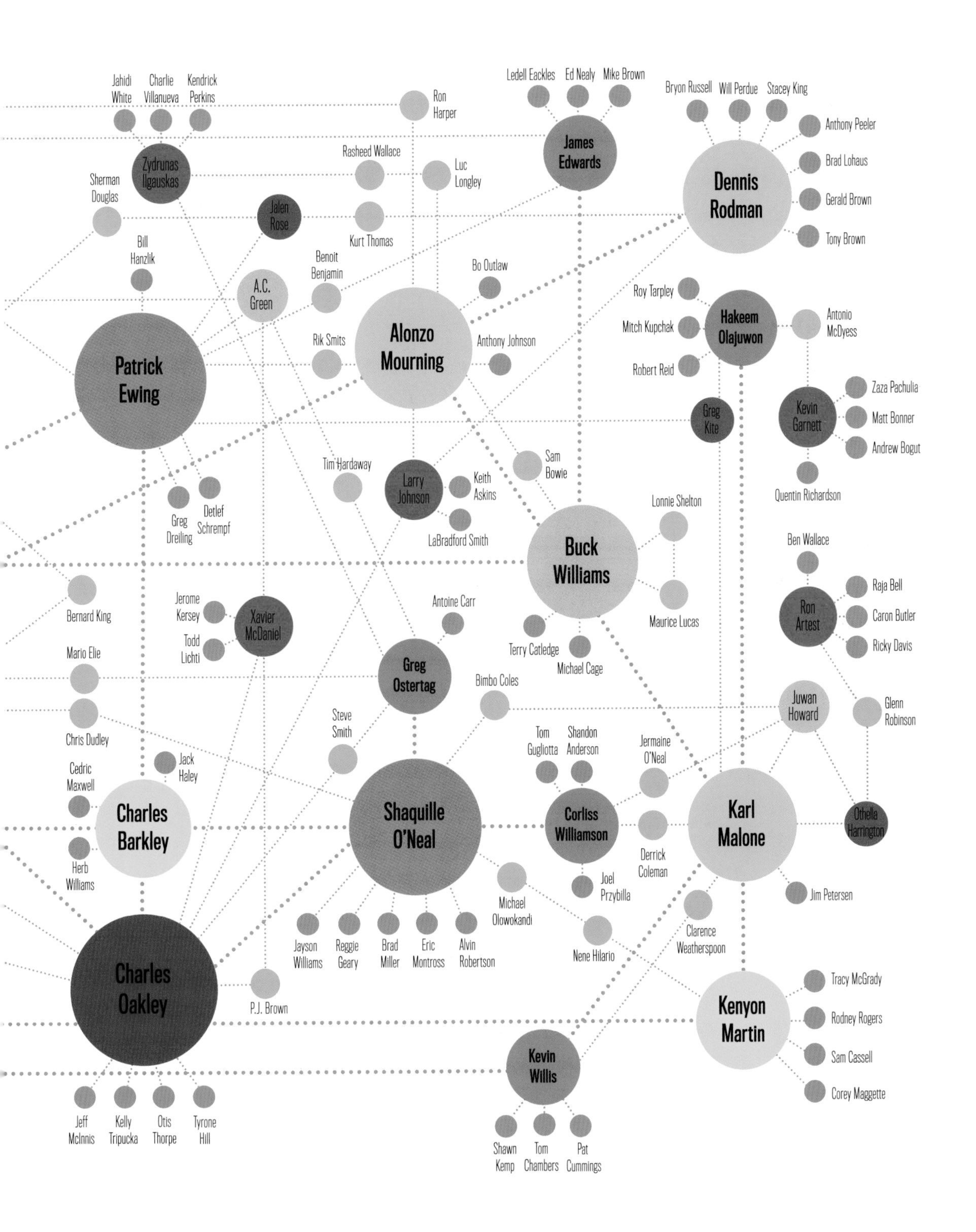

Jahidi White
Charlie Villanueva
Kendrick Perkins
Ron Harper
Ledell Eackles
Ed Nealy
Mike Brown
Bryon Russell
Will Perdue
Stacey King
Anthony Peeler
Brad Lohaus
Gerald Brown
Tony Brown
Zydrunas Ilgauskas
Rasheed Wallace
Luc Longley
James Edwards
Dennis Rodman
Sherman Douglas
Jalen Rose
Kurt Thomas
Bill Hanzlik
Benoit Benjamin
A.C. Green
Bo Outlaw
Roy Tarpley
Hakeem Olajuwon
Antonio McDyess
Mitch Kupchak
Robert Reid
Rik Smits
Alonzo Mourning
Anthony Johnson
Patrick Ewing
Greg Kite
Kevin Garnett
Zaza Pachulia
Matt Bonner
Andrew Bogut
Quentin Richardson
Tim Hardaway
Larry Johnson
Keith Askins
LaBradford Smith
Sam Bowie
Greg Dreiling
Detlef Schrempf
Lonnie Shelton
Buck Williams
Maurice Lucas
Ben Wallace
Bernard King
Jerome Kersey
Xavier McDaniel
Todd Lichti
Antoine Carr
Terry Catledge
Michael Cage
Raja Bell
Ron Artest
Caron Butler
Ricky Davis
Mario Elie
Greg Ostertag
Bimbo Coles
Juwan Howard
Glenn Robinson
Chris Dudley
Steve Smith
Tom Gugliotta
Shandon Anderson
Jermaine O'Neal
Jack Haley
Cedric Maxwell
Charles Barkley
Herb Williams
Shaquille O'Neal
Corliss Williamson
Derrick Coleman
Karl Malone
Othella Harrington
Joel Przybilla
Jim Petersen
Michael Olowokandi
Clarence Weatherspoon
Jayson Williams
Reggie Geary
Brad Miller
Eric Montross
Alvin Robertson
Nene Hilario
Charles Oakley
P.J. Brown
Kenyon Martin
Tracy McGrady
Rodney Rogers
Sam Cassell
Corey Maggette
Kevin Willis
Jeff McInnis
Kelly Tripucka
Otis Thorpe
Tyrone Hill
Shawn Kemp
Tom Chambers
Pat Cummings

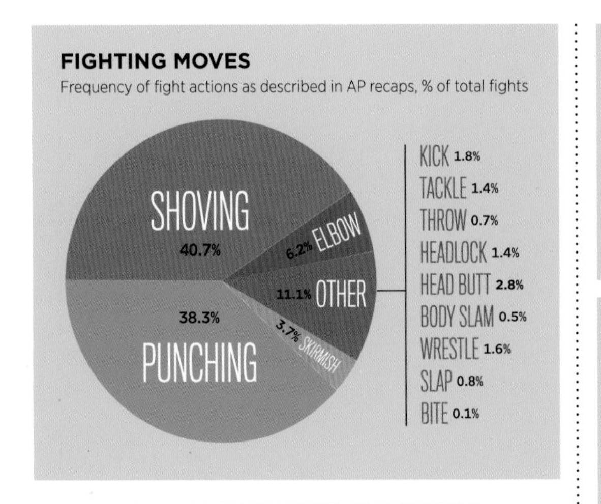

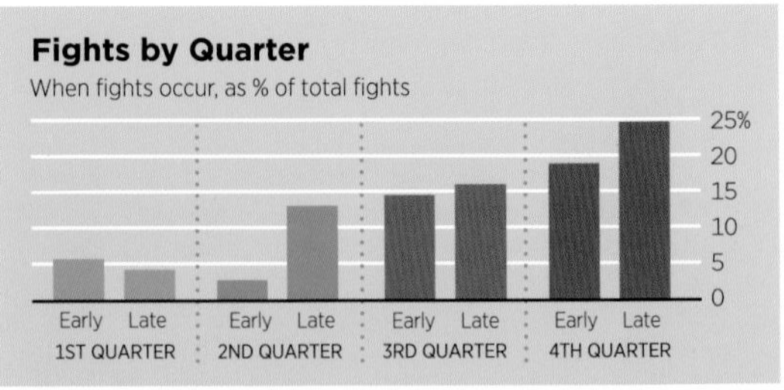

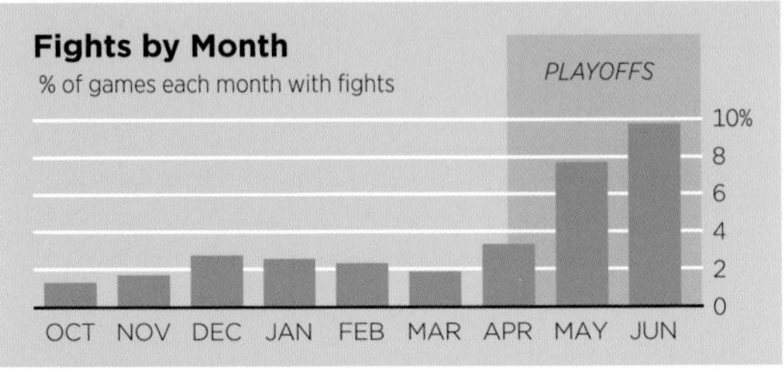

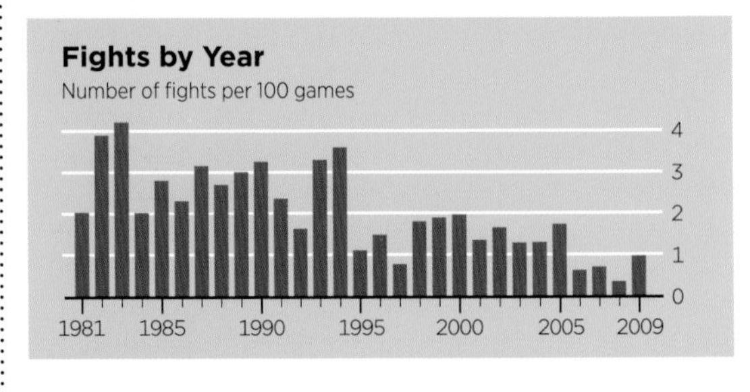

PLAYER WITH MOST FIGHT MOVES: ISIAH THOMAS

Few players can match the sheer variety of damage Isiah Thomas has doled out over the years:

- SLAPPED Sidney Green in the face, twice.
- KARATE-KICKED Doc Rivers in the head multiple times.
- JUMPED on seven-foot center Kevin Willis's back and tried to WRESTLE him to the floor.
- SLAMMED an open hand into former teammate Rick Mahorn's face following a SHOVING match.
- SUCKER PUNCHED teammate Bill Laimbeer in the back of his head during practice, BREAKING his own hand.

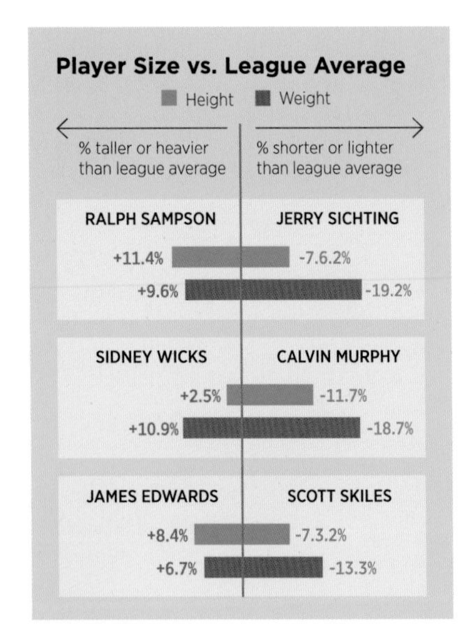

TOP THREE BIG MAN–LITTLE MAN BATTLES

15-INCH, 60-POUND DIFFERENTIAL: In Game 5 of the 1986 Finals, Ralph Sampson (7′4″, 228 lbs) went berserk when Jerry Sichting (6′1″, 168 lbs) elbowed the Rockets' center while fighting through a screen. Sampson started wildly throwing punches and hit Sichting twice. Larry Bird later quipped, "I still can't believe Ralph Sampson picked a fight with Jerry Sichting. Heck, my girlfriend could beat up Jerry Sichting."

11-INCH, 60-POUND DIFFERENTIAL: In a November 3, 1976, contest, the Houston pocket rocket, Calvin Murphy (5′9″, 165 lbs), became enraged at Boston center Sidney Wicks (6′8″, 225 lbs). Murphy leaped high into the air, latched onto a piece of Wicks' Afro with his left hand, and with his right hand proceeded to pummel his face.

11-INCH, 45-POUND DIFFERENTIAL: After a shoving match broke out between Indiana and Detroit's seven-foot centers on March 14, 1989, Scott Skiles (6′1″, 180 lbs) of the Pacers valiantly tried to break up the fight by jumping on the back of the Pistons' James Edwards (7′0″, 225 lbs) and unsuccessfully trying to subdue him with a headlock.

TOP THREE FEEL-GOOD FIGHTS

There have been many famous fights throughout the league's history, from Kermit Washington's infamous punch to the brawl at the Palace of Auburn Hills. But these weren't funny; they were sad and did incredible damage to the sport and everyone involved. Who wants to hear about that shit? Having exhaustively read up on fighting, basketball, and the combination of the two, we have tracked down three fights that aren't only totally hilarious—they also are absolutely guilt-free, and in some cases, sort of don't even involve two people. Enjoy!

TREE VS. MAN

LITTLE SHOP OF BIG MEN

APRIL 24, 1983

In a heated 1983 Hawks-Celtics playoff game, Wayne "Tree" Rollins elbowed Danny Ainge, who had been calling Rollins a sissy all game. Ainge proceeded to tackle Rollins and a team-wide brawl broke out, but Tree made sure to locate Ainge and exact a gruesome revenge: biting Ainge's middle finger. Undaunted, Danny picked himself up off the floor and chortled, "That big sissy just bit me." The following day, the *Boston Herald* ran the headline "Tree Bites Man."

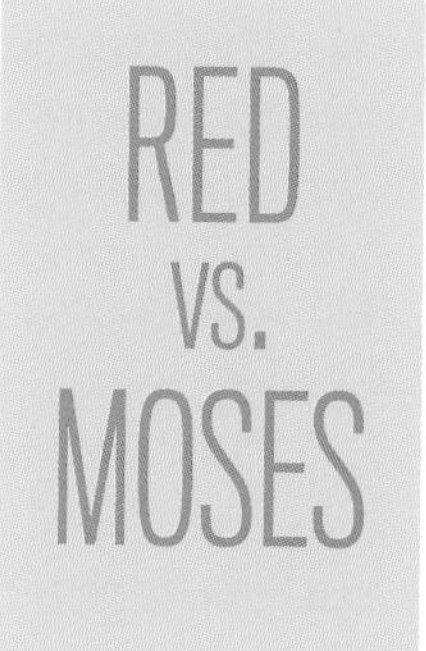

RED AUERBACH AIN'T NO ONE TO FUCK WIT

OCTOBER 16, 1983

Auerbach was known for mixing it up as a coach, and even as an executive he continued his hell-raising ways. During a 1983 preseason game, Red grew livid when Bird was ejected for slugging it out with 76er Marc Iavaroni. The sixty-six-year-old Auerbach rushed the court, berated referee Ralph Lembo, and then walked up to the 6′10″ Moses Malone, took off his glasses, and screamed, "Go ahead, hit me, you big SOB." Since this was in Boston, Moses politely declined.

CRUELTY TO ANIMALS

1992

The exact date has been lost to history, and it wasn't even really a fight, but the city of San Antonio will never forget the day referee Dick Bavetta beat the shit out of its beloved mascot, Coyote. The non-human party was asking for it, literally, so finally Bavetta obliged and popped him in the snout, knocking him to the ground. The crowd thought it was funny, but the man behind the fur was out cold and would need his nose reset after being removed on a stretcher.

FIGHTING WORDS

Charles Oakley liked to fight. And he liked to talk about it, too. These are a few of his stories.

JANUARY 16, 1998: "I guess [the fine] was fair, but it won't stop me. What I do next time could be worse." *—After a Pistons-Bulls brawl in which Oakley was fined $2,000 for "escalating the incident"*

DECEMBER 5, 1989: "We used to have respect for one another, but we don't now. Plain and simple." *—After a scuffle with the Philadelphia 76ers' Rick Mahorn*

FEBRUARY 7, 1994: "He tried to dunk the ball and I pushed him. He got emotional. It's part of the game." *—After a fight with the Miami Heat's Steve Smith*

NOVEMBER 2, 1996: "Oh, well, that's basketball . . . It used to be basketball. I don't know what it is now." *—After being assessed a flagrant foul for leveling the Nets' Kenyon Martin*

APRIL 3, 2001: "I don't think [getting suspended] hurt the team. I think the league hurt the team by putting them in Canada." *—On whether his one-game suspension for whipping a ball at Tyrone Hill's head had hurt the Toronto Raptors*

JANUARY 24, 2003: "You got to fight, that's part of leadership. Didn't nobody bleed. Things happen, the game kept going, and they won." *—After being ejected for fighting with the Hornets' P. J. Brown*

ASHES BEGET ASHES

Tales from the 1998 Lockout

BACK TO THE ESSENCE: Negotiations during the lockout occurred at the law firm Proskauer Rose, the employer of David Stern before he became the NBA's general counsel.

Western Civilization officially bottomed out in 1998. The noise on the radio was 'N Sync and the Backstreet Boys, Matchbox 20 and Third Eye Blind. *Seinfeld* ended, but *Friends* persisted. *Shakespeare in Love* was captivating our barely oxygenating hearts and awarded an Oscar for its troubles. Windows 98 was a massive event. Monica Lewinsky and Paula Jones dominated headlines and global terrorism was a distraction. In baseball, Mark McGwire and Sammy Sosa gave us vapid joy by tearing up the home run records with the help of human growth hormone and God knows what else. In *Back to the Future II*, 1998 was the year that Marty McFly Jr. was born.

The timing was perfect for the dreariest disappointment of all: the NBA lockout, which lasted from July 1, 1998, to January 20, 1999, cutting the season to 50 games and sullying the league's image. Just four years after Major League Baseball's strike, which nearly destroyed the national pastime, the NBA had its own work stoppage. The prosperity of the Jordan years finally burst at the seams, making way for an ugly dispute between employers and employees, a dispute from which some would argue the NBA has never fully recovered. The NBA owners looked like cartoonish money hoarders, a gaggle of Scrooge McDucks. Players also made fools of themselves, and all parties emerged looking greedy and unprofessional. The NBA's popularity slid, and every half-racist closet hoops-hater could forever point to the lockout to back up the stereotype that NBA players are selfish, overpaid, prima donna thugs.

BOTTOMING OUT: Because of the lockout, no NBA players could participate in the team that represented the U.S. at the 1998 FIBA World Championship in Athens. As a result, the team was made up of fairly obscure players, mostly from the CBA, but also from overseas leagues and the college ranks. The most well-known members were lesser Fab 5 member Jimmy King and Duke All-American Trajan Langdon. Coach Rudy Tomjanovich led this ragtag bunch to the bronze medal, even though the team had little time to practice together. Only Brad Miller was able to parlay the team's relative success into a long NBA career.

And to think, so much of the ensuing scuttlebutt was placed on the shoulders of a young, gangly Kevin Garnett, a faithful soldier to his team and a pawn in the economic lambada between players, owners, and Commissioner Stern. In the 1997–98 season, the Timberwolves—a franchise giddy over finally having a basketball player worth cheering about—gave Kevin Garnett an unprecedented contract extension, a six-year deal for $126 million. At the time it was the richest contract in professional sports history. And, wouldn't you know it, the only redeemable move that the Timberwolves made, after wallowing at the bottom of the standings for the first eight years of their existence, led to despair.

The contract alienated Garnett's teammate and running buddy Stephon Marbury, who then asked for a trade, which would ultimately lead him down a spiral of insanity. The Garnett contract and consequent lockout also directly contributed to the Timberwolves losing KG's costar Tom Gugliotta—and, in a rush to replace him, they illegally signed Joe Smith to an under-the-table contract. This move ultimately cost the Timberwolves three future draft picks as punishment and eliminated any remote possibility of obtaining a sufficient supporting cast for KG.

The Garnett Deal, as it came to be known, was frequently invoked as a scapegoat when the lockout began to take shape in June 1998. Morally capable, bright-eyed, and hardworking Kevin Garnett, perhaps the only man at the time deserving of such a contract—and indeed, in his tiny market, perhaps one of only a few who would have signed it—found himself the poster boy for a gigantic capitalist scramble over billions of dollars. The critical issue of the dispute became owners' desire to curb players' ever-expanding earnings—players' salaries had risen to an all-time high of 57 percent of all basketball-related income, which the owners sought to reduce to 48 percent—and the Garnett Deal became a convenient justification for the war they began to wage on the sport.

In a sense, the lockout was Stern's dream come true: an NBA that had truly been reduced to a seething boardroom. It was the culmination of the legalistic climate that had first taken root behind the scenes in the seventies. Media and fans followed the lockout season like its own kind of sport, and from that point on nothing would be the same. Instead of merely consuming game play and gawking, we now daydream about how trades will affect salary-cap flexibility, consider how a player's minutes and performance affect his signing bonuses, ponder whether injuries will make a player go "off the books," and anticipate whether the slightest breeze in the air will sway our favorite hometown player to opt out of the last year of his contract. This was the end of days. But, oh, what a barrel of monkeys those months visited upon the league.

BIG DOG'S BIG BITE: Before there was the Big Ticket, there was the Big Dog. When Glenn Robinson was selected first overall in the 1994 NBA draft, he initially asked for $100 million over thirteen years, but ended up signing for $68 million over ten years—still the largest rookie contract ever signed, since the rookie salary cap was instituted the following season.

WEIRD PIONEER: After having a career year (22.1 points, 8.1 rebounds, and 4.4 assists) in just his second season, Juwan Howard became the hottest free agent of the summer of 1996. He initially signed a seven-year, $101 million contract with the Miami Heat, but it was disallowed by the NBA because it violated existing salary-cap rules. Howard ended up re-signing with the Bullets for seven years and $105 million, becoming the first player in NBA history to sign a contract worth more than $100 million.

EWING ON THE HILL: Union president Patrick Ewing honed his skills with numbers as a summer intern for the Senate Finance Committee and Senator Bob Dole while a student at Georgetown.

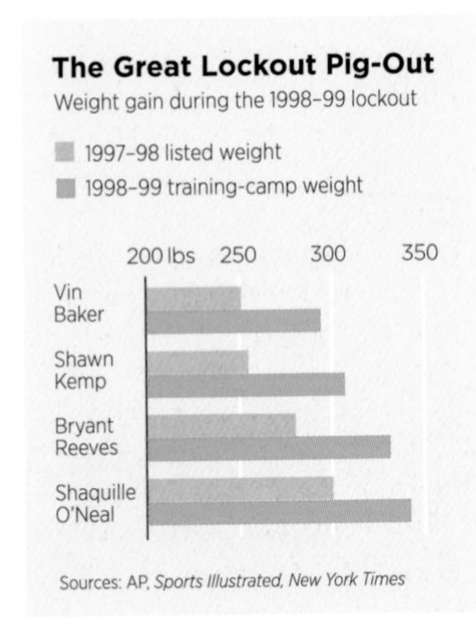

David Stern grew a "lockout beard." Patrick Ewing played Jimmy Hoffa as president of the NBA Players Association, famously remarking, "If you look at people who play professional sports, not a lot of them are financially secure. They make a lot of money and they also spend a lot of money." It should also be noted that as of November 1998, Ewing had lost more money as a result of the lockout than any other NBA player. Players got insanely fat during the downtime. Shawn Kemp never regained his game figure and essentially ate his career to pieces, Vin Baker sadly turned to alcohol, and Shaquille O'Neal backed out of a charity game when the shorts that the organizers provided him—size XXXL—did not fit him.

Perhaps more amusing—or depressing—than the lockout itself was that it also created one of the most forgettable basketball seasons of all time. In an act of ominous foreshadowing, the Los Angeles Clippers drafted Michael Olowokandi with the first pick of the first round. Olowokandi signed with Kinder Bologna in Italy to get some run during the lockout, then famously performed worse than anyone could have expected in the NBA, eventually exiting the league with the legacy of being considered the worst first overall pick of all time. Olowokandi's credentials also include giving less than a shit about basketball throughout his career, having a strange growth protruding from his head, and getting tazed by cops after failing to leave a Tiki Bob's in an orderly fashion on an off day in Indianapolis. But the Kandi Man was only the beginning. The 1998–99 All-Star Game was canceled. The shortened season also produced stunningly low win totals. The Vancouver Grizzlies won 8 games, the Los Angeles Clippers 9.

The labor dispute also contributed to Michael Jordan's second (fake) retirement, meaning that the Bulls dynasty was effectively over. NBA fans' sense of certainty and stability was rocked, and anomalies abounded. Darrell Armstrong miraculously won both the Sixth Man of the Year award and Most Improved Player. Mike Dunleavy coached the Portland Trail Blazers to an astonishing 35–15 record, winning Coach of the Year but losing in the Conference Finals to the San Antonio Spurs.

And then there was the famously wretched championship series, pitting Jeff Van Gundy's knuckleheaded Knicks against David Robinson's puritanical Spurs. The Knicks finished 27–23 and secured an eighth seed in the playoffs but clawed their way to the Finals by defeating the Miami Heat in the first round, a testament to the season's nonsensical ugliness. Patrick Ewing was injured midseason, marking the end of the glorious Ewing era in New York and paving the way for a regime of Latrell Sprewell, Charlie Ward, Larry Johnson, Marcus Camby, and Allan Houston that averaged a disgustingly low 86.4 points per game. Representing the Western Conference was an upstart San Antonio team that decimated New York 4 games to 1, beginning their run as the Dynasty of Dullness. The 1998–99 season did not make the most compelling argument for the league's post-lockout existence.

The extreme NBA cynic might ask whether the league ever recovered from the 1998 lockout. Charles Barkley, of all people, became the hovering voice of reason when he stated, "Everybody lost. We lost three months of the season and we did a disservice to the fans and the game." The betrayal of its fans was the least of the NBA's problems—the loss of the aesthetic beauty of the game itself was a far worse outcome. The lockout marked a clear schism between the high-octane, superstar-laden Dream Team era and a wavering period of uncertainty. A fascinating analysis of player salaries by economists J. Richard Hill and Peter A. Groothuis showed that in the two years following the lockout, a Robin Hood–style redistribution of wealth emerged in which the league's richest salaries—paid to the best players—diminished, while lesser players' salaries increased. Sadly, this also meant that middling players became albatrosses on their teams' payrolls amid the ever-looming salary-cap restrictions. In the immediate years following the lockout, a league of stars the NBA was not.

While the aftershocks of the lockout lasted well into the next decade, eventually the league recovered. The LeBron/Wade/Carmelo triumvirate emerged, the Steve Nash Suns brought on a renewed era of up-tempo offense, and the fans began to return. Good times are here again. And Garnett, his role in bringing about the lockout long forgotten, had served nobly in the wilds of Minnesota. In 2007, this wounded soldier at last got his Purple Heart with a Celtics team ready-made to bring a ring to himself and two other worthy vets, Paul Pierce and Ray Allen. Still, in very vivid and recent history, the 1998 lockout reminds us of how quickly things can go to pieces, and how quickly the game we love can reach its lowest lows. *—Dr. L.I.C*

TRULY OFFENSIVE: When players finally returned from the eight-month layover in 1999, they turned in one of the worst offensive seasons in history.

1. Only the Kings averaged more than 100 points per game (100.2), whereas seven teams would top that mark the following season.

2. Portland, Orlando, and Golden State all saw their leading scorer average fewer than 16 points per game. Somehow, the Blazers and Magic managed to win their divisions.

3. With little time to adjust, the rookie class turned in one of the most embarrassing All-Rookie teams ever. Matt Harpring was voted to the first team despite averaging only 8.2 points and 4.3 rebounds per game, and career stiff Michael Doleac found a spot on the second team with 6.2 points and 3 rebounds per game—even though it already had a center.

4. Just seven players shot better than 50 percent from the field, compared to nineteen in '97–'98 and fifteen in '99–'00.

5. On April 10, the Bulls scored only 49 points against the Miami Heat, a new low for the shot-clock era.

	2000	2001	2002	2003
NBA FINALS CHAMPION	LOS ANGELES LAKERS			SAN ANTONIO SPURS
FINALS LOSER	PACERS	76ERS	NETS	
MOST VALUABLE PLAYER	SHAQUILLE O'NEAL	ALLEN IVERSON	TIM DUNCAN	TIM DUNCAN
POINTS per game leader	Shaquille O'Neal **29.7**	Allen Iverson **31.1**	Allen Iverson **31.4**	Tracy McGrady **32.1**
REBOUNDS per game leader	D. Mutombo **14.1**	D. Mutombo **13.5**	Ben Wallace **13.0**	Ben Wallace **15.4**
ASSISTS per game leader	Jason Kidd **10.1**	Jason Kidd **9.8**	Andre Miller **10.9**	Jason Kidd **8.9**

THE NEW DEUTERONOMY

2000–2009

Like the eighties, the new century began with problems to solve. Jordan was gone, and in his place Allen Iverson—who fit every "thug" stereotype imaginable—was the game's most popular player. In the 2001 Finals, Iverson went toe-to-toe with the mighty Shaquille O'Neal–Kobe Bryant–Phil Jackson Lakers, a manufactured dynasty that accumulated three titles before falling to pieces. The Lakers proved to be far more interesting in their unraveling, as the Kobe-Shaq soap opera became one of the league's few reliable headline grabbers. Both stars would win titles again, separately, finally putting the feud to bed. The Spurs got three rings without anyone noticing. And while high school draftees and unknown imports supposedly lowered the quality of play, in 2003—as in 1984—a single draft class helped set the league back on the path to righteousness. That's when LeBron James, Dwyane Wade, Carmelo Anthony, and Chris Bosh came in. Factor in the revival of up-tempo basketball, and by the decade's end the game was finally fun again.

2004	2005	2006	2007	2008	2009
DETROIT PISTONS	SAN ANTONIO SPURS	MIAMI HEAT	SAN ANTONIO SPURS	BOSTON CELTICS	LOS ANGELES LAKERS
LAKERS	PISTONS	MAVS	CAVS	LAKERS	MAGIC
KEVIN GARNETT	STEVE NASH	STEVE NASH	DIRK NOWITZKI	KOBE BRYANT	LEBRON JAMES
Tracy McGrady 28.0	Allen Iverson 30.7	Kobe Bryant 35.4	Kobe Bryant 31.6	LeBron James 30.0	Dwyane Wade 30.2
Kevin Garnett 13.9	Kevin Garnett 13.5	Kevin Garnett 12.7	Kevin Garnett 12.8	Dwight Howard 14.2	Dwight Howard 13.8
Jason Kidd 9.2	Steve Nash 11.5	Steve Nash 10.5	Steve Nash 11.6	Chris Paul 11.6	Chris Paul 11.0

ONE SHINING MOMENT

The Realest Legacy of Allen Iverson

Allen Iverson is often credited with bringing hip-hop to the NBA. This is lazy, sloppy thinking. It's not as if the two had been blissfully unaware of each other before AI's rookie year—witness Shaq's multiplatinum recording career, or the oft-mocked comp *Basketball's Best-Kept Secret*. What's really meant is that Iverson's cornrows, reams of body art, do-rags, low-slung jeans, and perilously literal swagger made it impossible to ignore the demographic most associated with hip-hop.

Despite all that made Iverson unique as a basketball player—and there was plenty—what received the most attention were his body, his clothes, and his mannerisms. Iverson was reviled as a "thug," largely because he looked like the denizen of a back-alley dice game as imagined by BET. Supposedly, Allen Iverson was responsible for any rookie who looked, or acted, a little too hood for comfort. This presumes, though, that these kids had no friends, families, or cultural identities of their own. Say Iverson simply made it acceptable to share dark secrets with the world. That's quite different from planting the seed in the first place. He was one of the guys lucky enough to make it—the source of his appeal for many, and yet a point missed sorely by even some of his biggest supporters.

But what really made Iverson disruptive was his game. AI was the ultimate one-on-one player and an unrepentant ball hog. And that was that. In this acid rejection of so much received basketball wisdom, AI proved instantly provocative. A lightning-quick, relentlessly inventive, utterly fearless scorer, Iverson was unguardable without abundant help. Iverson's crossover was often pointless and theatrical, but that didn't seem to matter when it came to freezing defenders.

He wasn't neatly methodical like Kobe Bryant, but he was in some ways even more impressive—if Kobe saw the floor in terms of spots and options, Iverson carved it up anew each time he took

IVERSON VS. BULLS: During Iverson's 1996–97 rookie year, there was a palpable tension between the young upstart and the reigning kings of the NBA, the Chicago Bulls.

BULLS 115, 76ERS 86—NOV. 2, 1996: In just the second game of his NBA career, Iverson came out swaggering, which Ron Harper did not appreciate: "The guy is showing disrespect. You come into the league and you have to do something or your team has to do something [before you talk]. That's just immature."

BULLS 111, 76ERS 105—DEC. 22, 1996: Iverson talked trash with the Chicago bench all game long and eventually got into a shoving match with Dennis Rodman late in the game. Rodman commented, "Iverson came in there thinking he was Jumanji and was going to control the whole forest and the wilderness."

BULLS 108, 76ERS 104—MAR. 13, 1997: Iverson had one of the immortal NBA highlights, crossing Jordan over badly and hitting a jumper over him. After the game, Jordan conceded that it was "a great crossover move" and said, "It wasn't the first time he's done it and it won't be the last."

his man off the dribble. Henry Abbott has written about how Iverson's high school coach, Dennis Kozlowski, introduced the teen to psychocybernetics, the practice of visualization as a form of self-actualization developed to help plastic surgery patients. Kozlowski told his prized pupil, "I want you to play like you just tied your shoelaces—automatically. The way you do that is by having an image in your mind of what you do before you do it." That explains much of Iverson's game; point guards like Steve Nash discover new passing lanes, but Iverson used his vision to score from unpredictable angles.

SEARCH FOR A SECOND: During Iverson's first few years in the league, the Sixers unsuccessfully attempted to pair him with a secondary scorer. The failed sidekicks:

JERRY STACKHOUSE: Stackhouse was one of the best young scorers in the league when Iverson arrived. However, Stackhouse's scoring average dropped to 16 points per game in the first 22 games of their second season together and he was traded to Detroit.

LARRY HUGHES: Philadelphia drafted Hughes in the hope that he could be a bigger, more defensive complement to Iverson. But two high-volume scorers typically don't go well together, and he was traded to Golden State in his second season.

TONI KUKOC: Playing for a dismal Bulls team, Kukoc averaged 18 ppg before his trade to the Sixers. His average immediately dropped to 12.4 ppg in the season's final 32 games, then to just 8 ppg to start 2000–01. He was then dealt to the Hawks, where he saw his numbers rise to 19.7 ppg and close to 50 percent shooting.

But the paradox at the heart of AI was not only that he was so singular as to seem a fluke but that his perceived sins against the game were all in good faith. No player before or since has so sincerely believed in one-on-one basketball as a means to victory, imagining it fully while others had been unwittingly dragged into it by their egos. Iverson wanted the ball in his hands until the last possible second and seemed resistant to the idea that anyone else on his team could implement his plan for a possession. Iverson could only control the game if he employed his visualization/actualization technique, one that depended on both absolute concentration and—until he reached that climactic phase of shoot, foul, or dish—minimal intrusion from his less capable teammates. Yet it's important to bear in mind that, above all else, Iverson wanted to win. He just felt—and, it sometimes appeared, knew—that he had to think this way to be the truly unguardable player who could set an entire starting five quivering. Plenty of misguided talents have gone nowhere fast with this philosophy; most of the greats have had it in them, somewhere. For Allen Iverson, it was fundamental—if still problematic.

Feared as he was, Iverson proved to be more exception that proved the rule than a new beginning. He may have been the most popular player between Michael Jordan and LeBron James; he certainly had something to do with David Stern's forcing everyone to dress in suits for a month or two. But to suggest that Iverson set any kind of precedent is to ignore how utterly improbable, and irreplaceable, a figure he was. Fittingly, it all came down to a single bizarre season, one that his own team was hesitant to reproduce.

Iverson's 2000–01 almost didn't happen. The previous summer, the Sixers had thrown up their hands and decided to send their star to Detroit. However, as fate would have it (if you can't tell, this sort of divine intervention is a leitmotif of AI's story), the little-used big man Matt Geiger, a throw-in needed to make the money work, inexplicably had a trade kicker in his contract—a luxury usually afforded only to important players. Geiger didn't feel like moving and the deal fell apart. Iverson and the Sixers patched things up, with the expectation that the episode served as both a wake-up call and a further source of me-against-the-world motivation for AI.

Alas, more trouble lay ahead (the other shoe is never far away in AI's story). During the preseason, "40 Bars," the first single from Iverson's rap alter-ego Jewelz, leaked. With AI's notoriety at an all-time high, it couldn't have come at a worse time. The NBA was struggling with the perception that it was overrun by gangsters, thugs, and any number of other racial euphemisms. Stern simply did not need his number-one lightning rod boasting that "I know killaz that kill for a fee/that'll kill yo' ass for free, believe me." Iverson was most easily digested as the little man that could, the consummate underdog. Unfortunately, AI had zero interest in being anyone's Horatio Alger story.

Granted, this was before a single digital file could kill a career in seconds, so there was room for damage control. The single was buried, the album scrapped, and Iverson forced to apologize publicly for its content—specifically its homophobic slurs. However, from a public relations standpoint, this was David Stern's and the Sixers' doomsday scenario. "40 Bars" could not be neatly dismissed as a bored athlete booking studio time during the off-season. The single was pure Allen Iverson, three minutes of skittering, cocksure grit. Not that anyone felt like discussing it at the time, but Iverson's internal rhyme schemes were suprisingly intricate. Ever the exception, AI had virtually nothing in common with the amateurish athlete-rappers that soon became commonplace. Channeling the start-and-stop rhythms of his game, he had unmistakable style. Fittingly, the strongest evidence that Iverson had an aesthetic kinship with hip-hop also served to strengthen negative stereotypes about him, the genre, and where both were headed.

Given this backdrop, calling Allen Iverson's 2000–01 a fairy tale is a little strange. In fact, AI's always seemed a little too gruff for that kind of language. Maybe "vindication" works better; certainly "redemption" is out of the question. For one year, a team learned how to work with Iverson, and he learned how to work with a

THE JAZZ-O-METER

2000s RATING: Fake jazzy (10/100)

REBIRTH OF THE COOL: By the dawn of the twenty-first century, jazz's role in the NBA was largely as a signifier of cool. The Air Jordan XVII, released in 2002, was reportedly inspired by Michael Jordan's love of jazz and incorporated "jazz elements." The commercials, directed by Spike Lee, featured atmospheric empty gyms, a neo-bop soundtrack, and cats like Quentin Richardson and Darius Miles.

COVER SONGS: In 2009, the Miami Heat debuted a series of promotional posters and videos inspired by classic Blue Note cover art, giving each Heat player his own fake album cover.

JAM BAND: One of TNT's more memorable promos featured Chris Webber, Vince Carter, Ray Allen, and Vlade Divac performing as a jazz combo in some lucky family's living room. Carter, who played in his high school jazz band and stuck with it, took a sax solo that apparently he played himself.

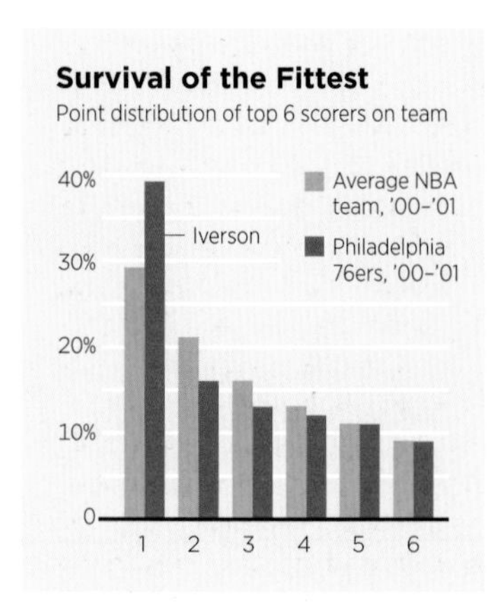

DIRTY WORK: When Larry Brown took over the Sixers in 1997, he surrounded Iverson with a group of players who realized their limitations and focused on the dirty work. Tyrone Hill was even that way off the court, naming his pet piranhas Rebound 1, Rebound 2, and Rebound 3, like some sort of backboard-obsessed George Foreman. Hill said that he came up with the names after watching how they fought for the goldfish he would drop into their tank: "It kind of reminded me of the way I felt going for a ball off the rim."

team. Of course, this involved surrounding AI with a collection of totally selfless role players who contributed primarily on defense. Larry Brown, known as the stodgiest coach in the league and a proponent of what he called "the right way," caved to and accommodated his star's idiosyncrasies—deformities, even. In turn, Iverson pushed himself even harder, winning the league's MVP and, more important, abruptly earning the respect of many of his former detractors. There was just no denying Allen Iverson; his team led the East all season, everyone was happy, and he had the blessings of one of the most revered coaches in the game. Suddenly he was a folk hero, a fount of populism who amounted to a grassroots Michael Jordan.

Finally, there was harmony between Iverson's startling ability, his desire to win, and the fact that basketball is a five-man sport. The Sixers even pulled off an upset of the indomitable Lakers, in L.A., in the first game of the Finals—which, considering that Kobe and Shaq had yet to lose a game that postseason and had just dismantled the Spurs, was about as big a moral victory as you'll find in sports.

And then the Lakers clamped down and asserted their championship fiat, winning the next four games to take the real prize. The next year, Iverson and Brown clashed; despite the formula they'd perfected in 2000–01, the Sixers insisted on trying to find real teammates for Iverson. Given their incompetence as a front office, this never worked out. But Iverson had his legitimacy; he had proven that the league had to take him seriously as a player.

That season is Iverson's legacy, and like the man himself, it stands apart. Because taken as a whole, AI's career ain't pretty. The Sixers were mediocre, but he made them too good to rebuild; they dealt him to Denver, where teaming with Carmelo Anthony proved only that Iverson really couldn't play well with another All-Star. Then came a lost year in Detroit; 2009–10 started with an abortive stint with Memphis, followed by a return to Philly that had the feel of a plea bargain or a mercy killing.

But in a way, all Iverson really needed was that single season—maybe even just that single win. He was never going to change the way basketball was played, or even—in the long run—the kind of athlete America was willing to accept. This put an especially plaintive, even morbid, spin on the "play like there's no tomorrow" cliché that defined his game. Iverson always knew that, at best, he'd get that one moment and then go back to being the league's problem child. At the same time, there was a sense that this high-water mark, whenever it came, might be the sum total of his legacy. Grim as that is, it's also what made Iverson so electrifying in his prime. Iverson was ultimately the basketball equivalent of Mobb Deep's 1995 *The Infamous*, with which late-teen MCs Prodigy and Havoc pull off a stark, haunting classic despite sounding like kids who were very much not counting on a future. Their rage, resignation, and every other emotion you'd expect is sublimated, the whole record a stylized acknowledgment that they plan on either dropping dead or staying young forever—if there's even a difference there.

That urgency and desperation was what made Allen Iverson compelling, but what he did with it in 2000–01 is why he's great. That was the only year Iverson made any sense, as well as that brief window when he beat back all the forces—including common sense—that conspired against him. He never found that synergy again, but it doesn't seem like he expected to, and he made only the slightest alterations to his game in an attempt to fit new contexts. However, what makes 2000–01 so monumental is that it happened at all. Not only was AI never supposed to exist in the first place, he most certainly wasn't supposed to take a team to the Finals and shock a dynasty in the making. Even as Iverson declined, millions of fans and players continued to look at him and see 2001, not out of sentimentality, but for the same reasons we never think of rappers as getting old. There was no plan past the present.

You can decide whether he died that season or vowed to stay young forever. Either way, it makes all that followed almost irrelevant—and, in a way, takes Iverson out of time and history altogether. —*B.S.*

LOCKS OF LOVE: No throwaway event signifies Iverson's cultural dominance among NBA players and fans quite like his arrival at the 2009 All-Star Game in New Orleans without his trademark cornrows. Iverson announced it was time for a change, jokingly citing President Obama's inauguration as inspiration. Video from the East locker room shows players and media gathered around Iverson, flashbulbs popping, and people as famous as Dwyane Wade ribbing AI on his new look with shouts of "Are you serious?" and "Thirteen years!"

SECURITY SLEEVE: In 2001, Iverson began wearing a sleeve on his right arm to combat the effects of bursitis in his elbow. Yet Iverson never stopped wearing the sleeve, leading Steven Kotler of *Psychology Today* to surmise that AI believed it would protect him from future injuries in a way similar to a placebo. For the most part, though, the sleeve became a fashion statement mimicked by players as notable as Kobe Bryant and Carmelo Anthony.

FAST-BREAK RENAISSANCE

The Kings, Mavs, and Suns Smash the Pedal

TRUE BELIEVERS: All fast-break coaches can't be painted with the same brush. There is a division between pragmatists like Rick Adelman and Pat Riley, who will run when the personnel and environment dictate, and the ideologues, for whom it is the only way.

PAUL WESTHEAD: From his first head-coaching gig with the Lakers to his current job with the University of Oregon's women's team, Westhead has been an unreconstructed run and gunner. He peaked with Loyola-Marymount in the late '80s, when the team set many NCAA records for offense behind its stars Hank Gathers and Bo Kimble.

DON NELSON: When it's all said and done, Nelson will likely be best remembered as the innovator of "Nellie Ball," which relies heavily on three-point shots and uses smaller, more athletic players to create mismatches on offense.

MIKE D'ANTONI: In his tenure as head coach of the Knicks, D'Antoni has remained true to his Seven Seconds or Less philosophy, but has been unable to duplicate the success he had in Phoenix.

It's no secret to fans that basketball skills have actually improved over time. The evidence is everywhere: NBA players as a community break their own shooting records every year. Fusty critics of the modern NBA sometimes decry the lack of fundamentals, but this is more a subjective stance against a certain style of play than a judgment about basic competence. Today's athletes do things every weekend that would have been earth-shattering accomplishments in the early years of the league. Things change: LeBron James's armory of turnaround jumpers, locomotive drives, and arcing three-pointers could not have existed without Jordan, Bird, Magic, and Baylor.

Yet these changes have also served to slow the game down over time. The prevailing theory goes that as all shots become easier to make, the need to earn "easy baskets" lessens in importance. If you have players who can hit threes, it's not as vital to get layups. As opponents score more efficiently, avoiding mistakes instead becomes a prime objective of each possession. Barring unassailable talent (MJ, who never had to take a tough shot because for him they were all easy) or synergy (Stockton-to-Malone), easy baskets tend to be created by ingenuity. Not all artistic experiments work, and for some reason a missed alley-oop fast-break connection is a greater crime than a bricked eighteen-footer. Risk is punished, both on the scoreboard and at the pulpit. The practical result of this moral framework is that league pace was in the toilet by the time the Jordan era ended in 1998.

Enter the Sacramento Kings, who up until this point had been terrible. In advance of the lockout-shortened 1998–99 season, Sacramento personnel boss Geoff Petrie assembled a murderous attack it's not clear even he understood. Remembering how brilliant Chris Webber's first foray into the prioritized fast break (as a rookie center for Don Nelson) had been, Petrie traded for Webber and drafted the world's premier hyperactive stoner and ultra-creative playmaker, Jason Williams, to lead the Kings to speeds unseen in nearly a decade. Vlade Divac, another deft-passing big man, and exemplary shooter Peja Stojakovic, drafted and stashed in Europe two years prior, came along for the ride, and the team changed the way people saw the NBA on the fly. Fawning *Sports Illustrated* spreads and last-minute additions to the national television schedule begat maximum mainstream exposure by the middle of the 1999–2000 season, as the Kings made the rest of the league scramble for the exits like they were in a bingo hall under a sarin attack. The unit's success at that point was overstated, simply because the local papers had never seen good before. But the Lakers still clobbered them when the time came, just as they always had.

IN APPEARANCE ONLY: During the Lakers-Kings first-round playoff series in 2000, Phil Jackson created a motivational video for the Lakers in which he spliced together footage of Edward Norton's character in *American History X* and Adolf Hitler, and juxtaposed them with images of Jason Williams and Kings coach Rick Adelman, respectively. Adelman said that Jackson had "crossed the line."

In its basic elements, the Williams-led fast break was little different from the standard Cousy fare: big man rebounds, big man gets ball to point guard, point guard gets ball up court and in scoring position for teammate. J-Will did all that, just with a little more flair. This is where Petrie earned his duchy, by trading Williams, the engine, tires, and transmission of the brilliant attack, for milquetoast game-managing point guard Mike Bibby. As expected, the Kings slowed down, with Bibby much less likely to scud an outlet three quarters of the court to a screeching C-Webb. But the Bibby-led Kings represented a far riskier experiment than the White Chocolate teams. By changing course at the point, the Kings shifted creative control to Webber and Divac, turning the fast break the team had just reintroduced to the world on its elbow. By deeding the offense to Webber and Divac, a new fast break was born, and a new era of basketball followed.

In Williams's final Sacramento season, 2000–01, he and platoonmate Bobby Jackson combined for 7.4 assists a game, while Webber and Divac totaled 7.1. The next season, with Bibby aboard and Jackson still in place, the point guards combined for 7 assists, but the front line jumped up to 8.5 a game. It was the basketball equivalent of Jimmy Garrison and Elvin Jones, the bassist and drummer of John Coltrane's classic quartet, staging a coup. They took a page from Pete Carril's famed Princeton offense, with Webber dominating from the high post during offensive sets. Carril's system had always been ultra-patient in college, and Webber's famous anxiety mutated the offense into a less cartoonish Harlem Globetrotter tour. C-Webb had no time for a series of backdoor cuts and often made the first idiosyncratic play he could. If Webber worked in Pollock-like brushstrokes, Divac

THROUGH THE BACK DOOR: The Kings have not been the only team to attempt the Princeton offense in the NBA, but their version, with Divac and Webber in the high post, has been the most faithful to Carril's collegiate system. Eddie Jordan, who coached with Carril for two years in Sacramento, has tried to install the offense in New Jersey, Washington, and Philadelphia over the past decade, with varying degrees of success.

provided the frame, putting a border around the canvas. C-Webb's crazy still made it to the gallery, as fawning viewers from Belgrade to Battle Creek can attest, but at least it was contained.

At the same time, Don Nelson had something brewing in Dallas. As White Chocolate reenergized Webber in Sacramento during the lockout season, Webber's former coach Nelson let Michael Finley shoot Dallas to a crummy record while studying the sleep patterns of new Maverick Steve Nash (then a fresh twenty-four-year-old) and supernal German rookie Dirk Nowitzki. Dallas of '99 is the ultimate NBA example of a chef fiddling through his pantry. By March of the next season (1999–2000), Nelson had a recipe: hefty helpings of Nash and Nowitzki, and all other seasonings to taste. It amounted to a resurrection of his old Golden State philosophy: Little people run, big people shoot. Nash became the permanent starter March 14, and the under-.500 Mavericks finished the season 15–5. The next year, Nash's fast-break offense—with Dirk's preference for jump shots—joined J-Will's Kings on the rocket to the future, busting up the stodgy Stockton-to-Malone routine in the playoffs before ceding to the Spurs.

Whereas Petrie pushed the Kings toward the surreal in 2001 (under the guise of getting religion with mild Bibby slowing things down a bit), Nelson bet the house on his vision of the seven-foot shooter. To go with his German prize, he folded in mystifying Chinese fugitive Wang Zhizhi and at midseason traded for Raef LaFrentz. The Kings unleashed their big men to create; the Mavericks demanded that their giants mimic Steve Kerr. Nelson's only big man who did typical big-man things that season was Shawn Bradley, as close to a white American sideshow the NBA had since the days of Maravich.

A team of behemoth gunners, orchestrated by a tiny Canadian hell-bent on setting up twenty-footer after open twenty-footer, was brilliant in its own way, even if Sacramento's symphony overwhelmed Dallas in the playoffs. The Kings had been transformed and beat Nelson to the promised land (a Conference Finals showdown with Kobe and Shaq), but Nelson kept his faith and banked on an improved Dirk going forward.

Dirk did improve, and the Dallas plan continued apace. As did the Sacramento version. Owing to the unique tools in use, copycats of either program failed to materialize, or at least to show themselves publicly. In the postseason, Webber's knee crumbled under the stress, and while the high-scoring series went on to attain cult-classic status, both of these experiments imploded suddenly: The Kings tried to make Brad Miller the new Webber, and the Mavericks sinfully traded for both Antoine Walker and Antawn Jamison. Pride goeth before the fall.

The Kings actually had some success—Miller was delightful playing off of Bibby, Divac, and especially Stojakovic—until Webber returned from a combination of microfracture rehab and a decade-late league suspension for taking money when he was in college. It took the Mavericks maybe two weeks to realize that Nash needed freedom instead of more mouths to feed, but the damage had been done, and Dallas bowed out quickly to the Kings amid Webber's most audacious (or ill-designed) power grab. Even during the 4–1 series win, Webb set the stage for a showdown with Peja (who happened to be an oblivious bystander through the whole situation) for top-dog status. When Webber finally publicly accused Peja of being soft, after the greatest performance of Kevin Garnett's life in Game 7 of the Kings-Wolves series, the dream died completely.

The Dallas dream died in July, when excessively personal owner Mark Cuban decided Nash's skills as conductor weren't worth the risk of a massive contract. But Nash carried the torch for the fast-break revival, bringing his talents to Phoenix to play for a new coach. Where Nash had matched with unrestrained gunners in Dallas, Mike D'Antoni would seek to pair the point guard with finishers closer to the Webber mold (minus the passing): a couple of freakish athletes known as Amar'e Stoudemire and Shawn Marion. Nash's predecessor, Stephon Marbury, had seen his partnership with Amar'e and Marion go awry, perhaps because Starbury really was not sane. Even so, Starbury really cracked the Amar'e code before being traded to the Knicks; D'Antoni knew it and saw Nash as the right executor of the plan.

To say it worked is quaint, maybe cute: The Suns made this offense into a hot rod, with Nash at the wheel. Setting up a transition three, as Nash did so often at the helm of the Mavericks, isn't as photogenic as tossing an ill-making alley-oop to America's brashest young men.

In the inaugural Seven Seconds or Less season, during which D'Antoni demanded his charges get a good shot up within seven seconds of getting the ball on every single possession, Nash averaged more assists than shots. Nash won MVP; D'Antoni won Coach of the Year; Stoudemire won a fat contract extension.

I AM CUBAN: Mark Cuban bought the Mavericks in January 2000 and immediately made his mark on the team with a series of luxurious purchases and tantrums:

1. Signed Dennis Rodman to a mid-season deal and allowed the Worm to stay in his guesthouse before the NBA deemed it a violation of salary-cap rules. Rodman played only 12 games and was eventually cut after disparaging Cuban's hands-on approach to ownership.

2. Employed ten assistant coaches; most teams have three or four.

3. Sent Don Nelson three or four e-mails every day filled with ideas to improve the team's performance.

4. Rushed onto the court during a February 2001 fight between the Mavs and Cavs. The fight started when Gary Trent scored a basket with a 19-point lead in order to break 100 points and win the Dallas fans free chalupas.

ME AND THE BEAN: Mike D'Antoni was a teammate of Joe "Jellybean" Bryant with Olimpia Milano, and Bryant's young son Kobe quickly found himself a favorite player, calling D'Antoni "one of my first basketball heroes." When Kobe entered the NBA, he chose number 8 as a tribute to D'Antoni.

Marion won universal acclaim while insisting he was underrated, forward Quentin Richardson won (temporary) relevance for the second time in his career; shooting guard Joe Johnson won the rights to his own team. And the Suns won a ton of games. This was basketball in its purest but most clearly belligerent form. And it became a standard by which all other up-tempo teams would be judged.

And imitations there were, unlike with the Kings and Mavericks. Seemingly everyone tried to replicate the Suns' magic—let us not forget Sam Mitchell's "100 FGAs or more" decree in Toronto, which lasted all of three weeks. Everyone basically failed, too. While Seven Seconds looked more feasible than the bonkers Kings or upside-down Mavs—if only because everyone's roles made sense, and because those types of players were more readily available than the heterodox big men of Sacramento and Dallas—it could only work with the single-minded devotion of all the actors at hand, and devotion ain't a transferable good.

The Suns reinvigorated the league, bringing back the spirit of the '02 Kings. But then fate struck another blow to basketball aesthetes by striking down Amar'e (knee injury) before the

What the Suns Hath Wrought

"Thou shalt not plagiarize" ought to be the NBA's top commandment, as these run-and-gun copycats of D'Antoni prove. Many tried to emulate Phoenix's screaming speed, but few succeeded. Of particular note are D'Antoni's early failed attempt at replicating his system in New York, and protégé Marc Iavaroni's dismal Memphis tenure. Here, team placement is based on dramatizations of quantitative measurement. Not shown: Sam Mitchell's short-lived flirtation with the mutant "100 FGAs or more" system.

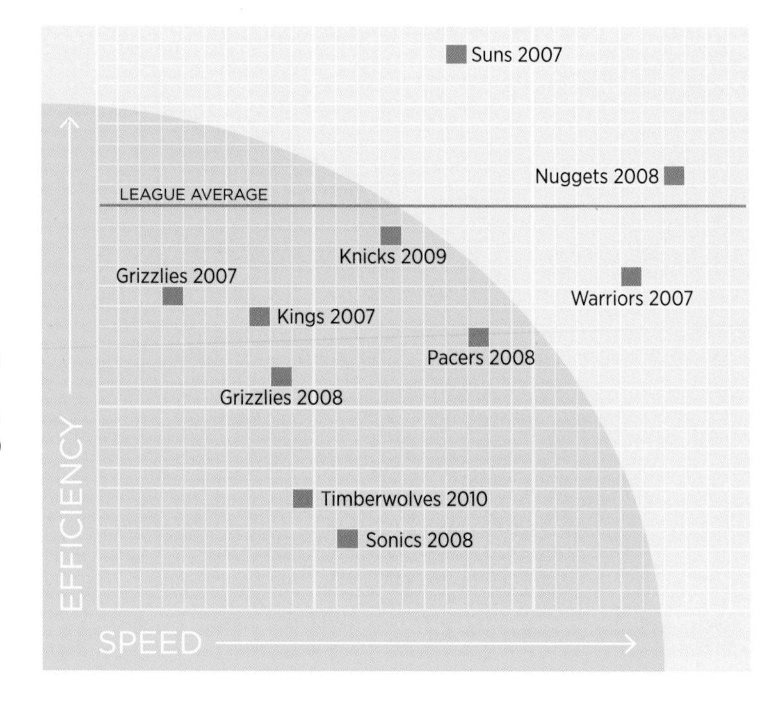

2005–06 season, leaving former Hawks backup point guard Boris Diaw to play center. The tall Frenchman Diaw had been a huge bust in Atlanta, but Suns boss Jerry Colangelo saw something in that sinuous body. With Johnson in line for a huge raise, Colangelo pulled the trigger and took on Diaw. Suddenly, the spirit of 2002 lived! Diaw resurrected Webber's philosophy, becoming the new predominant distributory pivot and unleashing a whole new wave of point-center obsession. If anything stood out (besides the dichotomy between his aloofness and his lightning-quick decision making), Diaw was far less concerned with scoring than any prior idiosyncratic big: The giant gunners like Dirk and Wang, of course, wanted to shoot as much as possible, while the men of Sacramento loved to set each other up for dunks or smooth post buckets. Diaw really just wanted to pass. That the Suns remained able to contend while shifting Amar'e the Conqueror's minutes to Boris the Dancer—all while leaving Nash's MVP MO untouched—is nothing short of amazing and quite possibly D'Antoni's greatest achievement. The personnel switch was as stark as that of the Williams/Bibby swap or Nash's ascension in Dallas. But the overall product remained extraordinarily similar: run, pass, score, run, pass, score. It was as if the team, and Diaw, had known all along.

Amar'e's return for the 2006–07 season didn't really complicate anything for anyone other than Diaw, who, when removed from the limelight, fell into a basketball depression (complete with a bonbon obsession) that shall never be cured. Nash-to-Amar'e regained stature, but few had forgotten. It seemed perfectly natural to refocus on the eternal pick and roll precisely because Diaw had fudged up so little. The Diaw era ended up being little more than a beautiful interlude, with the narrative reconnecting flawlessly. Only Robert Horry's body check on Nash in the playoffs—resulting in the weirdest suspension in league history, with the Suns losing both Diaw and Stoudemire for a critical game against the Spurs—caused the system to fail. (The following season's trade bringing Shaq to Phoenix closed the book on the Suns.) Fitting that outside forces—Dick Bavetta, Antoine Walker, David Stern—crippled each new fast-break coronation, each interceptor akin to Napoléon's Russian winter, or Hannibal's Alps. Speed kills, they say. But the Kings and Nash proved that there's more than one way to run and that the fast break can come back again. The legacy rides on. —*T.Z.*

SECRETLY CANADIAN: Steve Nash is not the only player from the Great White North in recent years:

RICK FOX: Fox lived in Canada for the first three years of his life. He played for his native country only once, in 1994. Canada was eliminated when Fox failed to score on an isolation play at the buzzer.

SAMUEL DALEMBERT: The Haitian-born center became a naturalized Canadian citizen in 2007 specifically to play for the national team. Then, in 2008, he was dismissed from the squad during Olympic qualifying due to a lack of effort.

JAMAAL MAGLOIRE: One of the most embarrassing All-Star selections ever, Magloire's a legend in his hometown, Scarborough, Ontario, where he was one of the first inductees into the Scarborough Town Centre Mall's Walk of Fame.

CARL ENGLISH: An undrafted free agent from St. John's, Newfoundland, English was invited to the Pacers' camp in 2003. Agent Harold Cipin mistakenly thought he had signed a guaranteed contract and boasted to the media that Larry Bird had fallen in love with English's game.

OBVIOUSLY CANADIAN: Todd MacCulloch and Bill Wennington, burly big men with no offensive skills.

Speed Saga

The revival of the fast break in the NBA may have been abrupt, but over the decade that followed it took on many forms and went by many names. This chart illustrates its evolution in the hands of the Sacramento Kings and Steve Nash's Mavericks and Suns. The Kings not only gave the world Jason "White Chocolate" Williams, but brought back the passing big man by making Chris Webber and Vlade Divac hubs of distribution. Nash saved the league from the Starbury era by reimagining Bob Cousy, purest of all point guards.

2000 2001 2002 2003

PLUS +

CREATIVITY AXIS

MINUS −

2000

MAVS

KINGS

NASH'S MAVS 1
Point guard as conductor, big man (Dirk) as gunner. Dissonant hair.

J-WILL'S KINGS
Point guard pushes, sets up big men and shooters. Cousy reborn.

2002

APEX!
Revolution realized.

KINGS MAVS

C-WEBB'S KINGS
Webber and Divac become the backcourt of the future.

NASH'S MAVS 2
Raef LaFrentz and Wang ZhiZhi complete the prophecy.

CREATIVITY COMPOUNDS:
Shown here are entirely interpretative diagrams of the interactions between players on these fast-break teams. Bubble size coincides with relative creativity quotient.

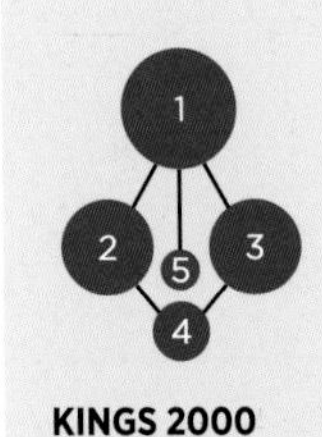

KINGS 2000
1. Jason Williams
2. Chris Webber
3. Vlade Divac
4. Peja Stojakovic
5. Corliss Williamson

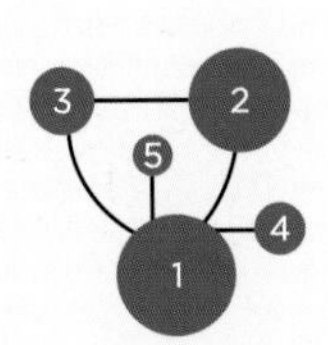

MAVS 2000
1. Steve Nash
2. Dirk Nowitzki
3. Michael Finley
4. Cedric Ceballos
5. Shawn Bradley

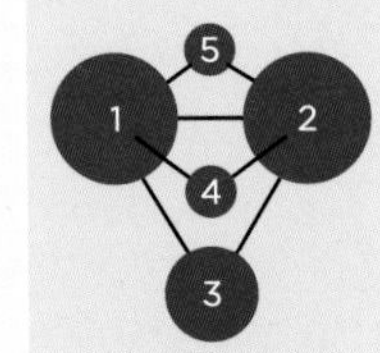

KINGS 2002
1. Chris Webber
2. Vlade Divac
3. Mike Bibby
4. Peja Stojakovic
5. Doug Christie

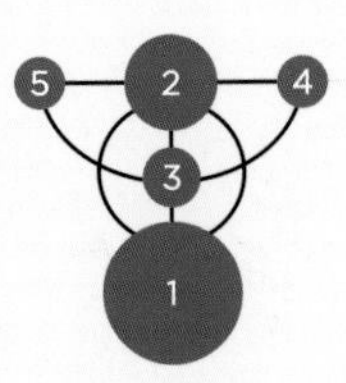

MAVS 2002
1. Steve Nash
2. Dirk Nowitzki
3. Michael Finley
4. Juwan Howard
5. Adrian Griffin

2004	2005	2006	2007	2008

IVORY TOWERS
Webber goes down, but Vlade and Brad Miller keep the faith.

KINGS

NASH REBORN
Hooking up with D'Antoni, Nash turns Amar'e into finest finisher in the land.

SUNS

SUNS

THE FRENCH REVOLUTION
Injury to Amar'e unleashes Boris Diaw, sparks new fantasy amid scientific communities worldwide.

SUNS

AMAR'E LIVES
...but Diaw dies. Another failure betokens a change of organizational philosophy.

MAVS

PANIC!
Nellie loses spirit, chases past with Jamison and Stackhouse.

REVOLUTION QUELLED
Trade of Webber and acquisition of Artest turns once-stylish team to standard fare.

KINGS

SUNS

ENTER SHAQ
Exit D'Antoni, exit global fan base.

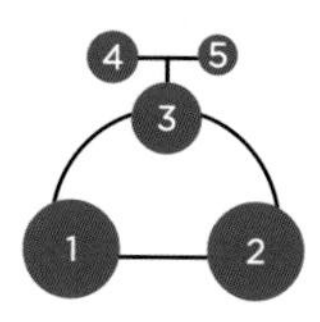

KINGS 2004
1. Vlade Divac
2. Brad Miller
3. Mike Bibby
4. Peja Stojakovic
5. Doug Christie

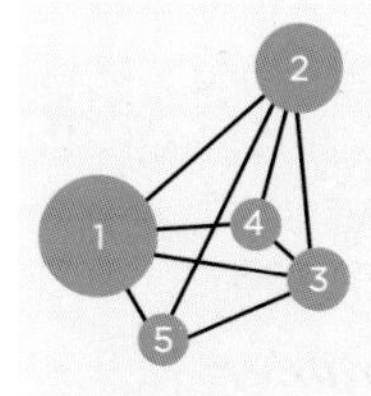

SUNS 2005
1. Steve Nash
2. Amar'e Stoudemire
3. Shawn Marion
4. Joe Johnson
5. Raja Bell

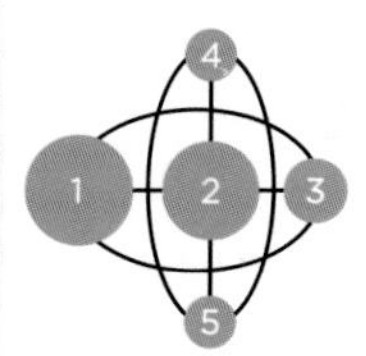

SUNS 2006
1. Steve Nash
2. Boris Diaw
3. Shawn Marion
4. Raja Bell
5. James Jones

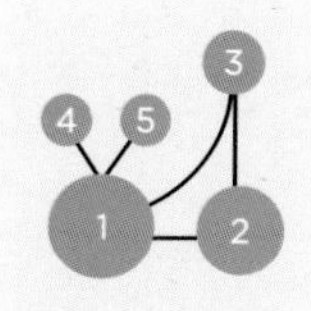

SUNS 2007
1. Steve Nash
2. Shawn Marion
3. Amar'e Stoudemire
4. Raja Bell
5. Leandro Barbosa

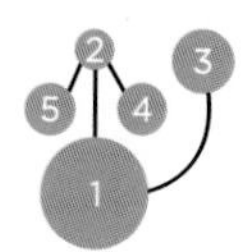

SUNS 2008
1. Steve Nash
2. Shaquille O'Neal
3. Amar'e Stoudemire
4. Raja Bell
5. Leandro Barbosa

BIG MAN BLUES

The Strange Love of Shaquille O'Neal

MISSING DON: Shaq's mafioso mural depicted DeNiro's character from *Goodfellas*, rather than Paul Sorvino, who actually played the role of the local mob capo. Presumably, this is because Sorvino, whose other roles include Henry Kissinger and Bruce Willis's dad on *Moonlighting*, doesn't exactly ooze street cred. However, if Shaq gave Sorvino a chance, he might find out that they have a lot in common. For instance, Sorvino is also interested in law enforcement and serves as a deputy sheriff in Pennsylvania.

In 2007, LSU alumnus Shaquille O'Neal showed up in Baton Rouge for the first home football game of the season. Shaq being Shaq, he showed up in a bus fit for a cross-country tour, complete with an end-to-end mural of himself presiding over some kind of fictive underworld super-summit, with Don Corleone, DeNiro's Jimmy Conway from *Goodfellas*, Tony Soprano, and *Scarface*'s Tony Montana in attendance. The message was silly, grandiose: Shaq was the don to end all dons.

Al Pacino's Scarface—a rap icon for his rags-to-riches story, love of grenade launchers, and knack for turning yay into mansions—was a generational given. But there's more to it than that. The drug lord Tony Montana is a self-help misfit convinced of his own destiny, emboldened by his humble beginnings, and now celebrated for his excess. Shaquille O'Neal is a "quotatious" giant beloved by all and a credit to the league. But his career tells a different story. Taken as a whole, it's a far cry from the hip-hop Paul Bunyan he'd spent years convincing the public he was. There's more Tony Montana to Shaq than he'd have you believe.

In the fraternity of NBA big men, O'Neal stands apart in his nonstop levity. You can spend days arguing chicken/egg, nature/nurture with this one; it's not hard to imagine what effect it might have on a young man to tower over his peers from puberty on. O'Neal has seemingly spent his entire career trying to overcome the off-court handicap of size.

SHAQONYMS: Superman, The Diesel, L.C.L (The Last Center Left), M.D.E (Most Dominant Ever), Osama Bin Shaq, Shaq Daddy, The Big Daddy, The Big Baryshnikov, The Big Cactus, The Big Shaqtus, The Big Galactus, The Big Deported, The Big Felon, The Big Banana, The Big IPO, The Big Maravich, The Real Deal, Wilt Chamberneezy, Dr. Shaq, and Shaqovic.

He wouldn't be the first athlete always angling for the spotlight. But O'Neal is at once lighthearted and uncomfortably deliberate. He assigns himself mind-bending nicknames and makes off-color jokes about opponents, like his disparaging reference to rivals "the Sacramento Queens." From the beginning, Shaq saw himself as an entertainer, which explains 1993's platinum rap album *Shaq Diesel* and film roles ranging from 1996's *Kazaam*, in which Shaq played a genie, to 1994's *Blue Chips*, an underrated look at corruption in college sports with Nick Nolte. Shaq had to stay in motion off the court. The more he did, the more control he exerted over his image. Anyone who stands in the way of Shaq's self-promotion, while not exactly in danger of being mutilated by a machine gun, has learned that O'Neal had a wrathful side. His current place in the American pop cosmology has been hard-fought, almost the opposite of his play on the court. If anything, the same thing that made him such an asset in games was, to O'Neal, a burden.

Shaquille O'Neal might have been Joe Frazier or George Foreman on the court, but he preferred the role of the garrulous, daft Ali off of it. In the post-Jordan NBA, smaller, more dynamic players are the unquestioned center of attention. Style-wise, they're the Alis, with inventive games that suggest a richness of personality. Shaq needs this kind of player to thrive, but always casts himself as the talker, the real celebrity, in these relationships. And while O'Neal has soft hands, nimble feet, excellent passing skills, and a few ball-handling gimmicks that make appearances in All-Star Games, his play tends toward elemental clangor.

Coming out of LSU as a junior in 1992, O'Neal was a new kind of center. Wilt, Russell, and, later, David Robinson had set a precedent of big men as more than lumbering monoliths, but Shaq's explosiveness around the basket rivaled that of guards and forwards. O'Neal's physical presence went beyond mere strength. His nickname "Superman" was descriptive, not boastful; he was gravity coming and going, capable of such immense expulsions of energy that the league had to alter the design of its hoops. This had happened once before, as a result of Darryl Dawkins shattering backboards in 1979. Shaq, however, did more than yank a rim away from a piece of glass. He brought down the whole basket, causing the structure to crumple like a piece of inferior engineering. When confronted with the force Shaq posed, it was just that.

The following summer, the Magic nabbed Penny Hardaway, the ideal match for Shaq's inside might. He also had no personality, which made him the perfect complement to O'Neal as both a player and public figure. The two grew together, and the Magic were a young team on the rise—cresting in 1995, when they knocked off Jordan's Bulls in the Conference Semis before falling to the Rockets in the Finals. Then a spate of injuries forced Shaq to miss 28 games and led Penny to take on more of a leadership role. The Magic lost in the Conference Finals that year to the Bulls, who were coming off an NBA-record 72 wins. It was Shaq's last

TRUE FU-SCHNICK: One of O'Neal's earliest nicknames was Shaq Fu, which came from his honorary membership in the Fu-Schnickens, his favorite hip-hop group and one of the first acts to make references to martial-arts films and Asian culture. Shaq made a guest appearance on the second Fu-Schnickens album, named one of his own albums *Shaq Fu: Da Return,* and lent his name and image to the video game *Shaq Fu,* a *Mortal Kombat* rip-off in which Shaq wanders into an alternate dimension ruled by a nefarious mummy while on his way to a charity game in Tokyo. The ridiculous nature of the plot and poor game mechanics have given it a reputation as one of the worst games ever.

IT'S ALL GREEK TO ME: Shaq has a long-standing and confused relationship with classical Greek civilization:

THE BIG ARISTOTLE: In 2000, coach Phil Jackson gave O'Neal a copy of Aristotle's *Nicomachean Ethics* in a wry attempt to improve his free-throw shooting by imparting Aristotle's teaching that "excellence is a habit." Shaq promptly dubbed himself the "Big Aristotle," but proceeded to shoot 16 percent worse from the line that season.

THE PYTHAGOREAN THEOREM: Shaq once stated: "I'm like the Pythagorean theorem. Not too many people know the answer to my game." When informed by Ahmad Rashad that the Pythagorean theorem was actually its own answer, the Big Euclid elaborated that most people would have to go to the library to look up the definition, and by the time they got back to the court, Shaq would have already scored.

THE PARTHENON: Asked after a trip to Greece if he had visited the Parthenon, O'Neal replied, "I don't know. I can't really remember the names of the clubs that we went to."

season with Orlando. He barely spoke to Penny when they were both members of the 1996 Olympic team, and Hardaway was the last to know that Shaq planned to sign with the Lakers.

Later in his career, O'Neal was fond of trotting out an analogy that cast himself as Don Corleone and his series of guard partners as his sons. Penny was Fredo, "who was never ready for me to hand it over to him." That O'Neal would come to this conclusion when Penny had taken center stage, guided the Magic to a 60–22 season, and then—with Shaq in tow—lost to arguably the greatest team ever, is a bit perplexing. It would seem the problem was exactly that Hardaway was all too ready, not to mention the beneficiary of the Nike campaign that had invented a personality for him. It's nonsense to suggest that Penny no longer needed Shaq, but he had certainly become too much of a threat, which is to say, too much of a guard in all imaginable ways.

On the Lakers, Shaq found himself teamed with a fledgling Kobe Bryant. The resulting soap opera featured its share of petulance on both sides, as Bryant worked his ass off and Shaq took it easy while practically guaranteeing the team a title if he stayed healthy. Thicker, if not quite as propulsive, than when he first entered the league, Shaq was now the immovable object realized. Fellow big man Yao Ming would later describe him as "a wall of meat." O'Neal was a load and a half, absolutely unstoppable when he got the ball deep enough. There was little artfulness to his play, but with the triangle focused on posting and reposting Shaq, it was usually just a matter of time before he sent the ball crashing through the hoop.

The Lakers won three straight titles as tensions simmered; in 2003, the Lakers were knocked off in the second round by the Spurs and decided to redouble their efforts by adding Karl Malone and Gary Payton to the mix. That summer, a Colorado woman accused Bryant of sexual assault, giving the world a glimpse of the perennial All-Star's secretive, dark, and neurotic side. While Kobe earned rave reviews for his ability to play in between court appearances, the new Lakers never gelled, Shaq and Malone broke down, and in that year's NBA Finals, they fell to a more pliant, impassioned Detroit Pistons team. This victory is celebrated as the big guy getting smacked by the workingman, but in retrospect it was inevitable. The Lakers had become a caricature of themselves between the addition of Payton and Malone, Shaq's lethargy, Kobe's drama, the Shaq/Kobe feud, and Phil Jackson's hands-off

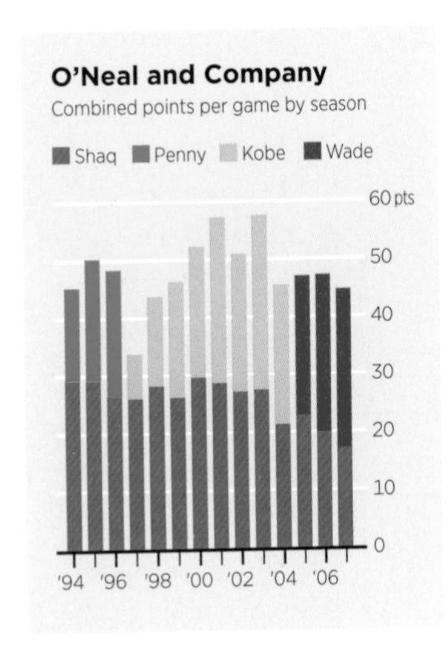

attempts to keep it all together; the Pistons were the spear that pricked the bubble.

Phil Jackson retired, O'Neal was dealt to Miami, and Kobe was left to wander through the wreckage. He also ended up shouldering the blame, cast as the ruthless, ambitious punk who ran a Hall of Fame center out of town. This interpretation fit what the public felt it knew about Bryant at that point. Although Shaq had issues with motivation and conditioning, Kobe just seemed like the one to cause problems. For all his brilliance on the court, if anyone was going to break the band up, it would be Kobe. Above all else, he was humorless, cold, and utterly unsympathetic. O'Neal, by contrast, was the league's clown prince, a cutup whose lapses in professional judgment could be excused with a grin and a quip. But between his good looks and, pre-arrest, innumerable endorsements, Kobe was able to effortlessly step into the celebrity's role—the thing Shaq had to try so hard to earn himself. Their feud wasn't just about tension on the court but also Shaq's resentment of Bryant's public figure.

In South Beach, Shaq held a rally with water guns and balloons that resembled a campaign appearance. He promised to bring a title to the city, a full-on public relations blast that temporarily made us all forget that he was beginning the downside of his career. Luckily, this was the year Dwyane Wade arrived as a truly frightening perimeter player. The Heat faltered in the 2005 playoffs when injuries curtailed Wade's rise. But O'Neal was credited with the renaissance, as much for his leadership and general aura as for his actual contributions on the floor. The following season saw the Heat get that title, the first in franchise history. Wade was now one of the biggest stars in the game, and Shaq even less of a factor than before. O'Neal seemed to recognize this, gushing that "if you watch the trilogy, the Godfather hands it over to Michael. So I have no problem handing it over to Dwyane." When Wade was awarded the Finals MVP by David Stern, Shaq stepped in and insisted on being the one who presented the trophy to him.

But the exact meaning of this gesture would prove to be murky. Shaq called Wade "the best player ever," but added that he "came to Miami because of this young fella . . . I knew I wanted to make him better." Injuries to both men derailed the Heat the following season, along with rumors of bad blood in the locker room; supposedly, in 2007, Shaq e-mailed friends a Photoshop job of

Wade's face on a woman's body. O'Neal was traded to the Suns in the middle of the 2007–08 season, and when the Heat and Suns met in Miami the following year, the two barely acknowledged each other. This was made all the more insidious not only by its eerie similarities to his post-break-up encounters with Kobe (the league's Christmas Day theater) but in that he decided to warm up to Bryant around this same time.

Shaq faced an even more direct threat in the person of Dwight Howard, the Magic center who resembles a young O'Neal and who has also dubbed himself the Man of Steel. Orlando also happens to be coached by Stan Van Gundy, O'Neal's coach in Miami before the championship. When their teams met in March 2009, O'Neal attempted to draw an offensive foul on Howard by falling to the ground. Van Gundy was as amused as anyone that the league's great man of mass could try and flop, and said so to the press. O'Neal castigated Van Gundy, calling him "a master of panic" hated by his players. He ripped Van Gundy's brother Jeff, another NBA coach without a title, and Magic assistant Patrick Ewing—a ringless Hall of Famer—as unaccomplished bums. He dismissed Howard himself as an inferior imitator. The Howard vendetta didn't stop there. Just before the 2010 All-Star Game, an aging Shaq went at the good-natured Howard again with renewed fervor, a man desperately holding on to his brand, which, as his game dwindled, was really the only foothold he had in the league.

The figures on Shaq's murals have become familiar, if not completely defanged. But watch any of them with fresh eyes, from start to finish, and you'll be reminded of just how unsettling they really are. So it is with O'Neal's career: He's always among the league's most dominant forces and biggest personalities. But just beneath the surface, there's always the trace of Shaq's less heroic side, the power-mad, insecure man who won't hesitate to take care of anyone who crosses him. That he's done so in the interest of not being seen as a brute is the truly bizarre irony of his career. —*B.S.*

A BETTER TOMORROW: Shaq was praised for ditching movies and music, but the reality is that he just took up way too many serious pursuits instead:

ACADEMICS: Shaq returned to LSU and received his BA in general studies in 2000, fulfilling a promise to his mother. Phil Jackson even let him miss a game to attend the graduation ceremony. Shaq also earned an MBA online through the University of Phoenix in 2005.

LAW ENFORCEMENT: O'Neal has been made a reserve officer in both Los Angeles and Miami and has also worked with the U.S. Marshals to crack down on online sexual predation. In 2005, he witnessed a hate crime against a gay man in Miami and helped the local police track the offenders over the phone.

REAL ESTATE: Since the housing crisis began in 2008, Shaq has started a program to buy the mortgages of Orlando homeowners in foreclosure and sell them back at a reduced rate. He makes a minimal profit off the deals.

IN PLAIN SIGHT

The Black-and-Silver Dynasty

From 1998 through the first decade of the twenty-first century, the Spurs dominated the NBA like some benign rat king, winning more consistently than any other team of their day. They were the stealth version of Auerbach's Celtics, remaining a constant even as they morphed from one incarnation to the next, though they were rarely recognized as clear-cut favorites. But the results speak for themselves: Four titles. Two surefire Hall of Famers in David Robinson and Tim Duncan, the latter of whom won a Rookie of the Year and then two MVP awards during the run. Multiple All-Star selections for their two unconventional stars Tony Parker and Manu Ginobili. And a Coach of the Year award for Gregg Popovich.

Executive R. C. Buford, who in 2002 succeeded Pop as general manager, had from the beginning of his involvement with the team been an innovator in international scouting, drafting Fabricio Oberto, Beno Udrih, Ian Mahinmi, and Luis Scola in addition to Parker and Manu. He also cleverly deployed the "veteran's minimum" and other salary-cap restrictions to sign near-burnouts (Michael Finley, Kevin Willis, and Glenn Robinson) in the twilight of their careers to play key roles for San Antonio. Buford developed such a Midas touch that we half expected to see Shawn Kemp don the black and silver—maybe not slimmed down, but certainly determined.

Yet San Antonio's legacy, lengthy as it is, is also strangely immaterial. This has been a problem from the beginning. The first title came in the lockout season, when they seemingly took advantage of the general disarray. Going back even further, the Duncan/Robinson frontcourt that won the first ring came about because, when Robinson lost a season to injury, the Spurs were terrible enough to win the Duncan sweepstakes (beating the lottery's odds to win the number-one pick in the draft), only to

THE LIGHTER SIDE: Despite their reputation as stern professionals on the court, the Spurs have one of the funniest locker rooms in the league. At times, we are lucky enough to get a glimpse:

LAFF-A-SHAQ: In the 2008 preseason, Shaquille O'Neal called the Spurs' habit of employing the Hack-A-Shaq technique "a coward move." In the first game of the regular season, Popovich instructed Michael Finley to intentionally foul Shaq five seconds into the game.

PITCHMEN: Their ads for Texas grocery chain H-E-B have featured Brent Barry, Bruce Bowen, and Manu Ginobili singing a cowboy song about delicious milk in a makeshift desert scene; Tim Duncan, Bowen, and Ginobili ensuring everyone that the fresh smell of their uniforms doesn't impede their manliness; and Duncan reciting beat poetry about brisket.

ESCARGOT, MY CAR GO: In February 2009, Ginobili informed the world via Twitter that he'd tricked George Hill into eating snails. His description: "His face was funny when I told him what it really was."

resume their regularly scheduled playoff-caliber performance the following year. Their matter-of-fact adaptability has allowed them to attain long-lasting greatness throughout the flux and ebb of the NBA; at times, it seems most appropriate to describe the Spurs in terms of what they exist in opposition to. During the era of the Spurs' dominance, three teams stand out as meaningful competition: the big-named, big-banked Los Angeles Lakers; the Pistons of Chauncey Billups, Rip Hamilton, and the Wallace Brothers, Ben and Rasheed; and the D'Antoni Suns, in all their run-and-shoot glory. Each of these proved formidable playoff rivals for the Spurs and in turn helped shape San Antonio's identity.

In 2003, the Spurs ended the Lakers' run of championships in the Western Conference Semifinals behind a spotless performance by Duncan and key contributions from up-and-comers Parker, Ginobili, and Bruce Bowen. The Lakers depended primarily on conventional stars, namely Shaquille O'Neal, Kobe Bryant, Phil Jackson, and triangle-offense guru Tex Winter. Duncan was seen as one of the premier big men in the league, if not a titan on the order of Shaq; Popovich, a great coach, but not an immortal like Jackson. What gave the Spurs an edge were contributions from three players who proved far more valuable than they had any business being. Can we call a journeyman defensive specialist known to be dirty (Bowen) one of the most important players on a dynasty? How about a flop-prone, late-twenties South American who played like his elbows were on fire (Ginobili)? What about a point guard who was neither a top-notch playmaker nor a model shooter, and whose main weapon was taking floaters in the paint (Parker)? The answer is that these labels said both too much and too little. Bowen was transformed from mere flunky to a reliable three-point shooter and game-changing defender, Ginobili from kicking fetus to glorious pest, and Parker from expendable French wuss to speed-demonic Casanova.

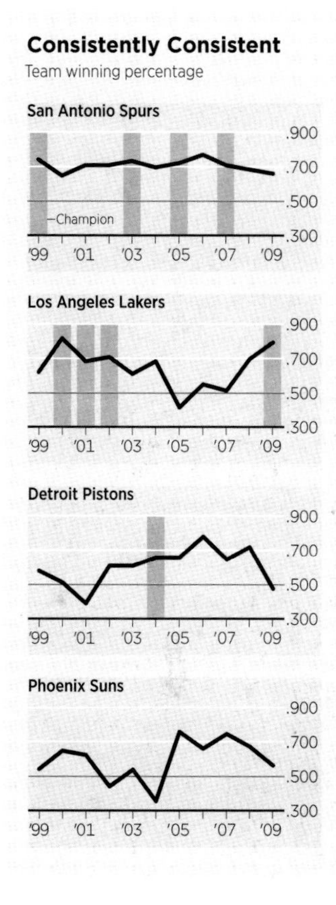

At the time, the Spurs came across as the anti-Lakers. Where Los Angeles stood for stardom, distraction, and riches, San Antonio represented collectivism, focus, and family. The teams' home cities reflected this dueling ethos, with Los Angeles as the glut of materialism, falsity, traffic, and self-presentation, while San Antonio represented immigrant struggle, homespun pride, and car dealerships. Their battles played out as classic morality operas, with the good guys, this time, wearing black.

From the Spurs' perspective, the most memorable contests came in the 2003 Conference Semifinals. Because of the expectations the Lakers always carried, and the thrashing they'd given the Spurs in years past, the series was watched intently by casual and serious fans alike. As Los Angeles went down in Game 6, Popovich pulled one of the most Popovichean moves of all time: He called a time-out with 2:26 left in the game to warn the Spurs not to celebrate their victory egregiously. It is here where we must consider the intent, not merely the outcome, of the action. Each of Popovich's acts, no matter how sportsmanlike, also carried with it an element of psychological purpose. Note that this is a coach who during his college years at the U.S. Air Force Academy underwent extensive intelligence training and even considered a career in the CIA. It is not that Popovich's warning to his players necessarily lacked sincere compassion for the losing Lakers but that it was also of great personal benefit to his team.

POPPO'S FIRST TEAM: Before heading to the NBA, Popovich coached for eight seasons at Pomona-Pitzer, a small Divison III program in Southern California. As head coach and chairman of the Student Life Committee, "Poppo" lived in a dorm, worked out of a closet, and led his first team to a 2–22 record, including a loss to a CalTech team that hadn't won a conference game in ninety-nine tries. He once told his players not to "move your head up and down like a sine wave." When Popovich left to become an assistant for the Spurs, he asked one of his players two questions: "Who is on the team besides David Robinson?" And, "What is an illegal defense?"

Perhaps Popovich also knew a thing or two about evolutionary biology, which makes quite a bit of noise over what is called costly signaling. This theory describes situations in which people act in a manner that is costly to themselves but serves some larger adaptive purpose. This explains why people do things that don't make sense from a rational point of view, like giving away money. The costly signaling explanation of such an act says that people give money away to establish a good reputation, to earn trust, and to reap the future benefits of this status. "Giving" in these theories takes on nastier names, such as competitive altruism or conspicuous consumption.

Popovichean endeavors such as calling a time-out to warn against celebration are textbook costly signals. Pop did not allow his team the public exuberance of celebrating a well-earned victory over an extremely worthy opponent. This short-term cost, however, gains him long-term respect from the media, referees, and future opponents. Other Popovichean costly signals include taking a time-out one minute into the game to "chastise" his team for a defensive "letdown," overtly praising his opponents, screaming at DeJuan Blair for pinning a block to the backboard (assuming it was showboating), and saying, after winning a thirteenth consecutive game in 2010, "We blew an opportunity to progress and get better . . . That's the goal, to get better every practice and every game, and we wasted that tonight . . . It doesn't mean a damn thing. What means something is getting better." Popovich doesn't teach, motivate, or manipulate. Rather, his actions reveal intentions—perhaps subconscious ones—to establish a moral high ground through intense humility and self-scrutiny, with the outcome of these tactics resulting in pure success.

The difference between the Spurs and the Pistons, whom they met in the 2005 Finals, hinged almost entirely on one of these subtle Popovichean points. Both teams prided themselves on defense and rebounding; both were fundamentally sound; both had unflashy stars, passed well, and shared the glory. Detroit's core of Rip Hamilton, Rasheed Wallace, Chauncey Billups, Ben Wallace, and Tayshaun Prince—the defending champions—inherited a certain nastiness from their Bad Boy predecessors. They still loved the spotlight; they just loved it as a team. They wanted to beat you up and put you down, and they were unabashed in making these their talking points before, during, and after the game. The Spurs, on the other hand, just went about their business, opening up a lead while you weren't looking, another testament to Popovich's psychological skill. In a seven-game series, the Spurs triumphed and the Pistons were never the same. The Spurs continued to shape-shift for years to come, while the Pistons never regained their championship swagger or dynastic hopes. The difference between upright and stubborn: One is portable, while the other carries in it the seed of its own demise. The Pistons' attempts to adjust their roster over the years have been big news, while the Spurs accomplish their makeovers without anyone's noticing until midseason.

The Spurs, who always seem to find a way to be everyone's rivals, were next cast in opposition to the Phoenix Suns—and, by extension, the direction in which the league was headed. The Suns were born out of David Stern's mandate to facilitate offensive play and increase scoring by instructing referees to put greater emphasis on defensive hand-checking fouls. These new priorities encouraged teams like the Suns to run the ball down opponents' throats, without care for hard-nosed defense or aggressive rebounding. This stood in direct opposition to the Spurs' methodical, defense-oriented, slow, grind-it-out style of play that the league was attempting to eradicate. The Suns represented motion, spontaneity, and birth. The Spurs represented industry, repetition, and death. Although the Suns' vision of the future was far brighter and more expansive, they were famously kept from the Finals by the Spurs in both 2005 and 2007, the Spurs finding ways to cap, match, and then exceed

HORRY BEFORE THE GLORY: Robert Horry has a distinguished résumé as a clutch shooter for the Rockets, Lakers, and Spurs. But sometimes things didn't go his way.

1995 CONFERENCE FINALS, GAME 1: Horry hits a jumper with 6.5 seconds remaining to give Houston a 94–93 win over the Spurs. *Before:* 5 points, 0–4 FG, 6 rebounds, 3 assists.

2001 NBA FINALS, GAME 3: Horry nails a corner three with 47 seconds left and hits 4 free throws in the final minute to help the Lakers to a 3-point win over the Sixers. *Before:* 8 points, 3–4 FG, 44 percent from the line in the playoffs.

2002 FIRST ROUND, GAME 3: Kobe Bryant finds Horry for a game-winning three with 10.2 seconds left to close out the series against Portland. *Before:* 5 points, 2–8 FG, 5 rebounds, 4 assists.

2005 NBA FINALS, GAME 5: Horry scores 21 points in the fourth quarter and overtime, including a game-winning three with 5.9 seconds left. *Before:* 0 points.

2007 FIRST ROUND, GAME 4: Horry drains a three with 30 seconds left to ice the game against the Nuggets. *Before:* 2 points, 1–2 FG, 6 rebounds.

SURPRISING INFLUENCE: Larry Brown is Gregg Popovich's primary mentor, the man who plucked him from Division III obscurity. However, the foundation for his offensive system comes from an unlikely source: Don Nelson. As an assistant with the Warriors in the early '90s, Pop refined his offensive principles. He even admits as much: "It's all either his play, or a variation."

the Suns' inevitable high point totals. Thus, fans were treated to Amar'e Stoudemire or Steve Nash putting on the offensive show of a lifetime, only to realize that the rest of the Phoenix team had been taken out of the picture altogether. Against the Lakers, the Spurs always seemed a lesser power. Taking on Phoenix, however, San Antonio finally assumed the mantle of league powerhouse, however elliptically. This team mattered to the league; they just refused to carry themselves like they did.

The Suns' 2007 loss was marred by an incident in which Bruce Bowen—already accused of dirty plays such as karate kicking Wally Szczerbiak and sticking a sneaker out under the foot of a jump shooter as he came down—casually threw a flailing Steve Nash into the scorer's table. During the Suns' enraged response to the incident, Amar'e Stoudemire and Boris Diaw broke league rules by leaving the bench area. Both players received suspensions for a critical game later in the series. This altercation defined the chippiness of the duels between these two teams and gave the Spurs—some say—an unfair advantage in a pivotal Game 5. Phoenix will never forget the incident, forever greeting Bruce Bowen's name with bellowing hatred. It also captures the Spurs' amazing versatility, playing heroes versus the Lakers and villains versus the Suns. But the epilogue to this series is perhaps the most intriguing, and telling, part of this rivalry. The Spurs were among the first wave of teams to periodically "go small," an emulation of the Suns' approach that—because of the iron fist of the Spurs—had never won a championship.

The Spurs were a lone constant in the NBA's complex and seemingly random universe. Losing stalwarts like David Robinson, Sean Elliott, Bruce Bowen, and Avery Johnson, and with a revolving cast of role players, Popovich and Duncan found the strength to remain steady. The difficulty in defining that formula is also what makes it so difficult to keep track of their legacy. Are they two separate dynasties? Three? Four championship teams that just happened to win out that year? Their importance seems to be primarily about when and how they won, not some credo written on the wall from Day One. The Spurs have been a necessary vortex, existing as a physical space where half-baked zone-defense schemes, perennial All-Stars with complexes, and gimmicky offenses are vacuumed up and dumped in the garbage. They achieved their success not by expanding what was possible but by limiting everyone else's attempts to do so. *—Dr. L.I.C*

ARBITERS OF AMAZEMENT

YouTube and the Democratic Archive

As its name suggests, the Shot—Michael Jordan's series-winning buzzer-beater against the Cavs during the 1989 playoffs—is iconic: "As the ball nestled through the net," confirms NBA.com, describing an image we all can easily visualize, "Jordan pumped his fists in jubilation, completing a video highlight for the ages." In time, the endlessly replayed Shot became representative of MJ's transformation from showman to champion and a metonym for the very idea of legacy—it's not just how dominantly you play the game, but how you're remembered.

Yet this version of the Shot is also, to some extent, a fabrication. The original CBS telecast cut immediately (and in retrospect, bafflingly) to the reaction of then Bulls coach Doug Collins; Jordan's celebratory histrionics only surfaced later, in archival footage. If the NBA is to be believed, the popularized version ranks with the moon landing and JFK assassination among the great live moments in American television history; this redux has become our memory of something most of us, watching Coach Collins tear around our TV screens, never saw.

Art in the Age of . . .

Where they saw the Shot (through 2009)

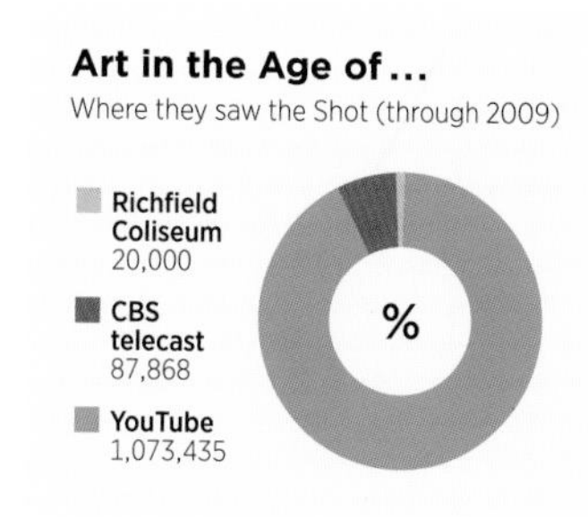

The Shot was featured among the NBA's "Where Will Amazing Happen This Year?" spots during the 2009 playoffs—as was a LeBron James dunk, a Manu Ginobili layup, and an alley-oop to Andrei Kirilenko, each slowed down, flipped to black-and-white, and soundtracked like the sad parts from *Amélie*.

The spots were solemn, bursting with meaning, somehow both stark and expansive, saying nothing and everything about these players and the sport they played. To call the clips highlights would be misleading; apart from Dr. J's staggering reverse layup, few were aesthetically or athletically "amazing." Rather, taking the Shot as a blueprint, they served as shorthand for larger narratives—of teams, of individuals, of the game itself. The goal of the campaign was to station these moments firmly, proprietarily, as commercials for an NBA product. As the Association has manipulated the import of Jordan's '89 game winner, so was this a perversion of nostalgia, wrenching moments out of context and playing them back as advertisements—effectively co-opting the personal experience of players and fans to reaffirm and sustain the NBA product. They also presented the potential for posterity as incentive to stay focused for all two and a half months of the playoffs: Don't change that dial, the ads suggested; you might miss out on what we later decide is history.

Since the whole business self-referentially recognized the league as the locus of "Where Amazing Happens," subsumed into this corporate agenda was the individual. Consider what the less blatantly commercial focus would have been had the choice of interrogatives been not "where" but "who." Not only would celebrating the *people* who made these moments happen have rescued poor Manu and Andrei from the generic, stuff-of-history, NBA-sanctioned Jordan model, but it would have also acknowledged that the Association's true organ of experience is much more human than what can be captured by a branding strategy.

The WWAHTY? campaign suggested that having experienced these scenes for yourself, awash in your own set of feelings, was secondary to the teleological packaging. But any fan's enjoyment (or misery, or bafflement, or envy) is always colored by his or her own subjectivity. We bring to professional basketball, and project upon its athletes, our own hopes, desires, fears, anxieties, and (sure, failed) dreams. For the league to try and tell us which moments are definitive and epochal seems not only counterintuitive but ignorant of the two-part engine, far beyond the NBA executive, that drives the game in the first place: players and fans.

But there's hope, a place where we find individualism—the "who" ignored by the league—rekindled, a place that reemphasizes the relationship between the great (and, occasionally, not-so-great) athletes of the NBA and those who obsess over them, a place that puts the power back in the hands of the people: YouTube.

It's on YouTube that WWAHTY? has spawned a legion of imitators. In the same style and with the same background music, these homemade approximations reclaim the subjectivity ignored by that thoughtless campaign. Take, for example, DWade3TV's version, which ends with "Where Will Amazing Happens [*sic*]

This Year?" superimposed in Arial bold italics over Dwyane Wade celebrating a regular-season game winner. Similar DIY spots have been created for Vince Carter, Derrick Rose, Joe Johnson, Allen Iverson, and countless others who didn't make the "official" cut but who *do* have legions of slighted fans who in turn have done something about it.

Much like the knock-off "Abibas" high-tops you might find in a Chennai market stall, there's something wonderfully fallible and defiant about these clips when contrasted with the NBA's slick production. And while it's sometimes hard to tell when the irony is intentional and the defiance inadvertent, it mostly doesn't matter. What's most important is that YouTube affords fans a venue to curate what they, not the league, consider "Amazing." Rather than having history defined from on high, this unauthorized alternative of who and what (and where) might be the only venue for this sort of agency. Most important, it serves as an archive of collective memory, a much more comprehensive document of what professional basketball means to its fans than the league's various CliffsNotes versions.

Basketball is a sport of continuous motion, or unbroken action, of games that must be seen from the start for that final buzzer-beater to make you leap screaming off the couch or hang your head in disgrace and shame. But the era of the highlight, as with all similar packaging of real-world content, forever changed the way the NBA was consumed. *SportsCenter*, as a convenient example, has since its advent in 1980 made the summary of games a project of fragmentation, and viewers have come to accept this as a means of understanding what happened around the league on any given night. What summarizing games in snippets misses, of course, is all the tension and nuance of the original: We get the final score and the big plays but, regardless how hysterical the accompanying narration, none of the *feeling* of the game itself. That feeling is, of course, always subjective, and nothing that can be transmitted without the totality of all forty-eight minutes (and all those off-the-clock minutes in between). While it was surely just as emotionally riveting at the time, who besides the odd nostalgic Cavs fan remembers Craig Ehlo's apparently series-clinching layup only seconds before Michael Jordan made the Shot? (Check it out on YouTube!)

But if fragmentation has become the process by which basketball is replayed, and so remembered, at least on YouTube what the

YOUTUBE SAVED MY LIFE:
YouTube has emerged as a new kind of historical document, one that rescues players from irrelevance:

SHAWN KEMP: On YouTube, he's still the same player who redefined the power forward position in Seattle.

ROBERT PACK: Over thirteen seasons, Pack was rarely more than a backup point guard. But he was one of the most ferocious in-game dunkers in the league, which is a skill you wouldn't know about from his pedestrian stat lines.

GOD SHAMMGOD: It's rare that people talk about someone who played only 20 games in the NBA, but Shammgod's handle is so legendary that he's become something of a cult figure.

SOCIAL FAUX PAS: Just as fans have been attracted by the participatory nature of online social media, so too have the players themselves. However, it took a minute for them to fully realize the ease with which a private thought can become an internationally published sound bite:

1. In July 2009, Stephon Marbury took a liking to uStream, a Web site where users can broadcast live video. In a series of marathon sessions, Marbury set new standards for bizarre athlete behavior, including eating Vaseline and broadcasting a car accident.

2. Shortly after the 2009 draft, rookie guard Brandon Jennings joined rapper Joe Budden on uStream for an interview he believed to be private. Jennings went off on any number of topics, including the other guards in Milwaukee, teams that passed him up ("Fuck the Knicks"), and Scott Skiles ("That n**** tough").

3. In August 2009, Michael Beasley put up a picture of himself on Twitter that appeared to show a bag of marijuana in the background. Within a few days, he had checked into a Houston-area rehab center.

game means to actual human beings, as opposed to the league or the networks, is being restored. Beyond the WWAHTY? rips, here fans celebrate and share not only the amazing, the remarkable, and the sublime, but also the banal and the ridiculous. It's a long, long season, and maintaining engagement often means having to nerd-out on the details; what's "Amazing" about the NBA, to many of us, certainly isn't limited to its career-defining moments. There aren't many of those, anyway, and the crystal-ball project of trying to identify them as they happen, without the value of hindsight, can be spurious, if not impossible. The Shot, after all, didn't become the Shot until Michael Jordan the guard became Michael Jordan the ultimate triumphant megastar and the NBA decided it was the birth of a legend.

"Amazing," for YouTube user marik1234, is "Nate Robinson breaks Jose Calderon's ankles." In this seventy-nine-second clip, Robinson sends poor, hapless Calderon flopping to the floor with a ruthless crossover, is fouled on the ensuing drive, and has his shot swatted away. It's a dead play, without any of the narrative weight we associate with the Shot—and never the stuff, for myriad reasons, of a WWAHTY? commercial. Fifteen years ago it would have been forgotten, lost and deleted from the league's official record. But marik1234 has ensured that the moment will live on—if not for eternity, at least long enough that a staggering 1.5 million viewers have watched the clip since its posting.

If that number is any indication, YouTube represents a new kind of communal mythmaking, one that resists the great dictatorial hegemony of the NBA administration in favor of something approaching democracy. Like any democracy, it's flawed (unfettered access can make the site something of a crazy train), but taken as an archive, hoops-on-YouTube offers a much more comprehensive understanding of how the game is played, watched, and remembered than those limited moments sanctioned by the league. And, fittingly, each post mirrors the remarkable self-expression so prevalent in professional basketball: Think what we learn or can at least speculate about marik1234 from his post—every portrait is a portrait of the artist, after all.

There's an assertion of autobiography, of stamping one's existence onto the world, in any creative gesture—be it a Nate Robinson crossover or curating (appreciating, recording, editing, posting, sharing) that crossover for mass consumption. YouTube is about fans appreciating the game on their terms: It allows the masses to contribute to the larger narrative of the NBA beyond the league's savvy marketing and even the players' own attempts at self-definition. YouTube renders meaningless the whole "this broadcast may not be retransmitted" legalese, a fitting demonstration of the limits of the league's jurisdiction over personalized experience, as well as how backward it is for a corporation to claim *our* game as *their* property. In a culture with increasingly fewer opportunities for the individual to trump the institution, YouTube has become a platform for fans to assert themselves and what they feel to be their personal relationships with the game and its players.

On one hand, YouTube represents an even more radical descent into pastiche, with seemingly random moments and insignificant games elevated to the same level as the ones that really made a difference. But if any official record of NBA games (or careers) is a fall from the paradise of fan subjectivity, then these bits and pieces become—however unwittingly—an attempt to restore the notion of individualized experience. After all, one fan's insignificance is another's "Nate Robinson breaks Jose Calderon's ankles"—or "Nate Robinson breaks Steve Blake's ankles," or "Nate Robinson breaks ankles of a boy in an exhibition in Málaga."

Who knows if YouTube will ever succeed in overthrowing its own ontology—there are scores of old games sitting on there, and none are as often viewed as the so-called mix tapes that abbreviate the careers of Clyde Drexler or Dominique Wilkins into a sequence of money shots, most of them dunks. However, what's key isn't that the wholeness of game-as-text be restored, but that the complexity and totality of the game's emotional truths are creeping back into fandom, and that fans now have a venue to share them.

While, if the Shot is any indication, the NBA's branding engine seems content to feed us an image we never saw as a way of remembering a moment that only gained significance in retrospect, at least the curations of marik1234 and his thousands of fellow archivists are helping create an alternate, potentially more honest record of the sport as it has always been played and consumed. And if fans continue to corrupt the league's attempts at memorializing professional basketball—as they have with the WWAHTY? rips—YouTube will not only challenge, but possibly even replace, the "official" document of what moves, frustrates, confuses, and amazes us about the NBA. —*P.M.*

THE 4 TYPES OF TWITTERERS:

Twitter in particular has become very popular with NBA players. While they take different approaches, they generally fall into four schools:

SERIOUS MEN: Willing to address any topic, no matter how sensitive it may be. They desire to communicate their lives to fans without a net.

Sample tweet: "This repuation of me being a jerk is growing so fast & it's so false. Articles can really make a fan think a certain way. That's sad. O well." —*Chris Douglas-Roberts*

COURT JESTERS: Never serious, constantly ragging on other players and people they see on the street. Often offensive, rarely boring.

Sample tweet: "Never trust a dude that drives with two hands... Idk y, that grind just seems a lil funnystyle." —*Marcus Williams*

CORPORATE PAWNS: Rarely tweet unless a major event happens. Most tweets are simply links to their personal Web sites, where you can read publicist-penned blog posts.

Sample tweet: "Reebok Statement - Reebok is thrilled Allen Iverson will be returning."—*Allen Iverson*

FRIENDS OF THE FAN: Tweet regularly, often with direct questions to fans about their favorite things. Always positive.

Sample tweet: "What yall think about these trades? I'm interested to see who goes where."—*Kevin Durant*

AFTERWORD

This book is far from a comprehensive history of basketball—professional or otherwise. It is, however, a project preoccupied with memory. YouTube functions as an archive for prosaic fan memories. Ad campaigns created characters that have outstripped, even outlasted, the players they were intended to market. At the most basic level, this book deals with what struck us as particularly memorable. That, above all else, is the criteria for inclusion.

As historian Yosef Hayim Yerushalmi wrote, "Certain memories live on; the rest are winnowed out, repressed, or simply discarded by a process of natural selection which the historian, uninvited, disturbs and reverses." In sports, history is winners and losers, statistics and dates; memory, which is where the stories start, is imperfect, stylized, personal. The phrase "history in the making," a standby in the discourse of sports, doesn't necessarily refer to having just seen history unfold (when do we not?) or even mark a particularly historic event. Nor is it a matter of "anticipation," the polite word for hype. It's present tense; it says, to whoever's listening, that whatever's happening in front of you will not be readily forgotten. When we watch LeBron James, we think to ourselves, *He might be the greatest basketball player ever*, and yet this alone does not make LeBron memorable. Otherwise, Tim Duncan would loom as large in the NBA imagination as Allen Iverson or Kevin Garnett.

Contrary to what the league may tell you, with a player like LeBron, "Amazing" is a continuous state, not a series of bullet points, fragments, and highlights. "Awe" doesn't do the experience justice, for that suggests mere shock, or the possibility of one day getting out from under it—of it ceasing to be personal. LeBron is such an overwhelming, even supernatural, presence in the sense that he's also creating memories that will haunt us and the sport indefinitely. Time and time again, LeBron pulls off a play that, much like his physique, seems positively indelible.

Nike's "Witness" campaign may have obvious religious overtones, but strip away the messianic tropes and you're left with a simple fact: When LeBron James plays basketball, you want to watch—to experience something that's not only important or impressive, but worth telling your grandkids, "I remember watching LeBron James," and being able to leave it at that.

Kevin Durant, just barely arrived into the superstar club, is in many ways the purest example of a memory maker in the league today. Like LeBron, Durant is an original—Garnett, but with the offensive arsenal of an at-his-best Tracy McGrady. (He's also longer, more astute, hungrier, faster, a better defender and shooter, and more explosive than anyone gives him credit for.) But while it's easy to explain what makes LeBron a sight to behold—he's almost terrifying in his ability, strength, and athleticism—with Durant, that quality is harder to pin down. What makes Durant so unique is that when he's on the court, you feel like you're bearing witness to *something happening*. He's not changing the game like LeBron; as a gangly scoring machine, he certainly has precedents. His numbers are astounding but not exactly mind-altering. And yet Durant just feels like one of the best players in the league, one who will only get better. There are no superlatives for what he does quite yet, and perhaps there never will be. LeBron is the orderly culmination of all basketball that has come before, assimilating and surpassing; Durant is at once more and less surprising. We can discuss LeBron quasi-rationally; with Durant, we're compelled to just shake our heads as he hits another dramatic three.

Not having been around for much of the material we've covered in these pages, we have had to speculate, borrow from others' accounts, and creatively interpret history—a process at best curatorial; at worst revisionist. But what remained constant—and what kept us honest—was a concerted attempt to honor the players, games, and stories we got to know along the way. Having a career recounted to you as an orderly set of momentous names, dates, statistics, and scouting reports is worlds away from knowing, as it must have been for anyone lucky enough to watch Elgin Baylor or Bill Walton play in their primes, that every second was worth remembering. These are memories we weren't around for, but we would like to think that, through the process of putting this book together, we can count at least some of those moments among our own. —*B.S.*

BIOGRAPHIES

FREEDARKO is a collective of like-minded NBA writers and artists whose blog has become a staple of basketball fandom on the Internet. www.freedarko.com

BETHLEHEM SHOALS is a writer living in Seattle. He contributes regularly to NBA FanHouse and is a founding member of FreeDarko. His work has also appeared in *Sports Illustrated*, *Slate*, *McSweeney's*, Deadspin.com, *SLAM*, and the *Nation*.

JACOB WEINSTEIN is a cartoonist, illustrator, and designer. His work has appeared in the *New Yorker*, *Tin House*, and *McSweeney's*.

J. GABRIEL BOYLAN is a music and art writer living in New York City. His work has appeared in *Spin*, the *Nation*, *Bookforum*, the *New York Observer*, *Vibe*, and elsewhere. For many years he was the lead singer and songwriter of Electric Light Orchestra.

BROWN RECLUSE, ESQ., is a law librarian living in Chicago. His writing on sports has appeared on Deadspin.com and UNC basketball message boards. He is very excited about the beginning of the Harrison Barnes Era.

DR. LAWYER INDIANCHIEF holds a Ph.D. in psychology and researches how people think about other minds. He has written about music, science, and sports for outlets such as the *Fader*, *Scientific American*, and *ESPN the Magazine*.

ERIC FREEMAN is a writer and editor from San Francisco. He writes for SportingNews.com and PlasmaPool.org. In his spare time, he enjoys reading long books and yelling at his television.

AVI KORINE is a screenwriter whose credits include the film *Mister Lonely*. He also writes about boxing for the *Sporting News*.

JOEY LITMAN follows basketball from St. Louis, where he attends law school. He writes the blog Straight Bangin', and he has contributed sportswriting to a host of Web sites, including ESPN.com. In his free time, Joey waits patiently for the Knicks to win another title and for Black Star to release another album.

PASHA MALLA is the author of *The Withdrawal Method* (stories) and *All Our Grandfathers Are Ghosts* (poems, sort of). His first novel, *People Park*, will be published in late 2011.

SILVERBIRD 5000 is FreeDarko's resident statistician, as well as the founder, editor, and sole proprietor of the only blog devoted exclusively to the English Revolution of 1640. He is currently completing his doctorate in sociology at Yale.

LANG WHITAKER is the executive editor of *SLAM* magazine. He appears regularly on NBA TV and has also written for *Sports Illustrated*, *Esquire*, *InStyle*, and *Antenna*, among others. His memoir about growing up as a fan of the Atlanta Braves is due out from Scribner in spring 2011.

TOM ZILLER writes about the NBA for FanHouse.com and SactownRoyalty.com.

RESEARCH ASSISTANTS

Benjamin Conway
Couper Moorhead
Greg Pietras
Gabe Stutman
Andrew Weatherhead

ACKNOWLEDGMENTS

Amelia Abreu
Benjamin Adams
Sherman Alexie
Liza Corsillo
Tommy Craggs
Charles Friedman and Patti Abbott
Mark Haubner
Paul Hirscheimer
Lakshmi IndraSimhan
Claude Johnson
Niamh McGuigan
Dave McMenamin
Andrew Nosnitsky
Mike O'Connor
Nathan Parham
Chris Parris-Lamb
Nick Trautwein
Jon Weinbach
Paul Waytz and Susan Gray
Josh and Johanna Weinstein
Patricia Weiss and Mark Staitman
Sarah and Iris Ziller

INDEX